Developing Advocacy for Children and Young People

of related interest

Supporting Children and Families
Lessons from Sure Start for Evidence-Based Practice in Health,
Social Care and Education
Edited by Justine Schneider, Mark Avis and Paul Leighton
ISBN 978 1 84310 506 0

Young Children's Rights
Exploring Beliefs, Principles and Practice
2nd Edition
Priscilla Alderson
ISBN 978 1 84310 599 2
Children in Charge series

Children Taken Seriously
In Theory, Policy and Practice
Edited by Jan Mason and Toby Fattore
Foreword by Mary John
ISBN 978 1 84310 250 2
Children in Charge series

Children's Rights and Power
Charging Up for a New Century
Mary John
ISBN 978 1 85302 659 1 (Paperback)
ISBN 978 1 85302 658 4 (Hardback)
Children in Charge series

Disabled Children and the Law
Research and Good Practice
2nd edition
Janet Read, Luke Clements and David Ruebain
ISBN 978 1 84310 280 9

Mentally Disordered Children and the Law
A Guide to Law and Practice
Anthony Harbour
ISBN 978 1 84310 576 3

Speaking Up
A Plain Text Guide to Advocacy 4-volume set
John Tufail and Kate Lyon
ISBN 978 1 84310 474 2

See You in Court
A Social Worker's Guide to Presenting Evidence in Care Proceedings
Lynn Davis
ISBN 978 1 84310 547 3

Developing Advocacy for Children and Young People

Current Issues in Research, Policy and Practice

Edited by Christine M. Oliver and Jane Dalrymple

Foreword by Cherie Booth QC

Jessica Kingsley Publishers
London and Philadelphia

First published in 2008
by Jessica Kingsley Publishers
116 Pentonville Road
London N1 9JB, UK
and
400 Market Street, Suite 400
Philadelphia, PA 19106, USA

www.jkp.com

Library of Congress Cataloging in Publication Data
Developing advocacy for children and young people : current issues in research, policy and practice / edited by Christine M. Oliver and Jane Dalrymple.
p. cm.
ISBN 978-1-84310-596-1 (pb : alk. paper) 1. Children--Services for. 2. Legal assistance to children. 3. Child welfare. 4. Children's rights. 5. Children--Legal status, laws, etc. 6. Social advocacy. I. Oliver, Christine M. II. Dalrymple, Jane, 1951-
HV713.D48 2008
362.7--dc22

2007040317

British Library Cataloguing in Publication Data
A CIP catalogue record for this book is available from the British Library

ISBN 978 1 84310 596 1

Printed and bound in Great Britain by
Athenaeum Press, Gateshead, Tyne and Wear

Contents

Foreword

I'd like to start with a question – why is it so important to listen to children and make sure they are involved in the decisions that impact on their lives? Many people, after all, would argue that it is adults' responsibility to make decisions in the best interests of children and that children themselves lack the life experience and knowledge to do this.

And, of course, adults must have a large input. But I would argue that it is in all our interests to make sure that we don't ignore children in these processes and indeed that we involve children as much as possible.

This is not simply because it is their interests, priorities, concerns and hopes that are being decided on – and if we are to get these decisions right it makes sense to know their opinion. We take this for granted if decisions are being made about ourselves. It is also because every society hopes and expects that its children will grow up to be capable and responsible citizens who contribute to the well-being of their communities. This development is not something, however, that occurs over-night, when the child suddenly reaches the age of majority. As with other aspects of growth and development, it is a gradual process that must be nurtured.

Bringing children up in a culture where they are consulted, involved and listened to and where respect is a two way process can only be of benefit to children, adults and society as a whole. Children make up nearly 25% of the population in the UK and are the primary users of many of our services – schools, health and leisure as well as our social services. Encouraging early participation gives children a taste for citizenship; it encourages fairness and tolerance; engenders respect for others; and thus reduces the danger of alienation in later years.

The benefits of involvement and participation for children and young people are well researched. They learn more about themselves and others; they learn to respect others' rights; they start to develop the capacity to exercise social responsi-bility; they develop interpersonal and practical skills and acquire new knowledge and skills. Perhaps most importantly they gain confidence in dealing with other people – both adults and children – and are able engage in reasonable debate.

As a human rights lawyer, I would also be a little remiss if I did not mention that a child's right to be listened to and involved is required in both international and domestic policy. Article 12 of the United Nations Convention on the Rights of the Child enshrines the right of children to have their views and opinions listened to and taken into account. In domestic policy the 1989 and 2004 Children Acts and the Every Child and Youth Matters agendas stress the importance of involving children and young people and places duties on agencies to ensure this happens.

But enshrining this right in law is not enough. Many children will need support to enable their voices to be heard – disabled children, younger children, those in care or custody, and those whose own parents are unable to act as champions for them will need additional support and help.

How important this is can be seen by looking at the position of children in care. The poor outcomes for this group are well documented and highlighted in the recent Green Paper *Care Matters: Transforming the Lives of Children in Care*. The achievement gap between them and other children is growing and the outcomes for them are even poorer than for those with similar backgrounds and characteristics who do not come into care.

When children come into care, their relationship with all the other systems and services they are involved with, such as schools and health services, is changed. They are no longer mediated by parents or guardians, so it is essential that they have access to people who can help them be heard and involved.

Despite guidance, policy and the best efforts of all working in the system, we are still very poor at ensuring that children in care have a real say in the decisions that are made about them. Children in these positions need help to ensure their voice and preferences are heard, which is why the role of advocates for children in care is crucial.

I should at this point reveal a personal interest. The role of an advocate for children is one that I perform myself, which is why I have found much of the research presented in this book so interesting. It's also important to remember that advocates can play an important part in awareness raising and training for staff to ensure that a culture of listening and participation is developed in the care system. We are all on the same side battling to improve life for children who have, through no fault of their own, been handed a very bad set of cards.

In recent years legislation and policy has required local authorities to involve children and ensure they have access to an advocate, when making a complaint for example.

But we have to go further. It is important that children in care are more widely involved in the services they receive and not only in the decisions that affect them individually. Research evidence indicates that services are more cost effective and have better outcomes when service users are involved in their design and development.

As adults we take it for granted that we make our own decisions or at least influence the decisions that are made about us. We have a duty and responsibility to ensure we give the same opportunity to children and young people so they continue to grow and develop into happy and healthy adulthood.

I believe properly trained advocates have a role to play in helping to build a culture where care providers put listening to the children's views and experiences at the heart of all their services.

But a willingness to listen to children and young people also requires a change of culture and an acceptance that all our children have a right to be heard and that we will all gain if they are.

Cherie Booth, QC

CHAPTER 1

Concepts, Public Policy and Research

Christine M. Oliver and Jane Dalrymple

Over the past decade or so, advocacy for children and young people has moved from the margins to the centre of public policy. Yet, advocacy is not widely understood as a concept or as a practice. Further, there is little research evidence placed in the public domain that can assist those curious about advocacy to find answers to any questions they may have. By drawing together the work of a number of researchers active in this field, we aim to begin the process of exploring advocacy from a range of perspectives – what it means, how it is practised, and what kind of impact it has on the lives of children and young people. We hope that policy makers, professionals working in children's health and social care, and all who work directly with children will become more aware of the advocacy role and its potential for promoting children's participation in decision-making and the development of genuinely child-centred services.

We use the phrase 'developing advocacy' to highlight our understanding of advocacy as an evolving and dynamic way of working with children and young people. We also explore the relationship between the theory and practice of advocacy, highlighting the ways in which understandings of the concept of advocacy influence practice, and vice versa. We take this approach for a number of reasons. First, advocacy for children and young people might be described as in the early stages of professional development. Consequently, many advocates acquire their skills 'on the job'. Yet, advocacy can be a highly demanding role and a set of guiding principles can help advocates to navigate the complexities and dilemmas of advocacy practice. Thus, we hope the book will help advocates to reflect on their practice, without necessarily offering a simplistic prescription or recipe for 'what works' in children's advocacy. Second, until recently, emphasis has been given to debates about the principles of advocacy. While this is of crucial importance, we also aim to provide descriptions of advocacy practice in order to provide some insight into how principles translate into practice and to provide the reader with a more immediate sense of what advocacy with children and young people entails.

We explore the increasing prominence given to advocacy for children and young people in public policy. The Adoption and Children Act 2002 gave advocacy statutory status for the first time and the Government's most recent proposals for improving the life chances of children in public care (DfES 2006) places advocacy centre stage. But, as we will see later, policy developments have yet to catch up with advocacy as it is understood and practised by most advocacy services and children's agencies in the voluntary sector. History shows that many radical ideas and forms of service provision have originated in the voluntary or charitable sector, only to be adopted, and often assimilated, into mainstream services. It is as yet unclear which direction Government policy in relation to advocacy for children and young people will take. It would therefore seem to be an opportune time to review how and why advocacy services for children and young people have developed in recent decades, and to identify some possible signposts for the future.

Advocacy for children and young people as a developing concept

Described as one of the oldest forms of support (Brandon 1995), the formal and best known development of advocacy is in relation to legal services where the role of an advocate in court (as a solicitor or barrister) is to represent the interests of their clients, speak up on their behalf and protect their rights (Wertheimer, 1996). As Chapter 10 shows, this definition of advocacy raises some interesting questions about the similarities and differences in roles and responsibilities between legal and non-legal advocates. Outside of strictly legal contexts, dictionary definitions portray advocates as people who act positively on behalf of someone else (Bateman 1995). Over time, advocacy for children and young people has evolved within a similar conceptual framework, but tends to place more emphasis on the notion of 'voice': advocacy is most commonly defined as a process of enabling children and young people to 'have a voice' about matters of concern to them (Dalrymple and Hough 1995).

Advocacy for children and young people draws on a number of historical roots. Some of its inspiration derives from the ideas and expertise developed by service user groups and movements in the late 1980s, particularly
those pioneered by people with disabilities and by survivors of the mental
health system. Service user groups identified links between forms of service
provision that were experienced as inadequate and stigmatising and wider
patterns of social inequality and discrimination. This led to what Beresford
describes as the 'emergence of new participants in social policy: service users
and their movements' (2002, p.496). In this context, advocacy developed as
a key tool in adjusting the power relations between service users and service
providers (Braye and Preston-Shoot 1995; Tunnard 1997), and as a vital
element in challenging inequality and oppression:

> When people are denied or unable to gain access to a fair share of what's on
> offer in society – when they are denied information or opportunities to take
> part in decisions concerning their lives – when they are dispossessed of
> insight, dignity, self confidence – then it becomes necessary in a caring
> society for more powerful people to act with integrity on their behalf or
> wherever possible to enable them to move to a point where they can retrieve
> control for themselves. (Advocacy in Action 1990)

This analysis suggests that those who suffer the effects of social inequality
may need someone to speak (act) on their behalf or support to enable them to
move towards a position of being able to advocate for themselves
(self-advocacy).

However, the service user movement has been largely adult-dominated.
While children's advocacy shares a common ethos with many adult forms of
advocacy, there are also important differences. Advocacy for children and
young people has developed with a specific focus on children in public care,
and children considered 'in need'. As a result, advocacy engages with discourses concerning the relationship between the social construction of
childhood and the concept of care – for example, whether children are perceived as active agents or passive recipients of care or even as care givers.
Historically, adults in their capacity as parents or welfare professionals, have
claimed to know 'what's best' for children in relation to their care, particularly for young children. However, notions of what constitutes adequate or
optimum care have changed over time, and the idea that children should
have a voice, and be listened to, has only recently gained acceptance. Even so,
it has been argued that the current zeitgeist in favour of 'listening' to
children and young people may be more a question of rhetoric than of reality

(McNeish 1999). In this context, advocacy offers a potentially important mechanism for translating children's rights to participation in decision-making into practice.

Advocacy for children and young people is also distinct from advocacy for adults in that it operates in the context of social norms concerning children's capacities to engage in decision-making. Children are widely perceived, biologically and cognitively, as immature but developing towards adulthood. As a result, there are debates about the age or stage at which children can, or should, be involved in decisions about their care. Further, some children, regardless of age, are more likely than others to be excluded from decision-making, such as children with disabilities. Chapter 7 provides examples of advocacy with children with disabilities, including children without speech. They illustrate the ways in which advocates have developed a variety of methods for working with children of varying capacities, underpinned in some cases by a clearly articulated rights-based model of advocacy.

Further, peer advocacy (that is, advocacy offered by someone who shares a common identity or experience) is a less common feature of children's advocacy compared with adult forms of advocacy. Given the double jeopardy experienced by children in public care – that they are both children and stigmatised for being in care – adult advocates are often needed to challenge adult-constructed decision-making systems. However, the involvement of adults as advocates for children raises important questions about the power dynamics of the advocacy relationship. Sensitivity to, and awareness of, the ways in which adult advocates can either empower children, or collude with professional or parental decision-making, is a key issue in advocacy practice. For this reason, authors describe and discuss advocacy practice in detail, highlighting the ways in which advocates attempt to work *with* children to construct a flexible and empathic relationship that takes account of their specific capacities, wishes and circumstances. Chapter 6, for example, uses in-depth case studies to identify the range of issues faced by young people in and leaving care and the complex dynamics that come into play between the young person, the advocate and other adults, including health and social care professionals.

If advocacy is about 'having a voice' or 'speaking up', then this suggests that children and young people who need advocacy are routinely silenced and marginalised by other, more powerful, individuals and decision-making systems. Thus, advocacy might be best understood as an empowerment practice. In the context of children's health and social care, a large and ever increasing number of adult professionals may be involved in decisions about an individual child's well-being. Increasingly, professional decision-making operates within the boundaries of formal assessment procedures and fora. Participating in such decision-making structures can be a confusing and intimidating experience for a child. Several chapters in this book investigate the role of advocacy in such contexts, including child protection conferences (Chapter 4), family group conferences (Chapter 5), reviews (Chapter 3) and in relation to formal complaints procedures (Chapters 8 and 9). However, as a result of such involvement, there is some debate about the extent to which advocacy is becoming increasingly proceduralised and thereby functioning as an adaptive, rather than radical, force of change for children. In Chapter 3, Jane Boylan highlights the potential limitations of advocacy and suggests that a critical perspective on existing advocacy provision for looked after children and young people is needed.

Discourses of children's rights, childhood and youth have been influential in contributing to understandings of children's agency and voice. In order to understand both the need for, and attitudes to, advocacy for children and young people, it is therefore necessary to consider contemporary debates about constructions of childhood alongside emerging perspectives on children's rights and participation in public policy.

Children's advocacy and public policy

A number of trends in national and international law, and changes in social policy, reflect and reinforce a renewed focus on the status and rights of children and young people. The 1989 UN Convention on the Rights of the Child represented a historic landmark, signalling an important shift in attitudes to children and their place in society. While globally, there are wide variations in children's status in law, in the family, and in their access to economic and social resources, the Convention established a set of universal rights for children and young people against which social progress on a local level might be measured. In particular, Article 12 upheld children's rights to participation in decision-making about matters of concern to them and provided an impetus and a justification for the growth of advocacy for children and young people.

The UN Convention of the Rights of the Child also influenced the spirit and substance of the 1989 Children Act. Heralded as 'the most far-reaching reform of child care law which has come before Parliament in living memory', (Mackay 1998), the 1989 Children Act established children's welfare as the central principle in decision-making, but it also set out the rights of children to be consulted on their needs and wishes. For some, the 1989 Children Act was seen as a vehicle for empowering children and young people to participate in decisions about their care (Smith and Woodhead 1999). Others were more cautious, citing the lack of whole-hearted support given to advocacy in the accompanying Guidance and Regulations (Timms 1995). Over time, the shortcomings of the 1989 Children Act in facilitating children's participatory rights have become more apparent, particularly in relation to children's access to, and use of, complaints procedures.

In theory, complaints procedures should enable children to voice their concerns to their 'corporate parent'. In practice, they have been widely criticised for being adult-oriented, inaccessible, lacking in confidentiality and difficult to negotiate without the support of an advocate (Aiers and Kettle, 1998; Utting, 1997). As a result, the Adoption and Children Act 2002 established a statutory duty on local authorities to provide advocacy for children wishing to make a complaint under the 1989 Children Act regulations. The relationship between advocacy and complaints procedures is explored in Chapters 8 and 9, which discuss findings from a Welsh Assembly Government-funded study of complaints against social services involving children and their use of advocacy services. Chapter 8 explores professional (social workers and their managers) attitudes towards advocacy providers and the likely impact of this upon day to day practice. Drawing on the same study, Chapter 9 focuses on the views of young people and argues that the findings challenge the assumption that the availability of complaints procedures and advocacy support services in themselves can provide an effective means of protecting the most vulnerable children from the worst abuses of our healthcare, social care, education or legal systems.

Advocacy for children and young people has evolved within both protectionist and rights-oriented discourses. These developments form part of a wider shift towards perceiving children and young people as active agents in their lives rather than merely passive recipients of service provision. At the same time, children's need for protection from abuse and neglect remains a powerful force. A series of investigations into child abuse in residential care, for example, highlighted that, without independent representation, children were not heard or believed, suffered isolation and lacked a means of redress (Utting 1997). Such findings provided an important impetus to the growth, and justification for, advocacy for children and young people. Some commentators concluded that children in public care should have a right to independent advocacy (Taylor 2000; Waterhouse 2000). In short, it was increasingly acknowledged that children in public care needed access to independent advocacy to protect their welfare *and* their rights (Oliver *et al.* 2006; Timms 1995).

From the mid-1990s, a number of key initiatives attempted to promote the benefits of 'listening' to children and young people, as well as a more specific focus on the value of children's advocacy. *The Quality Protects Programme* (Department of Health 1998) encouraged children's involvement in individual care planning and service development and, while it did not refer to advocacy specifically, funding made available to local authorities under the initiative led to a sudden increase in the number of advocacy services for children and young people in England.

In Wales, the policy mandate for the provision of independent advocacy for children and young people emerged as response to a number of investigations (for example, Carlile 2002; Clarke 2003; Jones 1999) as well as to the recommendations from the Report on the abuse of children and young people looked after in state care in North Wales, *Lost In Care* (Waterhouse 2000). The Welsh Assembly response to the recommendations of the Waterhouse Report was swift and the first UK Children's Commissioner was appointed in Wales in 2000 with recommendations from the Report used to inform the Care Standards Act 2000. The Welsh Assembly Government set in motion plans for children and young people in health, social care and education settings to have access to advocacy. Advocacy was subsequently prioritised in guidance (Welsh Assembly Government 2002) and a Task and Finish Group consisting of commissioners and providers was set up in 2002 by the Welsh Assembly Government to advise on the development of independent advocacy in Wales. The Welsh Assembly Government has since proposed that there should be a comprehensive integrated model of advocacy established in Wales (Welsh Assembly Government 2007).

As the number of advocacy services grew, attempts were made to ensure consistency in the quality of provision through the introduction of national standards for children's advocacy (Department of Health 2002; Welsh Assembly Government 2003a) and, later, by setting out guidelines for advocacy services providing support to children involved in complaints procedures under the provisions of the 1989 Children Act (DfES 2003; Welsh Assembly Government 2003b). The Children's Commissioner for England, set up under the terms of the Children Act 2004 and modelled on the role of the Children's Commissioner in Wales, reflected a growing acceptance that children need an adult champion (or advocate), able to promote the voice of children at the heart of policy development and service delivery.

Just as the 1989 Children Act has been seen as a catalyst to more progressive thinking concerning children's welfare and their rights, so legislation introduced over the last decade has been described as 'the start of the most ambitious cross-government policy agenda for children ever attempted anywhere in the world' (Aynsley-Green 2004). *Every Child Matters: Change for Children* (DfES 2004) established an agenda for achieving progress in the educational attainment, economic participation, health and well-being of all children and young people through co-ordinated children's services. Despite evidence that some progress has been made in improving the life chances of children in public care, this concentrated focus on improving the well-being of children and young people generally has had the unanticipated effect of widening the gap between children in public care and children living with their families. Consequently, new proposals have emerged to improve children's experience of the care system (DfES 2006). It has been proposed that the independent visitor scheme[1] could be 'revitalised' as a means of making 'independent advocacy' more widely available to children in public care. This means of extending advocacy has met with general disapproval on the part of children in care, advocacy services and children's organisations in the voluntary sector. The NSPCC, for example, is cited as stating 'in the strongest possible terms that the roles are not ones that could or should be merged' (DfES 2007, p.18). Several authors comment on this issue, reiterating the need for role boundaries to protect the integrity of advocacy as it is most widely understood. Nevertheless, it seems promising that, while the means for widening children's access to advocacy has yet to be finalised, the general principle that children in public care need access to independent advocacy has met with general acceptance.

The recent emphasis on the importance of listening to children and young people encounters a parallel and arguably contradictory trend: that of strengthening the authority of parents and family members in relation to decisions about the care and well-being of children (Oliver 2003; Piper 1998). In recent years, for example, there has been increasing interest in the role of family group conferences in mobilising the support of extended family members to reduce the risk or incidence of child abuse or neglect in the family. Government proposals to extend the use of family group conferences have met with near universal support (DfES 2007). However, there has been concern that children's voices may not be heard within family group conferences and that independent advocacy is needed to create a better balance of power. Chapter 5 investigates the role of children's advocacy on the processes and outcomes of family group conferences.

Overall, evidence suggests that achieving progress in children's participation in decision-making is not a question solely of legal reform, but also of creating change in organisational cultures and professional perspectives regarding children's participation in decision-making. Overall, progress in achieving children's participation has been uneven and professional resistance to children's participation is a key factor in this respect (Aldgate and Statham 2001). Chapter 11 highlights the need for cultural change and greater receptivity on the part of care providers towards listening to children and young people, and involving them in decisions about their care. Chapter 9 suggests that, unless we embrace the wider vision of children's participation and empowerment, public service complaints procedures and independent advocacy services will remain blunt instruments of protection and empowerment for all but a small minority of vulnerable children.

To be truly empowering, advocacy needs to have an impact on the lives of individual children, and on wider decision-making systems. Two broad models of advocacy can therefore be identified: case advocacy – work with individuals or small groups and cause or systemic advocacy – work with larger groups usually aimed at structural changes in relation to legislation, policy or practice. However, as in any practice which aims to promote change, advocacy at both the individual and the structural levels is inevitably interrelated (Mickelson 1995). The relationship between case and systemic advocacy is necessary as individual situations provide the data needed to promote change in legislation, systems and policies. Applying this model to advocacy with children and young people, we believe that if children and young people are to have access to adequate and relevant services, to be protected and to have a voice in the decisions which affect their lives, both case and systemic advocacy are important. In Chapter 11, the impact of advocacy at both levels is explored. This chapter also explores children's reasons for contacting an advocate and their satisfaction with the response they received.

Researching advocacy

Given the focus on power relations in advocacy, it is to be expected that researching advocacy is also a political activity. Over the last 20 years, more energy has been spent on defining advocacy principles and developing local services that incorporate those principles (Henderson and Pochin 2001) than on developing formal evaluative frameworks. Hitherto, only a limited number of studies have been published and much of these are in the form of 'think pieces' or small-scale studies of a single advocacy service (Oliver

2003). A number of more in-depth and systematic studies of advocacy for children and young people have been made in recent years, some on a national scale. The need for advocacy projects to be evaluated is important both to understand and develop advocacy practice and because of the need to be accountable to both funders and service users (Gould 1999).

While it has been suggested that evaluations are to be avoided unless done properly (Robson 1993), we believe that it is important to evaluate advocacy provision, partly since this is a necessary element of developing services and partly because it enables researchers to work together with advocacy services to find ways of developing practice. Evaluation research can be regarded as providing an account of advocacy to inform its future development as empowerment practice, which is one of the aims of this book. Parsons (1998) points out that if we are implementing or evaluating empowerment programmes then we need to understand the complexity of empowerment:

> No matter what kind of questions one wants to answer in evaluation, one must amplify the voice of clients in their perceptions of empowerment, their experiences as participants, and their perceptions of outcomes in themselves and others. (p.210)

If advocacy is defined in Parson's (1998) terms as an empowerment-oriented activity, then any evaluation of it has to amplify the voices of the population being studied. In this way participants are enabled to enabled 'to have a voice' and gain political power (in this case children and young people and their advocates). This can then be identified in research terms as providing a 'framework for engaging in [dialogical] relations whereby people pursue new and diverse forms of knowledge about social welfare, critique dominant ideologies, and challenge professional and bureaucratic power' (Sohng 1998, p. 92). The advantage of this approach is in providing the opportunity for all those involved in the process to contribute to narratives about the nature and purpose of advocacy. Through obtaining multiple and sometimes conflicting perspectives dialogue is possible, which may then be used to reach some consensus about advocacy practice. The disadvantage, though, is that it is the researcher who produces the final account and represents the voices – however empowering our aims are, researchers are in a position of power, able to use the articulation of a range of views to construct the nature of advocacy.

Advocacy services for children and young people are concerned with their voice and agency. An issue in devising a research methodology, therefore, is whether the research is aiming to hear the voices of young people or to hear the voices of advocates. Either way it could be argued that it is about 'voice'. Chapters 3 and 10 highlight the challenges that arise in undertaking research that is underpinned by a commitment to promoting children and young people's meaningful participation. In examining the dilemmas in representing the voices of children, Alldred (1998) states that discourses of 'giving voice' enable children to be active subjects rather than objects and that research is one way of providing a space for those whose opinions are rarely heard and to recognise them as subjects. She then identifies the tensions that can arise in the ethnographic study of children which challenge 'the general assumption that adults' benevolent attempts to represent children (as proxy or advocate) are necessarily always in their interests, and the simplicity with which it is assumed that what children say can be represented (portrayed) through research' (1998, p.151). There are two problems raised here: the first is the notion of 'giving voice', the second is that of representation.

The discourses of voice emanate from concerns that those who have been absent, unheard or silenced need a space to be heard. It could be argued though that there is an assumption of arrogance in the idea that we might be able to 'give' children and young people a voice. Maguire (2001) notes a caution by Noffke against the notion of 'giving' voice suggesting that 'we must see ourselves as part of the process of breaking apart the barriers for speakers and listeners, writers and readers' (1998, p.10). The notion of 'giving voice' has been challenged (Dalrymple 2003) and it has been suggested that enabling children and young people to 'come to voice' (hooks, 1989) is a more helpful way of understanding the practice of advocacy. Code (2000, p.192) suggests that *practices of advocacy often make knowledge possible* within the hierarchical distributions of autonomy and authority within western societies' (italics original). Such an understanding of advocacy means that children and young people in receipt of services may often require the guidance of adults to know what their experiences are. Advocacy makes 'truths available for negotiation' (Code 2000, p.189) with, by and for children, young people, their advocates and adults involved in their lives. Code states, 'Advocacy can counter-balance the patterns of incredulity into which the testimony of marginalised knowers tends to fall' (2000, p.189). For her advocacy is well placed to put 'knowledge into circulation where it can claim acknowledgement and working to ensure informed, emancipatory moral-political effects' (p.189).

Understanding the practice of advocacy as making knowledge possible enables response to ethical concerns against speaking for others. Arguments by writers such as hooks (1990), that the representation of oppressed groups by dominant groups can erase their 'voice', are powerful. Equally powerful is the recognition that 'not to speak about or for "others" encourages silences and gaps, which marginalise and exclude, while cementing the privilege of those with the more powerful voices' (Gillies and Alldred 2002, p.41). A number of authors in this collection have tried to manage this by including the words of children, young people and their advocates in their accounts. However, the discourse of 'voice' might be considered inherently problematic for children with disabilities, particularly children without speech (Oliver 2003). Given that all children, regardless of their level of disability, communicate in some way, through either gestures, body language or other means, 'voice' might be best considered a symbolic concept, inclusive of a wide range of capacities and modes of communication. Chapter 7 explores the dilemmas posed by the concept of 'voice' for advocates working with children without speech. Through this publication we have aimed to act responsibly, by trying to ensure that, in documenting advocacy experiences, the material presented contributes to knowledge in a way that does not further oppress and marginalise children and young people or erase their voices.

Advocacy services for children and young people: a potted history

Advocacy services for children and young people have developed along two parallel lines: as provided directly by local authorities, and as provided by voluntary sector organisations under contract to local authorities and other commissioning agencies. Either way, the increase in the number of advocacy services from the early 1990s onwards was closely associated with a burgeoning children's rights movement and the increasing emphasis given in public policy to children's participation in decision-making.

The first children's rights officer was appointed by Leicestershire Council in 1987. Subsequently, a number of similar posts were set up by other local authorities to provide information, support and advocacy for children in their care (Franklin 1995; Willow 1996). Most local authorities, however, contracted local branches of children's charities, such as the Children's Society, NCH (then National Children's Home), Barnardo's, and the NSPCC to provide independent advocacy for children in local authority care

(Franklin 1995). In a key development, two voluntary organisations, IRCHIN (Independent Representation for Children in Need) and VCC (Voice for the Child in Care, now called Voice), came together with support from ChildLine (a national telephone helpline for children and young people) to form a specialist national advocacy service, ASC (Advice, Advocacy and Representation Service for Children and Young People). In 1998, ASC and IRCHIN subsequently merged to form NYAS (National Youth Advocacy Service), a socio-legal agency that provides advocacy support for young people in any administrative or judicial procedures. NYAS and Voice are now two of the main national advocacy services in England. In Wales, Tros Gynnal, NYAS and the Children's Society are the largest providers of advocacy services for children and young people (Clarke 2003).

In England, the majority of advocacy services for children and young people were established between 1996 and 2000 (Oliver, Knight and Candappa 2006), mostly as a result of funding made available by the Quality Protects initiative (Department of Health 1998). This rapid development has produced a largely fragmented pattern of service provision (Clifton and Hodgson 1997; Department of Health 2000). Chapter 2 considers in more depth the ways in which advocacy services have developed and how this has set the scene for continuing debates concerning the independence of advocacy services and children's access to advocacy support. Currently, a minority of advocacy services are delivered directly by local authorities to young people in their care and a majority by national children's voluntary organisations. Advocacy services are also more available in some parts of the country than in others, raising important issues about equity of access. New strategies for delivering advocacy support are under consideration in England and Wales, including the potential for regional funding to promote the wider availability of advocacy services for children and young people (Oliver et al. 2006; Pithouse et al. 2005).

Advocacy services engage with children living in a wide range of settings, including children's homes and other institutional contexts, in foster homes, and in children's birth families. Recent research evidence also shows that, although most advocacy services have developed with a focus on looked after children, there is also a measure of variety in terms of their target audience, particularly in relation to age and disability (Oliver et al. 2006). It has been argued that children with disabilities (Morris 1998) and care leavers have a particular need for advocacy (Frost, Mills and Stein 1999), both as they prepare to leave care and once they are living independently. Chapter 2 considers the ways in which advocacy services attempt to meet the diverse needs of their users and highlight areas where services could be improved. Access to advocacy is considered both in its literal sense (the availability of local services) and in relation to the development of an inclusive model of advocacy practice.

Evidence also shows that, although most advocacy services have been funded by social services departments, advocates tend to work with a wide variety of service providers, including education, health, and mental health services and services for young offenders (Oliver *et al.* 2006). Advocacy services are therefore likely to have a continuing and important role in supporting children to express their wishes and concerns in the context of an increasing focus on partnership working and the development of integrated children's services.

References

Advocacy in Action (1990) 'A Model for User Consultation.' *Advocacy in Action Information Pack.* Nottingham: Advocacy in Action.

Aiers, A. and Kettle, J. (1998) *When Things Go Wrong: Young People's Experiences of Getting Access to the Complaints Procedure.* London: NISW.

Aldgate, J. and Statham, J. (2001) *The Children Act Now: Messages from the Research.* London: The Stationery Office.

Alldred, P. (1998) 'Ethnography and Discourse Analysis: Dilemmas in Representing the Voices of Children.' In J. Ribbens and R. Edwards (eds) *Feminist Dilemmas in Qualitative Research.* London: Sage.

Aynsley-Green, A. (2004) *What are the Implications of 'Change for Children' for R&D? Bridging the Gap between Politics, Policy and Practice.* Available at www.ihs.manchester.ac.uk (accessed 24 January 2000).

Bateman, N. (1995) *Advocacy Skills: A Handbook for Human Service Professionals.* Aldershot: Arena.

Beresford, P. (2002) 'Service users, social policy and the future of welfare.' *Critical Social Policy 21*, 494–512.

Brandon, D. (1995) *Advocacy: Power to People with Disabilities.* Birmingham: Venture Press.

Braye, S. and Preston-Shoot, M. (1995) *Empowering Practice in Social Care.* Buckingham: Open University Press.

Carlile, Lord A. (2002) *Too Serious A Thing: Review of Safeguards for Children and Young People Treated and Cared for by the NHS in Wales.* Cardiff: NafW.

Clarke, P. (2003) *Telling Concerns. Report of the Children's Commissioner for Wales' Review of the Operation of Complaints and Representations and Whistleblowing Procedures and Arrangements for the Provision of Children's Advocacy Services.* Swansea: Children's Commissioner for Wales.

Clifton, C. and Hodgson, D. (1997) 'Rethinking Practice Through a Children's Rights Perspective.' In C. Cannan and C. Warren (eds) *Social Action with Children and Families: A Community Development Approach to Children and Family Welfare.* London: Routledge.

Code, L. (2000) 'The Perversion of Autonomy and the Subjection of Women: Discourses of Social Advocacy at Century's End.' In C. Mackenzie and N. Stoljar (eds) *Relational Autonomy: Feminist Perspectives on Autonomy, Agency and the Social Self.* Oxford: Oxford University Press.

Dalrymple, J. (2003) 'Professional advocacy as a force for resistance in child welfare.' *British Journal of Social Work 33,* 1043–1062.

Dalrymple, J. and Hough, J. (eds) (1995) *Having a Voice: An Exploration of Children's Rights and Advocacy.* Birmingham: Venture Press/British Association of Social Workers.

Department of Health (1998) *The Quality Protects Programme: Transforming Children's Services.* London: The Stationery Office.

Department of Health (2000) *Learning the Lessons. The Government's Response to Lost in Care: The Report of the Tribunal of Inquiry into the Abuse of Children in Care in the former County Council Areas of Gwynedd and Clwyd since 1974.* London: The Stationery Office.

Department of Health (2002) *National Standards for Agencies Providing Advocacy for Children and Young People in England.* London: Department of Health.

DfES (2003) *Get It Sorted: Providing Effective Advocacy Services for Children and Young People Making a Complaint under the Children Act 1989.* London: DfES.

DfES (2004) *Every Child Matters.* Norwich: The Stationery Office.

DfES (2006) *Care Matters: Transforming the Lives of Children and Young People In Care.* London: DfES.

DfES (2007) *Care Matters: Consultation Responses.* London: DfES.

Franklin, R. (1995) *The Handbook of Children's Rights, Comparative Policy and Practice.* London: Routledge.

Frost, N., Mills, S. and Stein, M. (1999) *Understanding Residential Child Care.* Aldershot: Ashgate Arena.

Gillies, V. and Alldred, P. (2002) 'The Ethics of Intention: Research as a Political Tool.' In M. Mauthner, M. Birch, T. Jessop and T. Miller (eds) *Ethics in Qualitative Research.* London: Sage.

Gould, N. (1999) 'Qualitative Practice Evaluation.' In I. Shaw and J. Lishman (eds) *Evaluation and Social Work Practice.* London: Sage.

Henderson, R. and Pochin, M. (2001) *A Right Result? Advocacy, Justice and Empowerment.* Bristol: The Policy Press.

hooks, b. (1989) *Talking Back: Thinking Feminist, Thinking Black.* Boston: South End Press.

hooks, b. (1990) *Yearning: Race, Gender and Cultural Politics.* Boston: South End Press.

Jones, A. (1999) *Report of the Examination Team on Child Care Procedures and Practice in North Wales.* London: The Stationery Office.

Mackay, Lord (1998) Hansard HL, Volume 502, Column 488.

Maguire, P. (2001) 'Uneven Ground: Feminisms and Action Research.' In H. Bradbury and P. Reason (eds.) *Handbook of Action Research: Participative Inquiry and Practice.* London: Sage.

McNeish, D. (1999) *Rhetoric to Reality*. London: Health Education Authority.

Mickelson, J. S. (1995) *Advocacy*. Washington, DC: NASW Press.

Morris, J. (1998) *Don't Leave Us Out. Involving Disabled Children and Young People with Communication Impairments*. York: Joseph Rowntree Foundation.

Noffke, S. (1998) 'What's a nice theory like yours doing in a practice like this? And other impertinent questions about practitioner research.' Second International Practitioner Research Conference. Sydney, Australia.

Oliver, C. (2003) *Advocacy for Children and Young People: A Review of Literature*. Understanding Children's Social Care Series No 7. London: Institute of Education, University of London.

Oliver, C. (2006) 'Advocacy: Giving Young People a Voice.' In E. Chase, A. Simon and S. Jackson. (eds) *In Care and After: A Positive Perspective*. London: Routledge.

Oliver, C., Knight, A. and Candappa, M. (2006) *Advocacy for Looked After Children and Children in Need: Achievements and Challenges*. London: Thomas Coram Research Unit, Institute of Education, University of London. Also available at www.dfes.gov.uk/research or www.ioe.ac.uk/tcru (accessed 21 January 2008).

Parsons, R. J. (1998) 'Evaluation of Empowerment Practice.' In L. Gutierrez, R. J. Parsons and E. O. Cox (eds) *Empowerment in Social Work Practice: A Sourcebook*. Pacific Grove, CA: Brooks Cole Publishing Company.

Piper, C. (1998) 'Child Advocacy.' In Y. J. Craig (ed.) *Advocacy, Counselling and Mediation in Casework*. London: Jessica Kingsley Publishers.

Pithouse, A., Crowley, A., Parry, S., Payne, H. and Dalrymple, J. (2005) *A Study of Advocacy Services for Children and Young People in Wales: A Key Messages Report*. Cardiff: Cardiff University School of Social Sciences/Social Inclusion Research Unit; University of North East Wales/Department of Child Health; Wales College of Medicine.

Robson, C. (1993) *Real World Research*. Oxford: Blackwell.

Smith, C. and Woodhead, K. (1999) 'Justice for Children.' In N. Parton and C. Wattam (eds) *Child Sexual Abuse: Responding to the Experiences of Children*. Chichester: Wiley.

Sohng, S. S. L. (1998) 'Research as an Empowerment Strategy.' In L. Gutierrez, R. J. Parsons and E. O. Cox (eds) *Empowerment in Social Work Practice: A Sourcebook*. Pacific Grove, CA: Brooks Cole Publishing Company.

Taylor, M. (2000) 'Children must be seen and heard.' *Community Care*, 24 February 2000. Also available at www.communitycare.co.uk/Articles/2000/02/24/4958/children-must-be-seen-and-heard.html (accessed 21 January 2008).

Timms, J. E. (1995) *Children's Representation: A Practitioner's Guide*. London: Sweet and Maxwell.

Tunnard, J. (1997) 'Mechanisms for Empowerment: Family Group Conferences and Local Family Advocacy Schemes.' In C. Cannan and C. Warren (eds) *Social Action with Children and Families: A Community Development Approach to Child and Family Welfare*. London: Routledge.

Utting, W. (1997) *People Like Us: The Report of the Review of Safeguards for Children Living Away From Home*. London: HMSO/Department of Health/Welsh Office.

Waterhouse, R. (2000) *Lost in Care: Report of Tribunal of Inquiry into the Abuse of Children in Care in the Former County Council Areas of Gwynedd and Clwyd since 1974.* London: The Stationery Office.

Welsh Assembly Government (2002) *Framework for Partnership: Children and Young People's Framework Planning Guidance.* Cardiff: Welsh Assembly Government.

Welsh Assembly Government (2003a) *National Standards for the Provision of Children's Advocacy Services.* Cardiff: Welsh Assembly Government.

Welsh Assembly Government (2003b) *Providing Effective Advocacy Services for Children Making a Complaint* Cardiff: Welsh Assembly Government.

Welsh Assembly Government (2007) *Consultation on a New Service Model for Delivering Advocacy Services for Children and Young People.* Cardiff: Children's Health and Social Care Directorate WAG.

Wertheimer, A. (1996) *Advocacy. The Rantzen Report.* London: BBS Educational Developments.

Willow, C. (1996) *Children's Rights and Participation in Residential Care.* London: National Children's Bureau.

Endnote

1 Independent visitors have statutory duties established by the 1989 Children Act, which are defined as visiting, advising and befriending any child who has had no, or only infrequent, contact with their parents for over a year.

CHAPTER 2

Setting the Scene: Funding, Patterns of Advocacy Provision and Children's Access to Advocacy Services

Christine M. Oliver

This chapter aims to set the scene for some key debates in children's advocacy by describing some of the organisational characteristics of advocacy services as they have evolved over the past two decades or so. First, evidence from a telephone survey of advocacy services in England (Oliver, Knight and Candappa 2006) is presented to establish a rudimentary 'taxonomy' of advocacy provision for children and young people. This data provides a context for exploring the relationship between current arrangements for the funding of children's advocacy services and (a) the independence and sustainability in advocacy service provision and (b) children's access to advocacy, including the development of inclusive models of advocacy practice. In relation to the funding of children's advocacy, some key questions are: can advocacy services be considered genuinely independent of commissioning agencies? What is the impact of advocacy interventions on working relationships between advocates and professionals working in children's health and social care? Can advocacy services act with vigour and confidence if, as a consequence, their funding may be reduced or withdrawn? Are advocacy services provided directly by local authorities more or less independent than those delivered by the voluntary sector? Should advocacy services be funded in a different way in the future?

Questions of funding have implications, not only for the future development of advocacy organisations, but also for the children and young people they serve. To date, children's advocacy services have evolved in a largely ad hoc way; some parts of the country are relatively well-resourced, while others have no or limited provision. Some advocacy services target specific age groups, while others strive to offer a service to children from infancy to early adulthood. Consequently, children's access to advocacy support nationally is uneven. This pattern of service provision therefore raises important issues of equity and social justice. Is it fair, for example, that an eight-year-old child in care in one local authority has access to an advocacy service while a child in similar circumstances in a neighbouring authority does not?

Further, the question of children's access to advocacy relates not only to the availability of local services, but also to the extent to which advocacy services are sufficiently well-resourced in terms of staffing, skills and time to meet the diverse needs of their young service users. Findings from the survey are therefore investigated to explore advocate's views about the facilitators and barriers to developing models of advocacy provision that are socially inclusive. Finally, the implications of debates about the funding, independence, sustainability and accessibility of advocacy services are drawn together to highlight some potential directions for the further development of children's advocacy.

About the study

Children's advocacy services were recruited to take part in the telephone survey from two key sources: the membership database of Children's Rights Officers and Advocates and local authorities making statistical returns to the Department of Health on looked after children and children in need. Only those organisations that provided individual casework advocacy as their sole activity, or as part of a wider remit, were included in the survey. A total of 98 advocacy services for children and young people were identified. Seventy-five interviews were completed (a response rate of 77 per cent). While considerable effort was made to identify the range of advocacy services available to children and young people, it is acknowledged that the sample may not be representative of advocacy provision nationally.

The fieldwork for the survey was conducted between October and December 2003. As such it provides a snapshot of service provision at a specific point in time. Nevertheless, it is hoped that this data will provide an important benchmark for later studies and offer a picture of children's advocacy which, in its broad outline, continues to be of relevance to contemporary concerns.

Defining advocacy

The majority of advocates surveyed (80%) formulated their definitions of advocacy in terms of 'speaking up' on behalf of children and young people or enabling them to 'have a voice'. The role of advocacy in helping children to 'put their views across' by themselves was sometimes described as the 'ultimate goal' of advocacy. The adult advocacy role in this respect was sometimes described as 'amplifying' the young person's voice, or acting as:

> a megaphone for young people; listening to children and young people and repeating in a louder way using my power as an adult and a professional in an arena that might not be easy for young people to do that.
>
> (Susan, advocate)

While articulating broadly similar definitions of advocacy, some advocates also emphasised the importance of ensuring that children and young people's views are *actively listened to*, and taken account of, in decision-making. In terms of identifying guiding principles for advocacy, key themes were that advocacy should aim to be child-led and informed by a children's rights perspective:

> Our advocacy work is underpinned by the UN Convention of the Rights of the Child – Article 12 – and that children have rights to express their views and to have their views taken seriously.
>
> (Peter, advocate)

The decision about whether the advocate would speak on behalf of a young person, or support a young person to speak for themselves, was linked to the perceived self-confidence, ability or wishes of the child. In these circumstances, one advocate reported that 'you are guided by the child in terms of how far you represent, mediate or act as a conduit for their voice'. Others highlighted what advocacy should *not* be about: namely, an involvement in deciding what might be in the 'best interests' of the child. Providing advice, information and support to enable young people to negotiate bureaucratic processes were also highlighted as key functions of advocacy. Surprisingly, only a minority of advocates described their role as helping young people to gain access to needed services.

In summary, dominant understandings of advocacy among advocates comprised:

- *representing* young people's views
- *empowering* young people to speak for themselves (or *self-advocate*)
- providing *advice and information*
- fostering greater *accountability* on the part of service providers to children and young people
- helping young people to gain *access to needed services.*

Two key guiding principles for advocacy practice were identified, namely that advocacy should:

- be child-led
- operate within a children's rights framework.

A taxonomy of children's advocacy services

Funding

Turning now to the development of advocacy services for children and young people over the past two decades or so, findings from the telephone survey of advocacy services show that only a small minority (7%) were established before 1990. The majority have a more recent history, over half (59%) having been established in the four-year period between 1996 and 2000. After 2000, the pace of growth appeared to slow down (Table 2.1). This indicates that the funding made available under the Quality Protects initiative (Department of Health 1998) to promote children's participation in decisions about their care provided an important impetus to the growth in the number of children's advocacy services during the late 1990s. It is possible that the 2002 Adoption and Children Act, which places a duty on local authorities to provide advocacy services to children wishing to make a complaint under the 1989 Children Act, will have had a further impact on the number of advocacy services established since the survey was undertaken.

Children's advocacy has evolved within a tradition of voluntarism which, historically, has allowed for the introduction of innovative and radical approaches to enduring social problems – in this case, the persistent exclusion of looked after children and young people in decisions about their care. Survey findings showed that just over half (54%) of advocacy services were delivered by a national children's voluntary organisation (Figure 2.1) and almost a quarter (23%) were delivered directly by the local authority. A

Table 2.1: Advocacy services for looked after children and children in need, date of establishment, 1970–2003

n=75

Date	No.	%
1970–1975	1	1
1976–1980	1	1
1981–1985	0	0
1986–1990	4	5
1991–1995	10	13
1996–2000	44	59
2001–2003	14	19
Total	74	98

(n=1 no response)

fifth of advocacy services were delivered by local voluntary organisations (20% n=15).[1] Taken together, voluntary organisations provided more than three-quarters (76%) of the advocacy services included in the survey. The four national voluntary organisations most frequently cited (in order) were the Children's Society, NCH (then National Children's Home), Barnardo's, and the NSPCC. However, it should be noted that only the head offices of the former Voice of the Child in Care (now Voice), and National Youth Advocacy Service were included in the survey and that their profile in provision of advocacy nationally is therefore higher than the survey findings suggest.[2]

The majority of advocacy services surveyed (56%) received their entire funding from their host local authority. Almost a quarter (23%) of advocacy services were funded by a combination of core funding from the local authority, plus a contribution (typically between 20% and 30%) from the voluntary organisation delivering the service – an arrangement that the larger children's charities would find easier to achieve. A fifth of advocacy organisations (20%) relied upon a varied mix of funding sources, such as local authorities, health trusts, Connexions services, the National Lottery Children's Fund, and other charitable sources. Only one advocacy service provided by a national voluntary organisation was reported as relying entirely on resources generated by its own fundraising department.

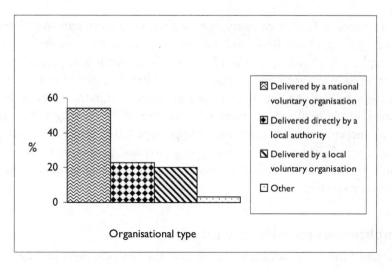

Figure 2.1: The delivery of advocacy services: organisational type – n = 75

Targeting of advocacy services

Commissioning agencies have had a key role to play in shaping how children's advocacy services are targeted. Findings from the telephone survey showed that the vast majority (85%)[3] were targeted at children in public care. Just under half (48%) of advocacy services interviewed offered advocacy to both looked after children *and* children in need. The term 'children in need' was variously defined as 'according to the provisions of the Children Act', disabled children in respite care, children involved in family disputes, and as children subject to child protection processes. On occasion, children and young people considered 'at risk' were also included in this group, such as young women at risk of sexual exploitation, young people seeking asylum, and homeless young people. Over a third (37%) offered advocacy for looked after children and care leavers *only*. A small minority of advocacy services (12%) were specialist services, targeted at disabled children and young people, and young people in secure juvenile justice or mental health settings.

The majority of advocacy services (53%) also utilised age group as a key criteria for defining their target group but there were also wide variations in the age groups cited. Some advocacy services, for example, reported that they targeted children from infancy to an upper age limit of 18 years, 24 years, 25 years or 26 years. Others set their lower age limit at 8, 10 or 11 years. A further category operated within a more narrowly defined lower and upper age limit, and was generally targeted at adolescents (for example, 11–18 years, or 12–17 years). These variations, particularly in relation to lower age limits, suggest that children's capacities to engage in decision-making are widely perceived as age-related, rather than as determined by adults' abilities to work with children of different ages and stages in an inclusive way. The setting of upper age limits tends to reflect the extent to which care leavers and young disabled people in transition to adult services are included within the spectrum of potential users of advocacy services.

Implications for advocacy practice

Current funding arrangements have important implications for the independence of, and children's access to, advocacy services.

Independence of advocacy services

The funding of advocacy services raises important questions about their ability to act with vigour and confidence without regard to the views of their commissioning bodies. Standard 6 of the National Advocacy Standards (Department of Health 2002) states that advocacy services should, as far as possible, be 'funded and managed in a way that ensures independence from the commissioning body, so that children and young people have confidence that their advocates will act for them and are free from any conflicts of interest' (p.10). While some advocacy services may be wary of funders' powers to constrain or limit the activity of advocates, it has also been suggested that funding contracts can provide a useful means for setting measurable objectives and targets and for clarifying the role of advocates (Children's Commissioner for Wales 2003). Ideally, funding contracts should include clear statements regarding advocacy's independence, and information on how potential conflicts of interest should be addressed (Baillie 2002; Henderson and Pochin 2001). It is notable that less attention has been paid to the potential for conflict of interest when voluntary organisations are contracted by a local authority to provide an advocacy service *and* to provide care services for children. It is as yet unclear how many of such voluntary organisations make arrangements for children in their care to obtain access to independent advocacy support from an alternative source.

The question of independence was considered at length by advocates working for externally commissioned advocacy services, and advocates employed directly by their local authority. Almost half (47%) of advocates interviewed acknowledged the impact of funding contracts (sometimes referred to as service level agreements) on their work, for example on the targeting of the service and in relation to monitoring and evaluation requirements. However, many were also quick to report that the influence was generally a positive one and that they perceived their relationship with their funder as a 'partnership' that enabled the advocacy service to participate in local decision-making fora and to have an influence on local policy developments. Indeed, in some cases, it was reported that the voluntary organisations delivering advocacy had more influence on the local authority than vice versa.

> Because we are funded by the local authority, we see ourselves as working in partnership, but also independently. The advantage is that we meet regularly with people who make decisions and give us a clear mandate for our actions. Social services accept our role, though sometimes they say we are a thorn in their flesh!
>
> (Gill, advocacy service manager)

However, a minority (17%) reported the influence of funding contracts as generally negative in their impact, citing excessive monitoring requirements, control of work plans and priorities, the setting of unrealistic targets, and restrictions placed on the groups of children and young people advocates were permitted to work with.

> With a smaller and less bureaucratic partner, we would be able to be more flexible and creative and there wouldn't be such a culture of suspicion about what we're doing.
>
> (Dorothy, advocacy service manager)

> We're renegotiating it [the service level agreement] and the local authority will put in specific bits of work they want us to do, which will divert time away from the advocacy service because of limited resources. But the local authority has blocked an advocacy referral because they said it would be in contempt of court, and we could not speak to them... There are serious questions concerning our independence.
>
> (Lisa, advocacy service manager)

Overall, findings were not conclusive on the perceived desirability (or not) of advocacy being delivered directly by local authorities (and the lack of independence implied by this arrangement). One advocate employed by a local authority expressed forceful views about the difficulties of her position:

> The service should be moved out of the local authority to protect the independence of the service. We are under enormous pressure to toe the party line. The role also becomes very confused being in-house.
>
> (Petra, advocate)

However, a second advocate challenged the assumption that services provided directly by local authorities are not independent, and that those provided by voluntary organisations necessarily are independent:

> I feel very irritated with the constant theme of independence. Voluntary groups are pushing children's rights so they would say it needs to be independent. But no one is fully independent. I have known some children's rights officers leave their job because they felt restricted by the service level agreement. I can understand why some people are concerned about in-house services, but if I'm allowed to be independent, I have more ability to be accepted. The local authority sees me as part of their trying to improve their services.
>
> (Kevin, advocate)

In general, the evidence suggests that the notion of organisational 'independence' represents something of a continuum rather than a rigid or fixed phenomenon. Some local authorities appear to perceive advocacy services as an extension of their own provision for children in their care, seemingly unaware that the advocacy role is to stand firmly by the child, regardless of the local authority's views or care plans for the child. Other local authorities appeared to have a greater capacity to protect the independence of advocacy services by establishing clear role and organisational boundaries, while also allowing for a collaborative approach to addressing problems and complaints raised by young people. Findings also indicate that the independence of advocacy services provided directly by local authorities can be enhanced or constrained by their location (in local authority premises, or in separate and community-based premises), by the degree of clarity (or confusion) in management structure and supervision arrangements, and by the extent of support (or resistance) on the part of senior managers and front-line staff towards children's participation in decisions about their care.

Working with health and social care professionals

A further factor having a potentially important impact on the independence of advocacy services concerns the ways in which both advocates and social care professionals respond to the conflict that is an inevitable part of the advocacy role. Indeed, Atkinson (1999, p.27) argues that 'the more separate and independent it [advocacy] is, the most likely advocates are to encounter resistance from services, and to experience the reality of institutional barriers'. Developing constructive professional relationships with social care professionals might therefore be expected to represent a challenging aspect of advocacy work. While our survey showed some evidence in support of this hypothesis, a majority of advocates (59%) reported a generally positive relationship with providers of children's services:

> There is mutual respect, but we're not too pally, which is as it should be.
>
> (Pat, advocate)

However, others felt that challenging decision-making while maintaining a positive working relationship with social work and other professionals represented one of the most difficult aspects of advocacy work. Over a third of advocates (35%) said that professional relationships could change rapidly from negative to positive, or vice versa. This was attributed to a number of factors, including differences in attitude between social work teams, or as a result of the differing views and personalities of the individual professionals involved, including the extent to which they felt personally and professionally attacked by advocacy interventions. One advocate described her relationship with the local authority in the following terms:

> Up and down. There are lots of different social work teams in the area and they are all quite different. The relationship is down to the perception of the social worker and how positively they view advocacy. Also, some specific cases can be challenging, especially about individual practice.
>
> (Linda, advocacy service manager)

A small minority described their relationship with providers of children's services as generally negative:

> It's difficult, and very difficult at times. Certainly social workers have said they take things personally. My argument is that the only way to improve the service is by registering complaints.
>
> (Catherine, advocacy service manager)

Nevertheless, survey findings indicate that professional relationships between advocates and staff working in children's services can improve over time: a majority of advocates (59%) reported that relationships had changed for the better or had been consistently good. This trend was attributed to the time and effort that was required to develop relationships of trust and to raise awareness of the advocacy role among social care professionals. The views expressed by advocates in our survey echo the findings of a study of advocacy in Scotland (including advocacy for children and young people) which identified professional resistance as common during the early stages, but that more productive working partnerships developed as staff became more familiar with the advocacy role (Lindsay 1997). This latter study also found that, in a minority of cases, tensions between advocates and social care staff were resistant to change, and that attitudes to children's participation in decision-making represented a key mediating factor. Similarly, findings from our survey showed that almost a fifth (19%) reported that professional relationships either were unpredictable or had deteriorated over time. Factors that contributed to pressurised or difficult professional relationships included high levels of staff turnover in social work teams, and a resistance to advocacy on the part of staff working directly with children and young people.

These challenges highlight a key question: how far can advocacy services act on children's behalf without fear of losing their funding? Almost half (48%) of advocates interviewed reported that they were confident that they would continue to be grant-aided by their current funder – most obviously those advocacy services that enjoyed a constructive relationship with their commissioning agency. However, over a quarter (29%) expressed uncertainty about their future funding, and a small minority (5%)[4] anticipated that their funding contract would be terminated. Insecure funding and short-term funding commitments were cited as contributing to difficulties in retaining advocacy staff, and might be seen as both a cause and a consequence of conflicted professional relationships and resistance to, or confusion about, the advocacy role.

> Our contract will be withdrawn at the end of March. The level of communication with the local authority is abysmal. We understand that they are going for an in-house service.
>
> (Trisha, advocacy service manager)

> Originally, the service was established until 2004 and then they told us we were extended for another year, but now it's uncertain and we are trying to get that agreed. We only get six-monthly commitments.

(Joan, advocacy service manager)

Thus, a degree of instability is a persistent feature of advocacy provision as one service is replaced by an alternative provider, or taken 'in-house'. This instability is likely to have an impact on the capacity of advocacy services to build relationships of trust with children and young people, and providers of children's services. It also has an impact on the promotion of advocacy support among potential service users.

Children's access to advocacy services

Current funding arrangements also have an impact on the targeting of advocacy services, and therefore children's access to them. As we have seen, the vast majority of children's advocacy services are targeted at looked after children and children considered 'in need', although there is also considerable variation in the criteria for access to advocacy support established by funders. Age is a key variable in this respect. Young children (variously defined as children under five, eight or ten years) were often placed beyond the remit of advocacy services. More informally, the placing of 'roadblocks', or the practice of gate-keeping, was also identified as a particularly strong feature of advocacy work with young children:

> Our youngest referral is 5 to 6 years old, and our biggest issue is allocating an advocate. We find roadblocks. We are told we can't talk to them, that 'we [social workers] have their best interests at heart', especially when a child is put up for adoption. Social services have said we don't want you visiting them.

(Mary, advocate)

Similarly, not all advocacy services were commissioned to work with disabled children or children involved in child protection processes. In relation to disabled children, some advocacy services perceived disabled children's teams as adopting an advocacy-oriented approach to their work and that, consequently, they could not provide any additional benefit. Providing support for children in child protection conferences was reported as a growing area of work for some advocacy services, but for others attitudinal barriers on the part of health and social care professionals represented an enduring problem:

> The local authority is not keen to support advocacy for child protection. They say it's inappropriate.
>
> (Ella, advocacy service manager)

A further factor that emerged as limiting access to advocacy concerned the tendency for some children to 'disappear' from the purview of advocacy services. Some local authorities, for example, routinely removed children from the child protection register once they entered the care system. In these circumstances, advocacy services working with looked after children reported that they had limited scope for engaging in child protection concerns because such children were no longer deemed by the local authority to be 'at risk'. Some looked after children 'disappeared' from the local authority list of looked after children when they entered a secure setting, such as a juvenile justice or psychiatric unit:

> We are not aware of any work with mental health services. When a child is in prison or a mental health establishment, they are taken off the LAC [looked after children] list. We have made contact with an advocacy service in a local mental health hospital, but these young people disappear.
>
> (Jackie, advocate)

Similarly, an advocacy service that successfully addressed the issue of homophobic bullying in children's homes suddenly found that this area of work was no longer required:

> We would like to pursue issues of sexuality, and we have a support group for young people experiencing homophobic bullying. But this work is now outside our contract area.
>
> (Rachel, advocacy service manager)

These external factors influencing children's access to advocacy may be further compounded, or limited, by the skills, knowledge and resources that advocates have to work effectively with children from a wide range of social backgrounds and with varying capacities to engage in decision-making. A review of advocacy services in Wales found that inadequate attention had been given to reaching children in public care who are doubly disadvantaged, such as children from minority ethnic backgrounds, disabled children and younger children (Children's Commissioner for Wales 2003).

Developing inclusive advocacy practice

Working as an advocate with children of different ages, ethnic origins, disabilities and genders requires a complex range of skills. The development of the *National Standards for the Provision of Children's Advocacy Services* (Department of Health 2002) was informed, at least in part, by a concern to promote advocacy services that are socially inclusive and anti-discriminatory. Standard 3, for example, aims to ensure that children who use advocacy services are not discriminated against due to age, gender, race, culture, religion, language, disability or sexual orientation. The National Standards also recommend that children should be enabled to work with an advocate of their choice. In the context of promoting equal opportunities, ideally, provision should be made to allow a child to work with an advocate of the same gender, ethnicity, disability or other shared identity, if they so wish. The composition of the advocacy workforce is therefore an important issue:

> Eighty per cent of our users in the last six months have been Black and ethnic minority children. We try to reflect this in the images we use on our publicity, and ensure that the staff team reflects different cultures.

> (Jean, advocate)

However, survey findings indicate that the vast majority of children's advocates are female (76%) and white (88%) and only a small minority of advocates described themselves as having a disability. Most advocacy services therefore have limited opportunities to offer children a choice of advocacy according to gender, ethnic or cultural identity, or disability. Over a quarter of advocacy services that participated in the survey were also single-worker projects (27%); lone advocates experience particular constraints in meeting the diverse communication and other needs of their service users.

Given these constraints, how, then, have advocates sought to develop a socially inclusive model of practice? Overall, findings indicate that advocacy services have attempted to respond to social diversity in the looked after population by:

- making *referrals* to specialist advocacy services
- making *links* with other specialist services, workers or voluntary organisations
- setting up *support* groups
- *recruiting* a socially diverse workforce

- producing relevant *publicity*.

A minority of advocacy services provided examples of initiatives taken to address diverse needs according to ethnicity, disability, gender, age, mental health and sexuality. Some advocacy services, for example, employed staff skilled in communicating with disabled children, while others learned such skills 'on the job' or compensated for their own lack of time or skills by drawing on local resources and specialist skills:[5]

> We tend to work with disabled children through their school as they have the resources that enable children to communicate, for example, with computers, or eye point cards.

> (Pat, advocate)

Only a minority of advocacy services worked with young children but the issues raised by advocates echoed many of the themes that emerged in working with disabled children, highlighting a lack of training or the time-consuming nature of the work. Nevertheless, a variety of means for working with young children was described, including the use of play and drama:

> We've planned a party for 0 to 14 year olds in foster care and respite care to introduce the idea of children's rights in a subtle way. For example, we have a puppet called Wish Wizard. Drama groups can be very empowering and they can provide an opportunity for children to meet us.

> (Uma, advocate)

Gender was almost universally discounted as an important consideration in the development of an inclusive approach to advocacy practice. Mental health issues were generally given less attention than other sources of social diversity and discrimination. Very little concrete action was reported in relation to young people with mental health problems, except in the case of specialist mental health advocacy services. Some advocates had lobbied to improve young people's access to local mental health services or made a conscious effort to liaise with specialist mental health teams or health posts, such as nurses for looked after children

> We have identified some work on mental health issues and there is a good LAC [looked after children] nurse; we are producing a new health information booklet and have done casework on psychiatric assessments and detention.

> (Kim, advocate)

In general, it would appear that, despite limited resources, a range of different strategies has been developed by advocacy services to meet the diverse needs of their users. However, progress has been uneven and there is a need to share good practice, and to make training in the development of socially inclusive models of advocacy practice more widely available.

Some conclusions and signposts for the future

Currently, there are wide variations between different local authorities in numbers of looked after children and children in need, and advocacy services are more available in some areas of the country than in others. Overall, the research reported on here shows that there is considerable variation in the children and young people targeted by advocacy services in relation to age group, disability and status as 'in need'. Children in out-of-area placements, residential institutions, and secure units have limited access to advocacy services. Children seeking asylum were also reported as experiencing particular difficulties in gaining access to advocacy support.

Arguably, looked after children and children in need should be entitled to a comparable standard of service wherever they live as a matter of equity. Both providers of children's services and advocacy services have an important part to play in this regard, and their collaboration could make a significant contribution to ensuring that children's access to advocacy services is a matter of choice, and not solely the result of chance. A key issue, therefore, concerns how advocacy services may be funded in the future. Should advocacy services continue to be funded in an ad hoc way, based on the principles of voluntarism and of local control? An argument in favour of continuing with current funding arrangements is that it might protect children's advocacy from the politically neutralising effects of assimilation into mainstream service provision. Alternatively, children's voluntary organisations might be said to have a vested interested in maintaining the current fragmented pattern of service provision, even though many children and young people may be disadvantaged by it. Additionally, a serious drawback of this approach is that children's advocacy would continue to develop, or decline, in a piecemeal fashion, ever dependent on the insecure and fluctuating financial resources of children's services.

Could a regional pattern of provision be preferable? This might entail commissioning agencies and advocacy organisations negotiating service agreements that ensure the wider availability of advocacy geographically, and in relation to *all* children in public care and children in need. An advantage of this approach is that the provision of children's advocacy could be extended to cover a broader geographical area and a wider constituency of children and young people. Militating against this trend, however, is the policy drive towards ever greater decentralisation which, while giving local authorities more control over the allocation of resources, also creates something akin to a 'postcode lottery' in the provision of children's advocacy and other services.

Perhaps the key and foremost question should be: is it time for children in public care to have access to advocacy as of right? It is acknowledged that the 2002 Adoption and Children Act, which places a duty on local authorities to provide advocacy services to children wishing to make a complaint under the 1989 Children Act, strengthens the formal status of children's advocacy by giving it a statutory basis. However, the terms of the Act may lead to the narrowing of the focus of children's advocacy towards formal complaints procedures, and away from the provision of support in more informal ways and in relation to everyday concerns. If such a trend develops it may be regrettable, since it is widely documented that children find formal complaints procedures alienating and that only a small minority seek to resolve their problems in this way. The recent Green Paper, *Care Matters: Transforming the Lives of Children and Young People in Care* (DfES 2006) highlights the potential role of advocacy in achieving greater parity between children in public care and their peers. However, the advocacy role as defined in the Green Paper is, at present, conflated with other roles (such as that of independent visitors) and is therefore far too elastic a definition to be considered 'fit for purpose'. An alternative strategy could be to retain the definition and role of advocacy as set out in the National Standards (Department of Health 2002), to give all children in public care access to an advocate as of right, and to provide a centralised source of funding as a means of securing genuine organisational independence from providers of children's services.

Debates about the current pattern of services provision also speak to wider concerns about the value and desirability of targeting advocacy services at specific groups of children and young people as compared with a universal model of service provision. The question arises: should advocacy services be open to *all* children and young people who express a need for advocacy support? Taking a pragmatic view, and given limitations on funding, it is perhaps both understandable and ethical that the needs of looked after children and children in need should be given priority. The disadvantage of this approach is that it maintains looked after children and children in need within a welfare model of advocacy service provision which might be perceived both as inherently stigmatising and as shoring up those children's services that are demonstrably failing to improve the life chances of children in public care. This approach might also be criticised for preventing looked after children and children 'in need' from joining with their peers to agitate for greater equality for all children as a social group.

Questions about the future direction of advocacy services should not deflect from current issues and concerns in advocacy practice. Findings show that organisational cultures can have a major role to play in shaping receptivity or resistance to the advocacy role and to children's participation in decisions about their care. In this context, the development of constructive working relationships between advocates and professionals working in children's health and social care is a key concern, at least under current funding arrangements. Nevertheless, a majority of advocates reported that working relationships were, on the whole, positive and improved over time. However, a considerable minority of advocates described working relationships with commissioning agencies as volatile and that this created insecurity with regard to the sustainability of advocacy services, with concomitant effects on their capacity to raise awareness of advocacy among potential users, and to develop relationships of trust with children as well as with providers of children's services.

Obviously, children in public care and children considered 'in need' do not represent a homogenous group; first and foremost, they are individuals with a particular set of personal strengths and their wishes for their future. They also represent diverse identities according to their age, gender, ethnicity, disability, sexuality or mental health status. Their personal circumstances may also vary widely: a Black child may be placed in foster care in a predominantly white rural area; a disabled child may be living at home or in residential care; a young person leaving care will have very different needs and personal resources compared with a very young child placed in foster care. This raises important issues about how an inclusive model of advocacy practice might be developed and shared. Findings show that advocates have identified many constructive ways of working with children experiencing multiple forms of discrimination, and often with very limited resources. However, there would appear to be room for improving advocacy practice in this respect, particularly in relation to Black and minority ethnic children, disabled children, young children and children with mental health problems.

References

Atkinson, D. (1999) *Advocacy: A Review*. Brighton: Pavilion.

Baillie, D. (2002) 'The Legal Context of the Advocacy Service.' In B. Gray and R. Jackson (eds) *Advocacy and Learning Disability*. London: Jessica Kingsley Publishers.

Children's Commissioner for Wales (2003) *Telling Concerns: A Report of the Children's Commissioner for Wales' Review of the Operation of Complaints and Representations and Whistleblowing Procedures and Arrangements for the Provision of Children's Advocacy Services.* Wales: Children's Commissioner for Wales Office.

Department of Health (1998) *The Quality Protects Programme: Transforming Children's Services.* London: HMSO.

Department of Health (2002) *National Standards for the Provision of Children's Advocacy Services.* London: Department of Health.

DfES (2006) *Care Matters: Transforming the Lives of Children and Young People in Care. Consultation document.* London: DfES.

Henderson, R. and Pochin, M. (2001) *A Right Result? Advocacy, Justice and Empowerment.* Bristol: The Policy Press.

Lindsay, M. (1997) 'Balancing power: advocacy in a Scottish health board.' *Research, Policy and Planning 15*, 2, 31–33.

Oliver, C., Knight, A. and Candappa, M. (2006) *Advocacy for Looked After Children and Children in Need: Achievements and Challenges.* Thomas Coram Research Unit/DfES. Also available at www.ioe.ac.uk/tcru and www.dfes.gov.uk/research (accessed 24 January 2008).

Endnotes

1   This does not include local branches of national voluntary organisations. Local voluntary organisations are defined as those originating in the locality, operating with the local authority or region.

2   See Chapter 6 for further information on the work of Voice.

3   Please note that figures add up to more than 100% as many advocacy services targeted more than one group.

4   Figures do not add up to 100% as responses were not recorded in 28% of cases.

5   See Chapter 7 for a more detailed exploration of approaches to working with disabled children.

CHAPTER 3

An Analysis of the Role of Advocacy in Promoting Looked After Children's Participation in Statutory Reviews

Jane Boylan

It is over 20 years since the publication of *Gizza Say?* (Stein and Ellis 1982), which exposed looked after children's exclusion and marginalisation from statutory review meetings. The research called for greater participation of young people in reviews and access to representation. Since then there have been a number of welcome changes to policy and practice pertaining to children's participation in reviews. Whilst there is broad agreement that children's participation in reviews is a good thing, the meaning of participation remains contested (Braye 2000). This chapter draws on empirical qualitative research undertaken with looked after children and young people to explore what they have to say about participation in review meetings and the impact of advocacy two decades on from *Gizza Say?* The chapter begins by locating children's participation in reviews in the context of wider moves to promote children's participatory rights.

Background and context for children's participation

There is wealth of research exposing the disempowering elements children and young people encounter in participating in decision-making arenas such as statutory review meetings (Boylan 2005; Buchanan, Wheal and Coker 1993; Franklin 1995; Lansdown 1997; Thomas and O'Kane 1999; Thomas 2000; Willow 1998). There is also a substantial body of knowledge concerning the case for, and the promotion of, children's participatory rights and the value of advocacy in this context (Boylan and Dalrymple 2006; Boylan and Ing 2005; Thomas and O'Kane, 1999; Utting 1997). It is therefore timely to access children's perspectives on their experiences of review meetings and the role of advocacy.

Increasing children's participation in decision-making is an important dimension of Government thinking. Government has to some extent sought to operationalise a number of measures that promote looked after children's visibility in decision-making and recognises the importance of children's perspectives. The National Child Care Strategy, Quality Protects (Department of Health 1998), the Government's Priorities for Children's Services (Department of Health 2001), and more recently the Children Act 2004, reiterated children's right to be listened to by service providers. Moreover there is an imperative to empower children and young people to shape and inform services that are responsive to what children and young people want. The need for disabled children to access advocacy has also been recognised in policy initiatives and The National Service Framework for Children, Young People and Maternity Services (Department of Health DfES 2004) emphasises the need to consult and involve young people. Standard 8 places an obligation on professionals to ensure that disabled children with complex communication needs are not excluded from decision-making. These developments have been a driving force in reforming children's services. There is now greater delineation of children's citizenship and participatory rights congruent with principles embedded in Articles 12 and 13 of the United Nations Convention on the Rights of the Child 1989. One of the key principles of the Convention is the promotion of young people's participation and their involvement in decision-making. Participation rights are promoted under a number of Articles: Article 12 (i) is at 'the heart of the participatory provisions' (Flekkoy and Kaufman 1997, p.32) which provide a qualified right to children, stating 'Governments shall assure to the child who is capable of forming his or her own views the right to express those views freely in all matters affecting the child.' Moreover, 12 (ii) clarifies this further:

> For this purpose the child shall in particular be provided with the opportunity to be heard in judicial and administrative proceedings affecting the child, either directly, or through a representative or an appropriate body, in manner consistent with the procedural rules of national law.

The reference to 'administrative proceedings' would include looked after children's statutory review meetings. In this regard, the opportunity for the child's voice to be heard through a 'representative' supports the case for someone to act as an advocate for the child. The Children Act 1989 and the Children Act 2004 require that looked after children of sufficient age and understanding are consulted about decisions concerning their initial placement and ongoing plans and decision-making (Brammer 2007; Fortin 1998).

Article 13 requires that children have the right to receive and impart information and freedom of expression. Article 10 of the European Convention on Human Rights (as incorporated into the Human Rights Act 1998) reinforces this aspect, providing: 'everybody has the right to freedom of expression. The rights shall include freedom to hold opinions and to receive and impart information and ideas without interference by public authority.' These Articles act as levers to promote children's rights to receive information in review meetings and for someone to act as an advocate for the child. The Convention places a moral obligation on researchers to enable children to have a voice in research. Whilst such developments are encouraging it has long been recognised that children may experience difficulty in exercising their rights or having them recognised by others. This has led to calls for advocacy provision and in the past ten years there has been a proliferation of advocacy services for children and young people.

Advocacy is now recognised as having an important role in supporting children and promoting their right to be involved in decision-making (Boylan and Boylan 1998; Boylan and Ing 2005; Dalrymple 2004). Advocacy is therefore inextricably linked with concepts of empowerment and social justice. However, the definition and meaning of advocacy is contested (Brandon 1995; Boylan and Dalrymple 2006; Flekkoy and Kaufman 1997; John 1996; Kagan 1997). For Melton (1987, p.357) advocacy should aim to:

> empower children, enabling them to make use of societal resources. Child advocates endeavor to raise the status of children and increase the responsiveness and accountability of the institutions affecting them. Advocacy consists of social action on behalf of children whether to increase their self-determination or to enhance the social, educational and medical resources to which they are entitled. Because it involves attempts to redistribute power to reallocate resources, child advocacy is inherently political.

Other commentators have described advocacy as a 'controversial and politically daring practice' (McCall 1978, p.56). The language of participation, empowerment and choice is evident in legislation and social policy

(Department of Health 2000a, 2000b; DfES, 2004), reflecting a wider shift towards inclusion of looked after children and young people. Whilst these are welcome developments, the wider context for children's participation is complex. The constitution of modern childhood holds assumptions about children's subordinate position in society and values passivity and compliance and so constrains children's autonomy and capacity to engage in decision-making. Dominant understandings of childhood determine the social status of children and to an extent led to the slow development of children's participatory rights (Franklin 1995, 2001). Advocacy is seen as a mechanism that counters young people's disempowerment and redresses the power imbalance between looked after children and social welfare professionals they encounter. There is now statutory recognition that looked after children should have access to an independent advocate; however, the legal mandate for advocacy is limited (Boylan and Braye 2006). The Children (Leaving Care) Act 2000 requires that information is provided about the provision of advocacy to children preparing to leave the care system, and the Adoption and Children Act 2002 places a duty on local authorities to provide advocacy services for children and young people using the representation and complaints procedures. It is in this context that the research was undertaken to explore and portray young people's participation in reviews and their experiences of advocacy.

The research

The marginalisation of children and young people's voices has traditionally been mirrored in their lack of involvement in research (Alderson 1995; Boylan and Ing 2005). Children have not been directly involved as research participants but as 'objects' of interest to the research community (Alderson 2004; Alderson and Mayall 1994; Beresford 1997). Traditional approaches to research reinforce the asymmetry of power relations between researcher and researched and contribute to the invisibility of young people's perspectives. Researchers have also been criticised for not directly involving children in discussions about research methods or ethics, generating a wider debate about the ethics of research with children. Assumptions about the extent to which children are able to 'rationally, knowingly and freely give informed consent' (Robson 1998, p.102) and concerns to protect children from being pressurised into giving their informed consent have in the past been used to exclude children from research other than via adult proxies (Beresford 1997). The rights of children to give consent are epitomised in the Gillick ruling. The legal distinction of the 'Gillick competent' child focuses not on the child's chronological age, but their ability to understand what giving informed consent means. Clearly there is a need to ensure that children and young people do not feel they have to take part in research or feel pressured into doing so by adults (including researchers). It should also be recognised that it may be difficult for children to consent (or refuse) against the wishes of their parents or carers. Clearly, the ethics of research with children and with adults need very careful consideration; this is reflected in both the literature (Alderson 2000; Boylan 2005; Boyden and Ennew 1996; Mayall, 1999) and the ethical guidelines and codes of conduct that have emerged (British Sociological Association 1993; Department of Health 2002; National Children's Bureau 1993).

A central concern for this study therefore has been to take steps to promote a collaborative approach that involved children and young people at the embryonic stage of the research. Consequently, during the very early stages of the research an initial consultative workshop with young people who had recently left the care system took place to discuss issues such as the research agenda and how the research should proceed and to consider ethical issues. Early negotiations with the young people indicated that workshops were an appropriate forum for discussion and planning the research.

Negotiating access with children's gate-keepers

The process of negotiating access to young people who may wish to be involved in the study was complex and time intensive. Initially senior managers and practitioners working with, and responsible for, looked after children understandably required reassurances about the research. Some staff were protective and wanted reassurances that safeguards and guidelines were being adhered to: in particular, that the children and young people were being respected and were clear about the nature of their involvement and their right to refuse consent and to opt out of the research if they changed their minds. Access therefore had to be carefully negotiated and re-negotiated with senior managers, unit managers, foster carers and individual staff acting as gate-keepers to the young people.

The initial approach to social services took the form of a letter to the Assistant Director of the local authority, which outlined the research and requested an initial meeting to discuss possible involvement in the study. A formal meeting followed this where the research proposal and the ethical basis of the research were examined. The turgid process of negotiating access to looked after children highlighted the reliance on those who exercised power over the young people. Pole, Mizen and Bolton (1999, p.48) reflect on this tension:

> At worst, these are structures that deny the agency of children, or at best temper it. The imperatives of our research, however, meant that we were prepared to work within existing structures and to engage in compromise which, by giving us access to children, would allow us to place them at the centre.

The concepts of power, participation and rights are embodied throughout the research and have inherently influenced the research approach and the relationships formed with young people during the research journey. Themes reflecting these concepts emerge from reviewing the literature and are central to the research approach and findings discussed later in this chapter. Awareness of the sensitivities to issues of power and participatory rights have framed the research approach and informed the methodology. Therefore, a methodology informed by participatory action research and feminism evolved. The approach adopted involved workshops, mixed gender focus group discussions, qualitative in-depth individual interviews and observation of statutory review meetings. These methods were developed and adapted for use with children and young people (Lewis and Lindsay 2000).

Initially, it was envisaged that a cycle involving a focus group, followed by individual interviews with focus group participants, followed by observation of the interviewee's review meeting, would take place. Consultation with young people had suggested that the design of this pattern of interaction might lead to greater trust and increased familiarity with the researcher. However, there were a number of practical and unexpected difficulties, which necessitated a change to the research strategy. First, it became apparent in the individual interviews that young people did not appear relaxed. The dynamic of the face-to-face interview had unexpectedly reminded some young people of previous interviews with a range of professionals including the police and social workers, with negative connotations. In contrast, the focus groups were experienced as 'fun and relaxing' and 'easy to talk in'. As a central aim of the research approach was to create an environment that was safe and relaxed in which young people felt able to talk freely, in discussion with young people the decision was taken not to undertake any further individual interviews.

A diverse group of children and young people were invited to participate in the study through the local authority and an independent advocacy organisation. Consent forms designed by the young people during the consultative workshop were obtained from all young people taking part in the research. The workshops, focus groups and individual interviews were taped, transcribed and analysed. A manual qualitative analysis (Ritchie and Spencer 1994) was utilised to analyse major themes across the interviews, focus groups and observed reviews. There was a concern at this point that young people were distant from the process of analysis. There was a danger that this would result in the young people having little or no control over the interpretation of the data gathered from them, or over the generation of knowledge yielded by their accounts. Participatory research should involve sharing with young people what we as researchers know and think. The initial analysis was fed back to young people for validation and discussion during a further day workshop. A subsequent workshop took place with the young people to plan the initial dissemination of findings. Suggestions for the dissemination strategy included:

- letters to Tony Blair or someone high up in Europe
- writing a play
- making a video
- designing a poster.

It was eventually agreed that initial dissemination of findings would comprise a video and role-play produced, directed and presented by the young people. All the fieldwork took place over a 15-month period, in one local authority in the West Midlands, and involved 39 looked after children with experience of living in residential children's homes or foster placements or who were living independently. The participants included young people aged 7 to 19. The characteristics of the young people were indicative of the authority's looked after population in terms of gender, ethnicity, disability and age. The research compares the experience of children and young people who had contact with an advocate and those who had not. Participants included:

- looked after children and young people who had not had any contact with independent advocacy services
- looked after children and young people who had used advocacy services and support during the review process.

Experiences of reviews

In England, looked after children's statutory reviews are regulated under the provisions of the Review of Children's Cases Regulations 1991, and the Review of Children's Cases (Amendments) (England) Regulations 2004. Reviews are central to the planning process for looked after children and should consider the local authority plan for the child and if the child's needs are being met. The Children Act 1989 and associated guidance requires that the circumstances of looked after children are reviewed regularly: initially within four weeks of placement, again three months later and thereafter at six-monthly intervals. The review is chaired by an independent review officer who is entrusted to monitor the plan for the child and who can direct that reviews be held before the required times. Matters for consideration, who should attend and the process of consultation prior to review are prescribed. The Children Act 1989 recognises children's capacity for participation in reviews in the context of their age and understanding. Section 22 (4) requires that:

> Before making any decisions with respect to the child whom they are looking after, or proposing to look after, a local authority shall as far as is reasonably practicable, ascertain the wishes and feelings of the child.

However, while the Act is clear about the requirement to give 'due consideration' to children's views, there is less clarity about the weight that should be attached to their views. This is reflected in the accounts of children and young people in this study who felt their views were not responded to or taken seriously.

During the group discussions and individual interviews, young people were asked about their general experiences of reviews and their experience and understanding of advocacy. What emerged from these discussions was the importance of being able to understand children's participation in reviews in the wider context of their lives. For example, a significant number of young people in this study felt they had been involved in the decision to enter the care system or where they had been placed, a process that was described repeatedly as 'arranging life around us'. Not surprisingly, therefore, all the young people recalled with great clarity how daunting their first review meeting had been. Their accounts described feeling ill-prepared for the meeting both emotionally and practically.

> I just didn't know what to expect, they just told me I was going. I didn't know mum was going to be there, and I didn't know what was going to happen or what I should do.

(Clare)

Reviews in the main were found to be disempowering experiences, domi-nated by adult decision-makers and 'strangers'. Most of the young people in this study had some limited awareness and knowledge of review meetings and most were regularly invited to attend. They were able to explain in broad terms the purpose of the meeting: 'to plan things about your future' or 'where you can live' or 'what happens when you leave care'. However, none of the participants had an awareness of a review process, or distinct stages of consultation, preparation, and post-review feedback. A number of young people were unsure why they had been invited to the meeting or who would be present. This compounded existing feelings of being alone, anxious and frightened about what was going to happen.

> You know you are on your own, all right, it's just you and all those people.

(Laura)

A recurring perception of reviews was that of a number of powerful adults, including carers, parents or social welfare professionals, coming together to discuss 'our' situation and make plans for the future. Several young people described their alienation and disengagement from the review process in terms of professionals 'arranging life around us'.

Access to knowledge and information about reviews

Those young people who had not had contact with an advocate felt ill-informed about their rights and their knowledge, and access to informa-tion about reviews was piecemeal. In residential placements young people were reliant on other young people informally sharing information about their review experience and knowledge of advocacy. Some residential staff, especially those defined by young people as 'good' key workers, were regarded as an excellent source of information. A number of young people had received good and accurate information about reviews from social workers who had been proactive in providing information. This was highly valued and went some way to demystifying the review process, particularly for those who had not attended a review meeting before. Young people in foster placements were largely reliant on foster carers or social workers as providers of information and knowledge. Some foster carers took time to explain what a review was, who might be there and what the young person might want to say. They often acted as informal advocates for young people. However, there appeared to be no effective universal system for ensuring young people received accurate and up-to-date information about the review process, or their participation. Promoting young people's participation in reviews requires that professionals and carers they encounter are aware of, and actively promote, their rights.

Many young people described feeling ambivalent about the purpose of the reviews. Those who had attended felt caught in a situation where there was 'no point in going', yet, at the same time, were aware that decisions would be made in their absence and so attended in order to try to maintain a degree of control over the decision-making process and their own lives.

Self-advocacy in reviews

A degree of scepticism existed as to whether young people's self-advocacy actually made any difference to review outcomes. Attempts at self-advocacy were not experienced as empowering; on the contrary they left some young people feeling completely powerless and very frustrated. This was compounded when they had been led to believe that their views and opinions were important and would be respected. In reality it was felt that the process was a denial of opportunity to influence plans and was tokenistic. This is illustrated through Martha's experience.

Martha

Martha, aged 14, had been accommodated under the provisions of the Children Act 1989 for six weeks and was living with foster carers. The foster home was 20 miles away from her parents, school, friends and social networks and supports. Prior to coming into care she had lived at home with her parents and siblings. Martha presented as a confident and articulate young women. Since coming into care Martha had limited contact with her social worker and was unclear about future plans. Martha's foster carers had talked to her about the forthcoming review meeting. In preparation, Martha had written down her wishes and feelings. Martha did not know whether or not her parents would be attending the review meeting (she hoped so). Her schoolteacher (who she liked) was attending and had already talked to Martha about the report she had written for the review. Martha was pleased the teacher had taken time to discuss this with her and felt that at least she would have a friendly face in the meeting. Martha's foster carer had encouraged her to raise issues that were important to her at the meeting and assured Martha of her support. Martha had not seen her social worker prior to the meeting.

At the meeting

Neither of Martha's parents were to attend the meeting. Martha's mum had five other children and so it was difficult for her to attend. Martha's father was unable to take time off work, but would have attended if the meeting had been held outside his working day. The review officer explained the review process to Martha, who listened carefully and attentively. Martha was invited to raise the issues important to her. Martha asked for consideration to be given to the following:

- I would like proper arrangements for seeing my family, especially Nan; we are really close.

- I need some schoolbooks, which are at home (Martha is concerned about falling behind at school).

- I would like to see my social worker more often.

- I would like a placement closer to my home, friends, family and school. Getting to school is particularly difficult – I have to leave the foster home at 6:30am in order to get to school on time.

- I would like future reviews to be held at a time when my mum and dad can attend.

- I would like to know when I will be going home.

The outcome

- The social worker agreed to arrange contact, but was unable to explain why arrangements had not been made six weeks into placement.

- There were no placements available closer to Martha's home and school but if one became available it would be considered.

- No decision was made as to when Martha might go home.

- The next review would be held in three months' time, at 4:30pm (Martha knew her mum would be busy with the other children and her dad would be at work).

- Martha's social worker left without arranging the next visit.

Martha had worked hard preparing for the review and formulating her views and opinions; prior to the review she had been confident that she would be listened to and the issues raised would be given serious consideration. However, Martha's views were not addressed and after the meeting she said she felt:

> There was absolutely no point in bothering with all that, they ignored what I had to say and just got on with what they had to do. I shall not go again, I won't.

Martha's account illustrates how disempowering the review experience can be. Martha felt alienated and let down by the process, which she perceived as primarily fulfilling an obligation to hold a meeting and to be seen to listen to children. Martha questioned the value of being consulted only to be ignored.

The need for representation and support – experiences of advocacy

Martha's account vividly demonstrates the need for representation and support in reviews to ensure that young people are listened to and taken seriously. A recurring message has been that young people's views continue to be ignored and marginalised. Some young people repeatedly ask for information or raise concerns that are not addressed. In one observed review meeting a young person asked repeatedly about contact with siblings and requested a photograph of his parents, but neither issue was addressed.

In contrast, those young people who had access to an advocate and were clear about what an advocate was perceived their role in a positive way. The qualities children value in an advocate are well documented (Boylan and Braye 2006; Boylan and Ing 2005). Reliability, honesty, confidentiality, independence and trust were repeatedly stated by young people as being central to a positive advocacy relationship. For some young people the involvement of an advocate was the first time they had experienced this kind of relationship. Of particular importance was the professional distance between the advocate and the local authority. Repeatedly, young people living in residential placements commented that the advocate 'did not go into the office' or 'talk about you with other staff'. This clear delineation of roles was seen as a real sign of the advocate's independence and a measure of the extent to which the children could trust and respect the advocate. The advocate was perceived by most young people as a powerful person, not constrained or influenced by the local authority. However, others questioned the true independence of any advocacy service that was commissioned by the local authority and felt strongly that this contractual relationship could compromise the independence of the advocate. Independent advocates, however, did play an important function in:

- preparing for the review meeting
- listening and encouraging
- promoting self-advocacy
- exploring young people's views, opinions and anxieties
- providing information about the review process
- exploring previous experiences of review meetings
- exploring the choices open to young people, the process of decision-making and avenues of redress
- providing answers to young people's questions
- providing information and support about the representation and complaints procedure
- 'standing up' for young people
- ensuring review minutes were obtained and were child-friendly.

Advocates had a crucial role in facilitating young people's exploration of how best to negotiate and navigate their involvement in review discussions. At no point did any of the young people express a desire to always get what they wanted. On the contrary, many young people wanted reviews to be fair, transparent and a place where decision-making was negotiated rather than controlled. The overwhelming impact of an advocate's involvement was the positive relationship and their influence on review outcomes. Essentially, the advocate was seen as a reliable, listening friend, someone they could 'talk to about anything' and whose involvement had tangible outcomes. As one young person explained:

> They are there to help and their wishes and feelings don't come into it; they may not agree with what the young person wants, but they still go along with it…because it's what the young person's asking for. So mum, and she [the advocate] walked in and I was really upset and she asked me what was the matter, and I told her, and she said she'd sort it out and she did!'
>
> (Sophie)

A discussion of review documentation and minutes of the meeting illuminates another important function of the advocate. Young people felt that without the advocate's involvement they had little if any control over what was recorded in the review minutes or indeed what was not. A recurring concern was that review minutes did not always reflect the young person's understanding of discussions that had taken place, any areas of disagreement or agreed outcomes. Young people appreciated practical and emotional support to challenge the accuracy of review minutes. Advocates were found to be helpful in checking if agreed actions from earlier reviews had been actioned, and if not how this would be remedied. In doing so, advocates were able to break a cycle in which young people repeatedly question without receiving a satisfactory response. Challenging policy and practice can be an effective way of strengthening the rights of individual children and in forming the development of best practice; it also reflects a subtle and observable shift in power relations.

The relationship young people experienced with independent advocates embodied a number of interrelated and multi-faceted components: trust, use of power, reliability and independence. The issues of power and control were central in the discussion about the role of advocacy in the review process and the promotion of children's participatory rights. The primary differences between independent advocates and other professionals involved in young people's lives appear to be a combination of being independent, being powerful, being reliable and being 'on our side'. The way independent advocates exercised their power was central to the relationship, as one young person explained:

> They're all scared of [the advocate] 'cos they know that she's got the power. When [the advocate] rings up, and says 'Well, [the young person] said this, she wants more contact with her mum' and they ignore it, they know that [the advocate] will go further than that. So they're all scared of [the advocate] and what she can do.
>
> (Vicky)

While young people did not speak explicitly of their own powerlessness, they were very aware of not always being listened to or taken seriously and were also aware that this dynamic appeared to change when an advocate became involved. They recognised that power and authority were essential prerequisites to participation in reviews and saw the absence of this as a significant barrier to their self-advocacy and effective participation.

Limitations to current advocacy provision

While there is much to be welcomed in aspects of advocacy provision for looked after children, commentators such as Boylan and Braye (2006) recognise the need for a critical advocacy perspective. Accessing advocacy was difficult for some young people and others were unfamiliar with the meaning of advocacy, its relevance and the services available to them. There did not appear to be any effective mechanism for all children routinely to be provided with information about advocacy services. Children and young people are without doubt disadvantaged if they do not have access to information about sources of support and redress.

Particular barriers exist for young people living in foster placements and disabled children who may wish to access information about advocacy. The exclusion of disabled children from participating in decision-making and the importance of having the skills to communicate effectively is well documented (Beresford 1997; Morris 2002). Morris concludes that there is little evidence that disabled children who are looked after have their wishes and feelings ascertained, despite the provisions of the Children Act 1998 relating to children's consultation rights. Access to advocacy is therefore important, however in this study disabled children were significantly less likely to access advocacy (Boylan and Dalrymple 2006; Department of Health 2002; Franklin and Sloper 2006). In this study disabled children were significantly less likely to attend review meetings or have the support of an advocate than were their non-disabled counterparts.

For those young people who had not had contact with an advocate, there was some confusion about who advocates were and how, if at all, they differed from other professionals that young people had encountered. A notable example was the confusion over the respective roles of independent visitors, the independent person and advocates, and under what circumstances they might each become involved in young people's lives. There is clearly a need to differentiate between advocacy and befriending. Advocacy provision in this study was independent, focused, issue-led and tended to be short term. In contrast, the befriending role of the independent visitor was long term and activity-based. The challenge is to ensure young people (and adults) are aware of the range of people who may be able to offer support and are clear about the parameters and distinctiveness of involvement.

The recent Green Paper, *Care Matters* (DfES 2006), recognised the importance of looked after children and young people having access to advocacy. The Paper proposes the role of the independent visitor be 'revitalised' and renamed as independent advocate. While the endorsement of advocacy is welcomed, there are some concerns. A valued feature of advocates identified in this study is their independence, specialist skills, knowledge and expertise. Particularly, advocates' confidence in challenging professional practice and policy on behalf or alongside children and young people. If the proposals in the Green Paper are implemented there is potential for their distinctive roles to become blurred and diluted. The independent visitor is an unpaid volunteer, whose role is to visit, advise and befriend the young person. However, not all children have access to an independent visitor; under the terms of the Children Act 1989. Local authorities are only obliged to appoint an independent visitor in certain circumstances: children who have infrequent contact with their parents or have not had a visit from their parents in the last 12 months qualify. A further caveat is that an appointment has to be deemed to be in the child's best interests. Furthermore, not all local authorities have been able to fulfill their obligation to those who do have an entitlement to an independent visitor (NSPCC 2006). In any event the role of the independent visitor was not envisaged as one that would provide formal advocacy (Department of Health 1991). It seems timely to reflect critically and thoughtfully on the increasingly proceduralised and routinised trajectory of advocacy developments for looked after children and young people.

Conclusion

Since Stein and Ellis (1982) called for greater involvement of young people in reviews, the participation of looked after children has moved up the policy and practice agenda in the UK. There is now broad agreement that children's participation in decision-making and access to advocacy is a good thing and contributes to positive and just outcomes. Most children and young people are now attending their reviews, with the notable exception of disabled children, particularly those with complex communication needs. However, the findings of this research suggest that complex barriers still exist that curtail opportunities for young people to participate in the review process, and access to advocacy is sometimes problematic. Bringing advocacy to the reach of all looked after children has to be made a greater priority.

The messages emerging from young people's accounts suggest that whilst most looked after children and young people regularly attend their reviews, without advocacy there is a high degree of dissatisfaction with their level of participation in the review process and outcomes, compounded by a notable lack of preparation and meaningful consultation. A significant disincentive to young people's participation was their lack of faith in review outcomes. There is a real danger that without the involvement of an advocate young people will become disillusioned and fatigued by the lack of impact their participation has on review outcomes despite their very genuine efforts to participate. Research suggests that the way to overcome barriers to young people's participation in the review process is complex. It requires parallel developments, as part of a wider participation strategy that promotes a culture in which children and young people are encouraged and to make and negotiate decisions on a day-to-day basis, rather than in enforced social environments (such as reviews) involving 'strangers'. If children are to participate positively in reviews, their agendas have to form part of the process and clearly there is a need for government and commissioners of advocacy to invest further in the provision of independent advocacy to meet the diverse needs and aspirations of looked after children and young people. The wider challenge is to embrace a fundamental ideological shift in the way we think about and respond to children and young people, combined with a change in attitude to one that recognises and respects children's skills, knowledge and aspirations to shape and inform their own lives.

References

Alderson, P. (1995) *Listening To Children: Children Ethics and Social Research.* London: Barnardo's.

Alderson, P. (2000) *Listening To Children: Children Ethics and Social Research.* London: Barnardo's.

Alderson, P. (2004) 'Ethics'. In S. Fraser, V. Lewis, S. Ding, M. Kellet and C. Robinson (eds) *Doing Research with Children and Young People.* London: Sage.

Alderson, P. and Mayall, B. (eds) (1994) Children's Decisions in Health Care and Research. Report of Social Services Unit, Consent Conference Series no.5. London: Institute of Education.

Beresford, B. (1997) *Personal Accounts Involving Disabled Children in Research.* Norwich: Social Policy Research Unit.

Boyden, J. and Ennew, J. (1996) 'Childhood and Policymakers: Comparative Study on the Globalisation Of Childhood.' In A. Prout and A. James (eds) *Reconstructing Childhood: Contemporary Issues in the Sociological Study of Childhood.* Basingstoke: Falmer Press.

Boylan, J. (2005) '"Reviewing Your Review"; A critical analysis of looked after children's participation in reviews and the impact of advocacy.' PhD thesis, University of Stafforshire.

Boylan, J. and Boylan, P. (1998) 'Empowering young people: advocacy in North Wales.' *Representing Children 11,* 1, 42–49.

Boylan, J. and Braye, S. (2006) 'Paid, professionalized and proceduralised: can legal and policy frameworks for child advocacy give voice to children and young people?' *Journal Social Welfare and Family Law 28*, 3–4, 591–607.

Boylan, J. and Dalrymple, J. (2006) 'Contemporary advocacy: Practice for children and young people.' *ChildRight 22*, 3, Feb., 28–30.

Boylan, J. and Ing, P. (2005) '"Seen but not heard" – young people's experience of advocacy.' *International Journal of Social Welfare 14*, 1, 2–12.

Brammer, A. (2007) *Social Work Law* (2nd edition). London: Pearson Longman.

Brandon, D. (1995) *Advocacy: Power to People with Disabilities*. Birmingham: Venture Press.

Braye, S. (2000) 'Participation and Involvement in Social Care: An Overview.' In H. Kemshall and R. Littlechild (eds) *User Involvement and Participation in Social Care: Research Informing Practice*. London: Jessica Kingsley Publishers.

British Sociological Association (1993) *Guidelines for Good Professional Conduct and Statement of Professional Ethics*. London: British Sociological Association.

Buchanan, A., Wheal, A. and Coker, R. (1993) *Answering Back: A Report by Young People Being Looked After by the Children Act 1989*. Southampton: CEDR, Department of Social Work, University of Southampton.

Dalrymple, J. (2004) 'Developing the concept of professional advocacy: an examination of the child and youth advocates.' *Journal of Social Work 4*, 2, 181–199.

Department for Education and Skills (DfES) (2006) *Care Matters: Transforming the Lives of Children and Young People in Care*. London: The Stationery Office.

Department of Health (1991) *The Children Act 1989, Guidance and Regulations, Volume 4, Residential Care*. London: The Stationery Office.

Department of Health (1998) *Quality Protects: Objectives for Social Services for Children*. Wetherby: The Stationery Office.

Department of Health (2001) *Children Act Now: Messages from Research*. London: Routledge.

Department of Health (2002) *Research Governance: Framework for Health and Social Care*. London: HMSO.

Department of Health (2002a) *Listening, Hearing and Responding*. London: HMSO.

Department of Health and DfES (2004) *Get It Sorted. Providing Effective Advocacy Services for Children and Young People Making a Complaint under the Children Act 1989*. London: Department for Education and Skills.

Flekkoy, M.G. and Kaufman, N.H. (1997) *The Participation Rights of the Child: Rights and Responsibilities in Family and Society*. London: Jessica Kingsley Publishers.

Franklin, A. and Sloper, T. (2006) *Participation of Disabled Children and Young People in Decision-making relating to Social Care*. York: The University of York.

Franklin, B. (1995) The Case for Children's Rights: A Progress Report.' In B. Franklin (ed.) (1995) *Children's Rights: Comparative Policy and Practice*. London: Routledge.

Franklin, B. (2001) 'The Case for Children's Rights: A Progress Report.' In B. Franklin (ed.) (1995) *Children's Rights: Comparative Policy and Practice*, second edition. London: Routledge.

Fortin, J. (1998) *Children's Rights and the Developing Law* (1st edition). London: Butterworths.

John, M. (ed.) (1996) *Children in Charge: The Child's Right to a Fair Hearing.* London: Jessica Kingsley Publishers.

Kagan, C. (1997) *Agencies and Advocates.* (n.p.): NWDT.

Lansdown, G. (1997) 'Children's rights and the law.' *Representing Children 10*, 4, 213–223.

Lewis, G. and Lindsay, A. (2000) *Researching Children's Perspectives.* Buckingham: Open University Press.

Mayall, B. (1999) *Children, Health and the Social Order.* Buckingham: Open University Press.

McCall, G.J. (1978) 'The Advocate Social Scientist: A Cross-Disciplinary Perspective. In G.H. Weber and G.J. McCall (eds) *Social Scientists as Advocates: Views from the Applied Professions.* Beverley Hills: Sage Publications.

Melton, G. (1987) 'Children, politics and morality: the ethics of child advocacy'. *Journal of Clinical Child Psychology 16*, 4, 357–367.

Morris, J. (2002) *A Lot To Say.* London: Scope.

National Children's Bureau (1993) *Guidelines for Research.* London: National Children's Bureau.

National Society for the Prevention of Cruelty to Children (NSPCC) (2006) *Independent Visitors and Advocacy.* Journalist briefing, Dec. London: NSPCC.

Pole, C, Mizen, P. and Bolton, A. (1999) 'Realising children's agency in research.' *Children and Society 12*, 3, 2–13.

Robson, C. (1998) *Real World Research: A Resource for Social Scientists and Practitioner Researchers.* Oxford: Routledge.

Russell, P. (1995) *Positive Choices – Services for Children with Disabilities away from Home.* London: National Children's Bureau.

Stein, M. and Ellis, S. (1982) *Gizza Say?* London: NAYPIC.

Thomas, N. (2000) Children, *Family and the State: Decision-making and Child Participation.* Bristol: Policy Press.

Thomas, N. and O'Kane, C. (1999) 'Children's participation in review and planning meetings when they are looked after in middle childhood.' *Child and Family Social Work 4*, 3, 221–230.

Utting, W. (1997) *People Like Us. The Report of the Review of the Safeguards for Children Living Away From Home.* London: Department of Health and the Welsh Office.

Willow, C. (1998) 'Listening To Children in Local Government'. In D. Utting (ed.) *Children's Services Now and in the Future.* London: National Children's Bureau.

CHAPTER 4

Advocacy in Child Protection Case Conferences

Jane Dalrymple and Hilary Horan

> I would say go with an advocate, because if you get scared they will help you.

The involvement of children and young people in child protection confer-ences is a relatively recent part of the child protection process. In fact it was only in the early 1990s that the involvement of parents in child protection conferences began to be recognised as important. A factor contributing to the recognition of the need to involve families in this decision-making process was the report from Cleveland Inquiry in 1988. Commenting on the treatment of children and their families by professionals who were investi-gating allegations of abuse in Cleveland, the report stated that the children who they were trying to help were often seen as 'objects of concern' (Butler-Schloss 1988) rather than people in their own right. Following this, a guide for inter-agency working in child abuse recognised the importance of including all members of the family – children and adults – in all stages of the child protection process and ensuring openness and honesty between families and professionals

Since then it has become apparent that the outcomes are likely to be better if children and their families are involved in decision-making. This is partly because, as later guidance stated, 'children of sufficient age and under-standing often have a clear perception of what needs to be done to ensure their safety and well-being' (Department of Health *et al.* 1999, p.77). Subse-quently there has been a general trend in UK policy that, recognising the right of children and young people to be involved in matters that affect them, requires children and young people to be involved in decision-making (Kirby *et al.*, 2003). The role of advocacy services in enabling this to happen is also becoming acknowledged:

> Advocates provide independent and confidential information, advice, representation and support, and can play a vital role in ensuring children have appropriate information and support to communicate their views in formal settings such as child protection conferences... (HM Government 2006, p.190)

Notwithstanding the government agenda, advocacy services have, in fact, been working for over a decade to provide advocacy support for children and young people to enable them to participate in the child protection process in a meaningful way (Scutt and Stephens 1995, quoted in Noon 2000; Wyllie 1999).

Although children and young people using social care services may be invited to participate in a range of decision-making for a (such as reviews, see Chapter 2; family group conferences, see Chapter 5) the significance of a child protection conference is considerable and as such can be daunting for young people, their families and the professionals involved. It is a specific decision-making process that takes place after an enquiry has shown that a child or young person is at risk of abuse or neglect. An initial child protection conference brings together family members, and the professionals involved with the child and the family to:

- bring together and analyse in a multi-disciplinary setting the information that has been obtained about the child's health, development and functioning, and the parents' or carers' capacity to ensure the child's safety and promote the child's health and development

- make judgements about the likelihood of a child suffering significant harm in the future

- decide what future action is needed to safeguard the child and promote their welfare, how that action will be taken forward, and with what intended outcomes.

(Department of Health *et al.* 1999, para. 5.53)

The professionals at the conference examine information gathered during the investigation and their previous knowledge of the family and analyse what it has shown about the risk of harm to the children. They will then decide if the child or young person's name should be added to the child protection register. This will depend on whether they think that there is risk of the child or young person concerned being harmed again through injury, abuse or neglect. The child protection register is a confidential list of children and young people who are believed to be in need of protection. A review meeting is held three months after the conference and then every six months following that to consider what changes have taken place since the conference – if the professionals involved think that the child or young person is no longer at risk, their name is removed from the register. If a child's name is added to the register, a child protection plan is drawn up to try and ensure the child is kept safe and to support the family. A group of professionals then work with the family, with a social worker being nominated as the key worker responsible for coordinating the child protection plan.

In September 2002 an advocacy service was set up in Wiltshire to help young people over the age of ten years old to participate in child protection conferences and their subsequent reviews. The aim of this service is to ensure that the views of young people have been listened to and taken into account, so that they can be meaningfully involved in the process. The hope of the project has been that, by valuing what young people have to say in the meetings, their concerns – which may not mirror those of their family or the professionals – are heard and that services reflect their identified needs. As discussed above, Government guidance is very clear about whether or not a child or young person meets the criteria for registration. This means that even if the meeting hears from the young person that she or he does not believe that they are 'at risk' their views may well be overruled by the professionals. The responsibility for the decision rests with the professionals involved – while therefore the young person may have a view, it is not their responsibility to assess whether or not they should be registered. The average time a child or young person is on the register in Wiltshire is about nine months.

Since the child protection process is so clearly defined it is perhaps inevitable that advocacy in child protection conferences is task centred. While, as Noon (2000) points out, the role may be described as 'subtle and complex' (p.9) the advocate has to focus on the 'specific tasks of enabling the young person to relate their views to the meeting, understand what happens at the meeting and feel supported when they attend' (p.9). Once the piece of work is completed the advocate has no need for ongoing contact with the young person or their family. An advocate will only be involved again if the young person wants support in the subsequent review(s). If a young person accepts advocacy support the role of the advocate in Wiltshire is therefore to:

1. ensure that the young person understands what the child protection conference is about

2. work with the young person to see how, when and where they want their information given to the child protection conference

3. talk to the young person about whether they want to attend the conference

4. support the young person through the process of the conference and ensure that their voice is heard

5. check out who is telling the young person the outcome of the meeting if they are not going to attend

6. 'debrief' and goodbye – unless re-involved in a subsequent review.

Using material from an evaluation of the Wiltshire project we will examine in this chapter the development of advocacy in child protection conferences and look at the challenges of supporting young people in these meetings. We will then discuss the contribution advocacy might make to safeguarding children and young people. The children and their families have all given permission for the material to be used although names/situations have obviously been changed to preserve confidentiality.

Evaluating the project

This is a small-scale study that evaluated the work of the project between September 2002 and July 2004. Wiltshire is a large rural county which at the time of the research was split into two areas for the management of child protection conferences. Each area has an administrator and independent chair. The advocacy service is provided by Barnardo's and is jointly funded by Barnardo's, Wiltshire County Council and a small local charity called The Peanut Trust. The Child Protection Advocacy Project was developed in consultation with staff from Wiltshire Social Services Department Children and Families teams (a consultation event was offered to all teams). Between September 2002 and April 2004, 134 families were referred for initial and review conferences where at least one child was over the age of ten years. This involved 268 children (a few under the age of ten were included as they were part of a sibling group). Of these, 13 parents and 4 children refused the service. The take-up rate of young people accepting the service was far higher than anticipated and so in the first four months there were ten families for whom the project was unable to meet the request for an advocate in time. Social Services Department withdrew the request for an advocate for two families. Overall, 231 children from 105 families used the service. The evaluation had three main aims:

1. to provide an overview of the development of advocacy for children and young people in child protection conferences in Wiltshire

2. to make recommendations for the future development of the service

3. to identify any research needs.

Within this framework the objectives of the evaluation were to:

- explore the views of young people who received an advocacy service

- explore the views of key professional participants involved in child protection conferences

- evaluate aspects of the participation of young people in child protection conferences

- monitor the development of appropriate advocacy support for young people attending child protection conferences

- make recommendations for the further development of the role of advocates for young people participating in child protection conferences

- make recommendations about the involvement of young people in child protection conferences.

The research team decided to try to talk to ten young people who had used the advocacy service to support them in their conference: advocates, social workers and other professionals and the two people who chair child protection conferences in Wiltshire. The researcher also attended advocates' meetings, read selected minutes of initial conferences and had ongoing informal contact with the project from its inception. All the families who had worked with an advocate were sent a letter explaining the study, and parents were asked to give written permission for any young person who agreed to be interviewed. All young people were given a feedback leaflet and the content of both this, and the letter sent out to young people was agreed with a young person involved with the Barnardo's project. Young people were given the chance to change their mind at any time if they agreed to be interviewed and the same confidentiality policy as that of the Advocacy Service was used. Young people who completed a feedback form received a voucher to thank them for their participation. Advocates were asked to complete a feedback form after each piece of work and social workers and other professionals were sent a similar form after each conference. Ethical approval for the evaluation was given by the Faculty Ethical Sub Committee of the University of the West of England.

During the evaluation 12 young people completed feedback forms and 13 agreed to speak to the researcher, although only 8 were eventually seen; 27 feedback forms were completed by advocates and 6 advocates were interviewed. Two other professionals/social workers completed feedback forms. One independent chair was interviewed at the start and the end of the project. The other was interviewed at the end of the project. The researcher also attended five advocates' meetings and read the minutes of ten initial conferences where young people and/or their advocates attended the meeting.

Setting up the advocacy service

Two years into the project the involvement of advocates in child protection conferences was an accepted part of the child protection process. However, the start of the project was slow and difficult for several reasons. The process was discussed and debated by the Area Child Protection committee, the Head of Safer Care, the Children's Services Manager for Barnardo's and the Children's Rights Officer for Wiltshire. Unfortunately, the Children's Rights Officer who was involved in helping to set up the project changed jobs and there was a gap for a while until his replacement arrived. There were also delays in obtaining police checks for the newly trained advocates. Administrative support was initially provided by the Children's Rights Service, whose administrator found that the high take-up rate meant that she did not have the time available to manage it effectively and so the administration transferred to Barnardo's. Processes were set up and social work teams were sent information packs about the advocacy service once the project was launched. A team of advocates, who work on a sessional basis, is now established. The team is varied and all the advocates had experience of working with children and young people before starting to work with the project although most were not trained social workers. They all attend a two-day training course and shadow other advocates before taking on advocacy cases themselves. They receive regular supervision.

The form of advocacy used in this project can be described as proactive case advocacy. When the decision to hold a child protection conference is made the young person involved and their parent(s) are sent separate invitations to the conference by the independent chair. Information about the advocacy service is included with the invitations and the advocacy service is alerted to the conference. It is therefore an 'opt out' service – the advocacy service is not in the gift of the social worker – and all children over the age of ten are offered the service. An advocate contacts the family involved and, if they agree, arranges to visit them. The young person, the parents of the young person or the person with parental responsibility may refuse advocacy involvement but it is always offered. Parents have to give their permission for the advocacy service to be involved. If the young person chooses not to attend the conference, advocacy is still offered as an advocate can take their views, wishes and feelings to the meeting. Often this will take the form of a report that the young person writes with the advocate who will then read it out at the conference. One of the dangers here is that advocacy in child protection conferences may become proceduralised: it becomes an expectation that young people will produce reports for meetings which, it has been argued, should only happen if it is appropriate for the person concerned (Boylan and Wyllie 1999). The Wiltshire advocacy service checks carefully that the child or young person *does* want advocacy support and negotiates with them how information is presented to the conference.

Advocacy practice

Although this is a small study we feel that the messages from the young people, their advocates and other professionals can contribute to developing theory and knowledge about advocacy practice in child protection. In the following section we will look at what they said before considering some case examples in order to examine the development of advocacy within the decision-making process.

1. Young people's views: enabling participation

Generally speaking, young people identified their parents and advocates as the key people involved in helping them to *prepare for their conferences*. The process of thinking about the meeting and what they might want to tell people seemed to be important in helping young people to feel more relaxed about the process:

> She asked us to say what we wanted to say in our own words and gave us confidence to speak up if we felt we wanted to.

Going to a child protection conference is scary for young people. Some were frightened that their family would be split up afterwards, that they would be taken into care, that they would be put on the register or, in one case, that they would be taken off it: 'The bad bit was when they said that I was still on the pottekshen [protection] register.' One young person was terrified that his father would be arrested and leave their home.

Advocacy support helped because:

> the advocate was there to speak on our behalf, made it less scary and that things are going to be sorted out now it has happened. She gave a lot of confidence. I just sat there quietly like a little lost sheep. The kids – they feel intimidated. It was a scary meeting – [the young person] was so nervous she laughed.
>
> (Parent)

Young people who attended their meeting did feel that they were included:

> [The chair] was brilliant at the meeting. He told me what was going on as well as my advocate.

And eight young people felt that they were listened to, even if it was only because of the outcome:

> I think they did [listen] because our family is getting some help now.

However, young people also graphically described how they and their advocate did not feel listened to:

> I don't think they did really take notice. The advocate pointed out things wrong in the report. Wasn't til the end that [the advocate] got our points across. She was trying to do it in the middle but couldn't get a word in.

The mother of one family felt the same way:

> I think the children should have been listened to first – it would give them a clearer view of why things are happening as they are. The agencies made up their minds without taking into account what the kids felt. They were not valued – I thought they just wanted to hurry up and get to the register list and just go home... The kids' views don't count. I was glad they went because they have the right to be heard.

Nevertheless for this family, and for other young people, being included made a difference because:

> They knew what we wanted to say and they could talk about it. We think it helped change their mind about putting us on the child protection register.

However, one young person answered *yes* and *no* when asked if being at the conference made a difference:

> Yes, because they listen, and no, because it made no difference.

Knowing that the advocate was there to speak for those who decided *not to go to their conference* also made things easier, although not knowing what was being said could, of course, raise anxieties. Whether or not the young person chose to attend, without exception, all were positive about *their advocate* for a range of reasons – the advocate:

- listened to them
- explained things
- gave them confidence to speak/spoke for them/helped them to write their views
- helped them to feel comfortable in the conference.

> She helps you, like if you get your words mixed up, like I do now, then she'll like write it down properly...and just take care of everything for you 'cos your mum can't always speak for you...'cos you've got your mum's point of view, your sister's point of view, your Nan's point of view and then [the advocate] just puts it...

However, one young woman commented on the fact that if she saw more of her social worker she would not have needed an advocate:

> Being independent is not so important – my social worker could advocate for me.

Although there was no plan to include parents in the evaluation there were a number of comments about the fact that an advocate had also helped them through the process:

> She gave us all confidence, including our mum, to say how we felt and spoke for us with passion. I give her 100% because she really calmed them down – I could have done with one myself actually.

2. Advocates' views: issues and dilemmas in promoting participation

Advocates generally spent between half an hour and three hours with young people helping them to prepare for the conference. Most tried to see the young person at home and also arrived early for the conference so that they could see them again on the day. Some young people chose to see their advocate at school and this could be arranged if requested. Issues for advocates at this stage included dealing with young people's fears. Lack of privacy when meeting with the young people, however, was identified as a problem – usually advocates met young people in their own home, or had to find a space away from other people attending the conference on the day. Some advocates offered to give the young person a lift to the conference, which they also saw as giving them a chance to answer any last minute queries, check if there were any changes to their material they wanted to make and calm their nerves. Initially, advocates felt that there was an element of suspicion about their role by other professionals; however, towards the end of the evaluation advocates felt more accepted and valued within the child protection process. An ongoing problem for advocates though was that they did not receive the social worker's report in time. Most of the advocates felt that being able to go through the social worker's report before the meeting was essential, although one advocate suggested that it is not impossible to work without the report. All the advocates also felt that giving young people information about the conference was a key part of their role:

> Inclusion via information is an important part of the advocacy role in child protection. This should be the social worker's role but it is difficult – young people only see the authority hat.

Advocates stated that the service helps young people to understand why decisions are made and enables them to feel better about themselves. On the whole advocates felt more comfortable about supporting a young person in the conference than reading what they had to say – as one explained:

> The chair asked me things about the young people and I felt uncomfortable answering without them there. I found it difficult.

Many also felt that when a young person attends a meeting it has more of an impact than if what they have to say is just read out. Professionals are more careful about what they say and young people also have the experience of hearing positive things said about their lives. However, there was a strong feeling that conferences are not child-friendly and that what young people have to say does not really make a difference to the decision-making:

> At the meetings where the young people have been there, on the whole they haven't been ignored. But you don't get the feeling that it is a meeting for the child – it is more about the parents. If you are reading out a report for the young person or they are speaking you feel they've been given their time and that's it. No one says 'wow, that's really interesting' or makes much comment. There is almost a cold response to it – as if they've got to let them speak, so let them and move on.

The task-focused nature of the work means that once the conference is over the advocate has completed their work, particularly when the young person has attended the meeting. In situations where the advocate has spoken for the child most prefer to tell the young person themselves what has happened, rather than leave this to the social worker, for example:

> I really think it is important to tell the young person that I said what they wanted me to say and what I heard other people say about them. You *should* go back if they have talked to you about what they want you to do.

Many advocates find it hard to finish the piece of work at this point, especially if a young person is upset about the outcome. Some commented on the length of time between the conference where a young person is registered and the review meeting (three months, six months), as so much would happen in that young person's life that they would have to re-establish their relationship.

3. Views of the independent chairs involved: impact of participatory approach

Most of the information in this section is from the independent chairs although some social workers also provided feedback. The chairs were positive about the service and pleased that advocacy support was available for young people. As one said, 'By and large very little harm is done and quite a lot of good by having advocates.' Clearly all families are different and all conferences are different. But since guidance about the purpose of a child protection conference is clear there is little likelihood of any young person persuading the professionals involved that the risk is lower or of coming up with a way to reduce any identified risk. Consequently the chairs recognised that those whose experience was that the contribution of the young person did not appear to make a difference to the decision were probably right.

However, for them it did not therefore follow that young people should not be part of the process. There seemed to be no doubt that the participation of young people improved as a result of the advocacy service. The most important question that the independent chairs felt that young people and advocates could help with was in thinking about what needed to change – what did families or agencies have to do in order for the risk to be reduced? Advocates can help children feel safe to say things; to have a chance to drive forward plans. Often parents don't recognise the effect of their behaviour on children and so the contribution of young people can focus other people on changing what is possible. The combination of a young person and an advocate working together was described as 'powerful and poignant' and to that extent it could have a significant influence on the planning. Certainly the presence of a young person and/or their advocate could structure the way a conference was run, which meant trying to make the process as human and interactive as possible. Young people appreciated the efforts of chairs in this respect:

> The chair was brilliant – he said about a holiday. He asked us girls what we were going to do when we left school. The chairman said there was no need for the school welfare officer – they were digging in further than they needed to. He told the welfare officer off.

One chair suggested that it is less important how many people attend a conference or whether the young person has an advocate, but it is important that the young people should have their views heard in the meeting:

> We are looking at what needs to be changed. I want to know if the social worker has *seen* and *spoken* to the children. So I ask who is representing the children's view. That is the way forward. It is important to get social workers and core group members to get the views of the young people – they are as important as the views of the parents.

The power relations in a conference are very real and obviously not all young people understand the process. However, whatever their age, it was felt that young people who have an advocate 'have a different slant on things' – that is, they can say what they want. There was an awareness that often young people are part of a household where they have lived in a situation for a long time. They attend the meeting because they want to help. But they also take on responsibility for what has happened – they see themselves as the problem and by attending they are trying to improve the situation. So the role of the advocate has been described as helping them to realise that it is not their responsibility that the conference is happening. However, it was recognised that this could be a dilemma for advocates as the young person may be saying something to reassure the conference, which could mean that they are less likely to get the best outcome.

A good advocate in child protection conferences was described by one professional as:

1. someone who is able to allow a young person to give their views in a proper way – asking them what the issue is for them

2. someone who gives more of a structure to the questions

3. Someone who is there to help young people through the process

4. someone who helps prepare young people for a conference.

Discussion

It is important not to underestimate that a child protection conference is experienced as 'scary'. Boylan and Wyllie (1999) indicated in their research of a local advocacy project working with young people in child protection conferences that there was need for 'more radical change required in relation to planning and decision making generally so that children can be involved, not as victims, but as participants from the outset' (p.67) if advocacy is to be viewed as a process and dialogue. Advocates then were particularly helpful in attempting to lessen the scariness of the process, initially by preparing young people for the meeting. When young people did attend a meeting it had an effect on how the meeting was run. What young people said also had a powerful impact on the adults at the meeting, who were often unaware of the reality of their lives.

We found that young people are able to give a vivid picture of what is happening in their lives. This is often both an assessment of their situation, which gives clues about their vulnerability and resilience, and a chance to identify which services might be needed to make their lives better. Research into the conduct of in-depth assessments of families in child protection cases indicates that often reports provide a partial rather than holistic representation of children with very limited accounts of the complexity of their lives. Children are often described in relation to their parents (how they respond to or interact with them), so that what people at the meeting come to know about them are partial aspects of their lives 'mediated through adult perspectives and actions' (Holland 2001, p.237). The young person's contribution is therefore likely to be significant and crucial in helping to make positive changes in their lives, as the following case study indicates.

Susi (10) and Nicky (12) have been on the child protection register for nearly a year under the catagory of emotional abuse. The concerns centred on their mother's heavy drinking and her violent relationship with her boyfriend, Joe. The girls decided they would use an advocate to help them express their views to their review child protection conference (the advocacy service was not available when they were first registered). The girls also decided to talk to the advocate together – they were given a choice of having different advocates or seeing the same advocate together or separately. They decided to attend their conference but to get their advocate to read out their wishes and feelings for them. This is part of what they wrote:

> We don't think that we are at risk living with our mum.
>
> There has only been one time since the last meeting when there was a fight at our house and we weren't there when it happened. When we came home, the police were there but Joe had left. There used to be lots of fights when Joe was there but he has been gone about eight weeks.
>
> The nicest thing about living at our house is that our mum loves us. We have lived in our house for nearly eight years and it feels like home. Mum doesn't get into fights with the neighbours anymore and she keeps herself to herself.
>
> Mum has cut down on her drinking and now only drinks about a litre of cider a day instead of the three litres that she sometimes used to. The drink just calms her down and stops her having a go at us or getting violent with other people. We don't think that her drinking puts us at risk. Our dad will always collect us for a bit if we want him to.
>
> Mum does crosswords in her big book with us. When we use a big word she says we must have eaten the dictionary for breakfast.
>
> Lots of families have arguments and we don't think our family is more at risk than anyone else.

Susi and Nicky assessed accurately the changes achieved over the past few weeks – Joe leaving, a lessening of violent incidents and the reduction in their mother's drinking. They are realistic about their situation – their mother needs some drink to get through the day – and have identified an escape route if necessary: their father will come and get them. The warmth in their family unit also comes across – 'it feels like home' – and they are confident their mother loves them. Another positive is the comment about doing the crosswords with their mother. The girls' resilience shines through in a way it would be hard to access from a social worker's or teacher's report. Susi and Nicky were, in fact, kept on the register – mainly because of concerns about how recent the improvements were and fears that Joe would return again (a pattern over the past year). However, their parents and the agencies were all impressed by their input to the conference. It strengthened their father's resolve to remain in contact when he heard how important his involvement was to the girls. Their mother was delighted by their positive comments as she felt she had let them down over the years. She said that it made her more determined to keep up the progress she had made.

While the young people's views might not make a difference to the immediate outcome of the conference decision, in the longer term they should make a difference to how plans are made about their future. For instance, Susie and Nicky were left on the child protection register but the plan incorporated a commitment from their father to respond quickly to any request for help from the girls and an agreement that if their mother was having a bad day she could ring him and the girls would spend a couple of days with him. Prior to the conference their father's involvement in a formal child protection plan had been minimal as their mother had previously told the social worker he was not that interested in his daughters.

A second example demonstrates that part of the process of influencing the meeting can be in actually identifying key people to attend – which in turn may have an impact on the decision-making process. For example, a child protection conference was being held for Zac (age 12) because of concerns about neglect as a result of his mother's drinking. Zac told the advocate that he wanted his older brother, who no longer lived at home (and had not been invited), to be at the meeting, for two reasons:

1. he had been the subject of a child protection conference himself as a child and understood the stress of living with their mother's heavy drinking

2. because Zac wanted to live with his brother if he could not live at home.

The advocate arranged for the brother to be invited and consequently the family were able to talk openly to each other in the conference. Although the advocate felt that the registration decision would have been the same if the brother had not attended the meeting, the way the family talked to each other helped the professionals understand how the family communicated and the efforts the brother was willing to make to support both Zac and his mother. The impact of the brother on the family's functioning had not been identified in any of the reports and an advocate or social worker reading out a report from the young person would not have had the same impact. The family were really involved in the decision-making and assessment of how well Zac's mother was doing to improve her parenting. This was also a two-way process because Zac also needed to change some of his behaviour – and if Zac had not been at the meeting that would not have been so clear to him.

Conclusions

Research indicates that children and young people are wary about talking to adults and, when they do have problems, find it difficult to access formal agencies (Butler and Williamson 1994; Hallett, Murray and Punch 2003). When faced with a professionally led decision-making forum such as a child protection conference they are unlikely therefore to seek help to contribute to this unless a service is proactively offered. The children and young people we spoke to who worked with an advocate clearly found that this enabled them to negotiate and address the issues being raised by the professionals – who might then be more able to understand the reality of their lives and what might help them to cope and be safe. Parton (2006) suggests that if we really want to ensure that children and young people feel safe we have to go beyond hearing their voices to giving them more control over what happens once they have been enabled to raise them. In the current system of child protection conferences the decision-making rests entirely with the professionals. The process of the conference is a difficult one – both young people and their advocates had mixed feelings about their level of involvement and impact on decision-making. If, however, advocates can enable children and young people to contribute to an understanding about the difficulties they are facing, and how they manage those difficulties, then this is the first step towards enabling them to be involved in any planning processes and consequently to ensure their safety and build on their resilience. As young people grow in confidence they may become more confident in asking for and accessing resources that they feel would be useful. This then can have an impact on changing adult/child relations:

> ensuring that children and young people can realise and individualise themselves according to criteria and outcomes which they determine, rather than those which are generated by adults or, more to the point, by the

various systems and procedures which are designed to promote and safe-guard their welfare.

(Parton 2006, p.182)

We can see from this evaluation therefore that, while there are challenges for advocates and young people in enabling their genuine participation in child protection conferences, advocacy can make a contribution to protecting them and to ensuring that their participation in the process is meaningful. Further research is needed however to identify what happens after the conference and to ascertain how much control children and young people within the systems are really having over their own lives and how this would impact on improving their well-being.

References

Boylan, J. and Wyllie, J. (1999) 'Advocacy and Child Protection.' In N. Parton and C. Wattam (eds) *Child Sexual Abuse. Responding to the Experiences of Children.* Chichester: Wiley.

Butler-Schloss, LJ E. (1988) *Report of the Inquiry into Child Abuse in Cleveland (the Cleveland Report).* London, The Stationery Office.

Butler, I. and Williamson, H. (1994) *Children Speak: Children, Trauma and Social Work.* Harlow: Longman.

Department of Health, Home Office and Employment, D. F. E. A. (1999) *Working Together to Safeguard Children: A Guide to Inter-agency Working to Safeguard and Promote the Welfare of Children.* London. The Stationery Office.

Hallett, C., Murray, C. and Punch, S. (2003) 'Young People and Welfare: Negotiating Pathways.' In C. Hallett and A. Prout (eds) *Hearing the Voices of Children: Social Policy for a New Century.* London: Routledge Falmer.

HM Government (2006) *Working Together to Safeguard Children: A Guide to Interagency Working to Safeguard and Promote the Welfare of Children.* London: The Stationery Office.

Holland, S. (2001) 'Representing children in child protection assessments.' *Childhood 8,* 322–339.

Kirby, P., Lanyon, C., Cronin, K. and Sinclair, R. (2003) *Building a Culture of Participation: Involving Children and Young People in Policy, Service Planning, Delivery and Evaluation.* London: Department for Education and Skills.

Noon, A. (2000) *Having a Say: The Participation of Children and Young People at Child Protection Meetings and the Role of Advocacy.* London: The Children's Society.

Parton, N. (2006) *Safeguarding Childhood: Early Intervention and Surveillance in a Late Modern Society.* Basingstoke: Palgrave Macmillan.

Scutt, N. and Stephens, J. (1995) *Social Services – NSPCC – Y.E.S. – Child Advocacy Project.* Plymouth: Devon Social Services Department.

Wyllie, J. (1999) *The Last Rung of the Ladder: An Examination of the Use of Advocacy by Children and Young People in Advancing Participation Practice within the Child Protection System.* London: The Children's Society.

CHAPTER 5

At the Table or Under the Table? Children's Participation in Family Group Conferences – A Comparative Study of the Use of Professional Advocates and Family Supporters

Sophie Laws and Perpetua Kirby

In recent years there has been increasing interest in the use of family group conferences (FGCs) in decision-making for children, and in the provision of independent professional advocates for children around the UK. Each of these developments has been driven by a distinct shift in thinking – first, a concern to assist members of extended family networks to contribute towards the welfare of children, and, second, the recognition that children's own voices need to be heard in decision-making processes that affect their lives. These trends come together where professional advocates are employed to support children within FGCs.

FGCs aim to bring together as many members of the extended family and friendship network around a child or children as possible, to address one or more specific questions. They are sometimes used in an attempt to avoid a child becoming 'looked after' in local authority care by identifying support within the extended family, but more often the question being considered by the FGC concerns ways of supporting the immediate carer/s. There are three stages to the conference: first, the information-giving stage, attended by family and professionals (for example, social workers, educational welfare officers and teachers as well as the FCG coordinator), in which professionals outline their concerns and what support they can offer; second, private family time in which the family members work by themselves to make their plan. In the third and final stage the family share their plan with professionals and an agreement is reached about taking the plan forward.

Generally, children are more likely to attend FGCs than they are child protection Conferences, and the majority are positive about the process and their ability to take part in it (Ryan 2004). However, a number of studies have identified concern from practitioners and other adults that children may be expected to take on too much responsibility and be troubled by attending FGCs (e.g. Paterson and Harvey 1991; Rasmussen 2003). Concern about how children are heard within FGCs has also been influenced by the wider move in children's services, discussed throughout this book, to provide children and young people with advocacy support in order to assist them in having a real say in decisions made about them. There, is however, a tension between the ethos of the FGC and the use of professional advocates to support children in decision-making. The issue then is who is best placed to support a child or young person in such a process. The use of supporters from within the extended family as advocates for children appears to be more congruent with the attempt to mobilise extended family help more broadly. But many FGC projects now involve professional advocates to support children and young people in these meetings.

Drawing on research carried out mainly between October 2004 and October 2005 with one final case studied in March/April 2006 (Laws and Kirby 2007), we will examine the relative merits of professional advocates and family supporters for children in FGCs. We begin by exploring the extent to which children influence outcomes from FGCs and their perception of the process. We then examine people's understanding of advocacy and consider the advantages and disadvantages of both family supporters and professional advocates. This leads into a discussion about family decision-making, advocacy and power. Finally, we summarise the learning on how to support children's effective participation in FGCs. All the people involved in this research realised that they were developing innovative practice. The managers and practitioners involved in the research were courageous in their openness to learning from these experiences.

Family group conferences and children's participation

FGC practice originally developed in New Zealand from a Maori tradition, and FGCs are used in many countries round the world, for a variety of purposes – including as a form of restorative justice as well as in child welfare. In the UK, FGCs can be seen as an attempt to mitigate the overwhelming force of state intervention where there is concern for a child's welfare. The assumption is challenged that where there are problems in caring appropriately for a child the whole of the family network surrounding them is also 'dysfunctional' or likely to be abusive. Evidence of children's powerful attachment to their birth family, often in the face of great difficulties, has been influential. Further, there has been a loss of confidence in the success of state-provided care to effectively ensure children's safety and welfare.

The research literature on FGCs reflects trends in theory and practice over the last few years with a gradual increase in the focus on children's effective participation within them. In the late 1990s research summaries stated that only young people over 10 or 12 usually attend. They made no mention of professional advocates for children, although the use of family members or school-friends was mentioned as an option used in some cases (Marsh and Crow 1998, 1999). A more recent survey of international FGC practice (Nixon *et al.* 2005) found a similar picture: variable practice in terms of the presence of children and young people at conferences, with children under ten excluded as a matter of principle in some programmes. This survey did not look at the provision of professional advocacy, presumably because it is rare internationally.

An important theme of commentary in this period focused on the way in which FGCs might operate in relation to the balance of power between families and the state (Lupton and Nixon 1999). The obvious difficulty with the idea of empowering 'the family' is the problem of what constitutes 'the family' and the question of the power inequalities that are present within families. Nixon (2001) noted that a key criticism of FGCs was that they 'could reinforce power imbalances in families'. He cited Pennell and Burford's (2000) suggestion that 'the use of supporters and advocates for vulnerable children and adults at the conference preparation stage can do much to ensure vulnerable individuals have a voice'.

Interest in children and young people's right to have a say in decisions about them has increased greatly over the last few years. Children's participation can be taken to mean a whole range of things, from taking an active part in decision-making to simply being present (Kirby *et al.* 2003). In relation to FGCs it is important to unpack the question of children's attendance and how it relates to whether the views of the child are heard and taken into account. An overview study which summarised the messages, themes and findings of more than 25 research and evaluation studies on family group decision-making (Merkel-Holguin, Nixon and Burford 2003) found that 'children's involvement and participation vary considerably'. It was reported that 'some researchers express concern that children's perspectives and contribution might be overlooked or restricted at FGCs and that...this might make children more vulnerable'. The authors suggest that research is needed 'to more carefully explore the actual benefits and costs to children of being more fully involved in FGC, learn what methods effectively and safely engage them as participants' (p.8).

An important issue affecting the choice of advocacy support to the children relates to the principle of family time in FGCs. The practice of ensuring that part of the time spent in the FGC involves only family members, without any professional presence, is widely seen as a key element of an FGC (Lupton and Stevens 1997; Merkel-Holguin *et al.* 2003). One of the impulses behind this research was a concern that the involvement of professional advocates might undermine a core value of the FGC process by disrupting the ability of the family to take responsibility for its children.

Sample and methods

The research, commissioned by Brighton and Hove Children's Fund in partnership with the Brighton and Hove Daybreak FGC Project, used a primarily qualitative and participatory methodology with a small quantitative component. We examined the Daybreak Brighton and Hove FGC Project, which involved specially trained professional advocates provided by the local independent advocacy service (Youth Advocacy and Participation) and, for comparison, Daybreak FGC projects in Hampshire, Southampton and the Isle of Wight where family supporters are more often used.

Practice nationally in terms of support to children within FGCs is quite diverse. The Brighton and Hove Daybreak FGC Project has offered an independent professional advocate to children involved in its FGCs since its inception in 2003. These advocates meet with children and young people in advance of the conference, support the child during the meeting, and visit the child after the FGC to make sure that they understand the plan. In other areas it is not unusual to find professional advocates who otherwise work as coordinators for FGCs and are employed by the FGC project itself.

Although the use of professional advocates is spreading fast, a more widespread practice amongst FGC providers has been to suggest asking a member of the extended family to act as a 'family supporter' to the child. Other approaches have been to invite a professional already involved with the family – for instance a school-based learning support worker, or a member of the child's peer group – to act in this capacity. Whatever the offer, some children and young people refuse advocacy support and choose to speak for themselves.

Before starting the case study research, focus group discussions were held with advocates and coordinators, and with children and adult family members with experience of FGCs, to gain their advice on shaping the research.

A set of criteria was established for cases that could be included in the sample and potential families and children were sent a leaflet providing details of the research. Families were also offered an incentive of a £10 voucher per child if they took the time to take part in the interviews. There were considerable delays in identifying suitable case studies however – very few families were referred to the research team and it took a long time to recruit families to the study. This is typical of research involving a comparative sample – those involved have less sense of ownership of the research. Other barriers in all projects included families where it was difficult to seek consent for the child/ren's involvement from the person with parental responsibility. We asked those closest to the children to talk through the research and ask if they were happy to take part.

Ten families were included in the case study research. We compared the experience of six families using a professional advocate, with three that had a family supporter, and one family in which the young person had refused the offer of a professional advocate. Within each family, the following people were interviewed:

- one to three children
- two close family members who attended the conference
- the FGC coordinator
- the professional advocate/s *or* family supporter
- one or two other professionals who attended the meeting.

Altogether, 83 individuals contributed opinions, including 66 interviews (either face to face or on the telephone). This included children and young people aged between 3 and 14.

Our aim was to listen to the opinions of a range of people who took part in FGCs, but also to ascertain whether the things that children wanted were put into FGC plans and made to happen. Did having a say in their FGC improve the children's lives? And what was it like for the children to take part?

Collecting appropriate information to assess the work of the advocates and supporters was a complex process. In every case study, participants' views varied. Indeed, a number of individual respondents, including children, gave both positive and negative evaluations of the same advocate's work. Where possible we asked children to draw themselves with their advocate and then talk about it. In some cases we showed them a page with different faces showing different feelings and asked some questions using this. We asked how much they felt they had told the advocate, offering a choice of pictures illustrating 'I told her a lot' and so on. Children were also asked whether they would want the same advocate again, if they were to have another FGC. We had some concerns here about the validity of responses. With younger children it was not always clear whether they had understood the questions. With some older children concentration seemed to be an issue.

Outcomes of children's participation

We approached the question of outcomes in these difficult family situations in a number of different ways. Asked if they were happy with the FGC plan, most children reported confused or mixed feelings. Only two children said that they were happy, and one was not happy. We looked particularly for evidence of children being able to influence the agenda of FGCs, as well as their decisions on the pre-set questions. There was a clear pattern by which the chance of a child getting her or his view into the plan and then acted upon was stronger when a professional advocate was involved. For example, there was evidence of eight of the ten children having a say, in that points in the plan referred to issues that had been raised by them. Of these, in two cases, young children's views (given through a professional advocate) were taken into account in making the key decision of the FGC. However, in some other cases the points that children had succeeded in adding to the plan were about relatively minor issues. Children had a clear impact on the key decisions within the plan in only three cases, all with professional advocates. In the two cases where there was no evidence of the child's influence, the children had family supporters.

We also tried to find evidence about any longer term outcomes in the children's lives. In the majority of cases, the consensus amongst respondents saw positive change on some aspects. In six out of ten cases there were specific outcomes that were a result of the input of the child concerned. Examples of desired outcomes that were met included contact with members of the extended family, more contact with parents not living with them, and changes in their parents' behaviour:

My mum's got better and my dad he more rings me now…like when she's meant to turn up at things like [arranged contact meetings] she has been doing that now, she never used to come, she has now. She's stopped being naughty, she's stopped drinking, she has probably one beer every week now…normally she'd have one every day.

(Child, age 8)

There were also many examples of changes desired by children that were either not agreed by the FGC or did not happen in practice although they were agreed.

A child's eye view of a family group conference

We have looked above at practical outcomes, but it is important to note that, from children's point of view, this may not be the most important aspect of an FGC. In keeping with other research findings (Bell and Wilson 2006; Holland and O'Neill 2006), we found that children sometimes choose to attend more because they want to see parents or family who they rarely see than because they have made a decision that they want to attend. One five-year-old, for example, was reported by the advocate to have changed her mind and decided to attend the FGC when she heard that her parents would be there.

The perspectives of children were radically different from those of the adults involved. Even in cases where the child/ren's views were by all (adult) accounts heard and taken into account, their experience of the meeting could be negative. One 8-year-old child chose a face that described the FGC as 'annoying…because there was lots of speaking. So I just ran off after an hour or so, and went under the table'. A 9-year-old child's drawing excluded all her family members, although for her too the main excitement of the meeting, before it happened, had been the chance to see her family. She drew only herself and the coordinator, and when prompted as to anyone else who might have been there, wrote 'That's all' across her picture. This girl had hoped that someone in her extended family would remove her from foster care and look after her, but all those present had said they could not.

A painful issue for children at FGCs, identified by adult respondents, was the sense that it could be humiliating to have their difficulties aired publicly. In several cases the child's own behaviour was a key issue for the FGC. Other research has raised the concern that children may be present alongside people who have abused them; that they may 'feel trapped' by the status being given to the family's authority in decision-making; and that they may witness arguments and conflicts (Holland and O'Neill 2006). Commentators have doubted whether children's voices could be heard in an adult-dominated forum. Children talking to Holland and O'Neill also identified FGC meetings as an opportunity for confrontation of family members 'telling me/my mum off'. Young people feared being confronted themselves but at times welcomed it in relation to others.

In terms of young people's overall experience of the FGCs, Holland and O'Neill make the point that it is not to be expected that this would be a wholly positive experience, and they look at a range of risks and benefits to young people of attendance. In their sample of young people aged 6 to 18, a small minority reported mainly negative emotions on this matter, in one case identifying a gap between the expectation (created by professionals) that he would be able to be a powerful person within the FGC and his actual experience in private family time. Others were upset by family conflict at the FGC but nonetheless valued the opportunity to participate. But the majority of the young people in that study found the experience positive on balance. It is possible that the somewhat older age range of this sample accounts for the rather more positive picture – younger children may give replies that reflect a wish not to be in a situation to need an FGC more than reflecting on their participation, given that one is being held.

Understandings of advocacy roles

Overall, there were problems for some adult FGC participants in understanding the advocate's role in half the cases we studied with a professional advocate, and in all those with a family supporter. For example, there were people who saw professional advocates as making an assessment rather than representing the child/ren's views:

> [The professional advocate is] someone who is going to help [the mother] – because she needed some help with them…to make sure that things are being done properly, you know, within the family… I don't know what her role was in the meetings, though I know she went to [the children's house] to see how the children were and all that. She had to discuss what she thought – were the children happy?
>
> (Family member)

There were participants present at FGCs with family supporters who did not realise that they were supposed to have been supporting the child. However, in many of these cases there were other family members who understood very well the intended role of the advocate:

> To be there for the child to say what they want without the pressure of what the child thinks the grown-up wants to hear. They can say what they feel, they're not going to upset one person or the other.

Respondents could accurately distinguish a social worker's role from that of a professional advocate, though one family member thought they were similar to a guardian ad litem (now children's guardian).

Some of the children in this study had understood the role of the advocate, and actively used them to make their views known:

> To help me, and if I don't want to say anything in that family conference, she can say it for me.

One four-year-old child, when the advocate arrived for her second visit, came to the door, took her hand and led her to his toy trains. He laid out trains to show himself in the middle with his parents close on either side. He seemed to have decided to tell her something important about how he wanted things to be.

However, other children were less clear; advocates were seen, for example, as there to 'sort out' theirs and others' lives. In Bell and Wilson's (2006) study, two of the children said that their advocates had been helpful, but others were vague about whether an advocate had been involved or not, 'either because they did not remember or because they were unclear of their function'.

Family supporters – pros and cons

The key benefits of the involvement of a family member or friend to advocate for a child arose from their existing relationship with the child, and with the family. For example, asked about the skills used by a family supporter, a coordinator said that it was more an attribute than a skill, that the family supporter 'knew X very well, understood his behaviour very well, and could explain this [to others in the family] in a non-threatening way.' This child was 'painfully shy', and they prepared a statement by passing notes back and forth under his door. It seemed unlikely that someone unfamiliar, like a professional advocate, would have been able to gain his trust sufficiently to present his view to the same extent. In a second case the coordinator said of the supporter that, 'She knows and loves that child'. She thought that the supporter had done an excellent job, supporting the child within the meeting and interpreting his behaviour to others. A family supporter's understanding of the family situation could also be an asset – particularly, for example, in a situation where there was a large extended family and a variety of difficult issues.

The presence of family supporters in FGC family time would not be disruptive of the family group. The use of family supporters is also in tune with the value of FGCs in building up the sense of the responsibility of the extended family for the welfare of its child/ren.

However, we found that the 'service' provided by family supporters to children was less consistent than that provided by a professional advocacy service. One family member, for example, said the fact that another member of the family was supposed to be playing this role 'sort of came to light' after the meeting. Preparation with the child before the meeting was an important factor in whether or not the child's views were heard at the FGC, and only one of the family supporters did any preparation (although it should be noted that she showed great skill in how she did this). In two of the three cases we studied, at least some participants felt that the family supporter had not really 'done the job'.

> Everyone more or less said what they thought about the child and what could be done. [The family supporter] herself didn't speak, nobody really spoke for the child that day, everybody just mainly gave their opinions on what, the best way what could be done for him.
>
> (Foster carer)

The whole family in attendance at the FGC in one case refused to take any responsibility for the child, and the fact that she was represented by one of the family meant that her voice was not heard at all clearly. While the coordinator noted that the supporter had 'had a few quiet times with the child during the meeting, without being reminded', which he appreciated, the family supporter herself did not articulate the child's point of view when asked about it in our interview, but explained her own opinion. In all the three cases we studied, the family supporters spoke up on behalf of other adult family members to whom they were close, compromising the idea that they were there to help the child to be heard.

Other problems concern the choice of who, within the family, might be able to undertake the advocacy role. FGCs may be convened quite quickly, for unavoidable reasons, and in these situations coordinators may not necessarily be able to assess the capabilities of a family member. A child's own choice of supporter can also be motivated by a number of factors. A problem mentioned by several families who opted for a professional advocate was that a family member might not be trusted to give an unbiased account of the child's view, where there was strong family conflict. In one case, for example, the child had in the past alleged sexual abuse by a family member, and this was strongly denied by some members of the family including the father, who persistently raised the issue. The family supporter chosen by the child was her father's sister, whose loyalties are likely to have been split. It is also interesting to note that the family supporter seen as most skilled by some participants was nonetheless said by an external professional to have 'fuelled the problems within the family' when she 'got sucked into' family disputes. So, however keen they may be to help, there are clearly inherent tensions for a family supporter, in that they are likely to have their own opinion to represent as well as the child's:

> Her views were important and she was torn between what to do. Going out with the child or giving her own views.

> (Coordinator)

A related problem identified by participants was that a child could be aware of the possibility of hurting the feelings of the family supporter themselves in expressing their views:

> When I said to [the child] in the meeting that his father would like to see him… As soon as I was out of the room he said that he didn't want to see his father. He's a sensitive child and he didn't want to upset me.

> (Family supporter)

Is there evidence that greater support for family supporters from coordinators could overcome the drawbacks discussed for family support? We have identified that there was one case where the family supporter displayed strong skills in supporting the child. This coordinator said that she felt she had not assisted the family supporter enough. She had met this family supporter only once ahead of the FGC and this was at the family's home with parent and child present too. In this instance success in undertaking the advocacy role was clearly due to the skills of the person concerned. Coordinators had not been able to provide a great deal of support to family supporters in any of the cases we studied, for a number of reasons.

It would appear then that, where family supporters were used, the chances for a child of getting good support depended on the strengths within a child's own family and social circle. The weaker the family's support for the child, the less chance the child had of finding someone to help them effectively.

Professional advocates – pros and cons

It was at times a challenging task to ascertain children's views in these family situations, and professional advocates were seen to bring strong skills in gaining children's trust and in preparing for the FGC. They spent an average of three meetings preparing for the FGCs, and also made a follow-up visit to ensure that the child understood what had happened. Advocates talked about spending quite a lot of time with the children just getting to know them – playing football, going to the park, for a pizza – and listening to and reflecting what children said.

> We did some work together, drawings, she talked about what was important to her. When we had done everything to her satisfaction she wanted to show me her room and her things... She was just chattering I would say. Then she said to me in the middle of all of it, 'I don't want to lose my mummy.' I said to her that sounds like something really important to you would you like me to write it down so I tell everyone else?
>
> (Advocate, about a 5-year-old girl)

Many family members valued the independence of the professional advocates. Two felt that if family members had conveyed the child's point of view others might have challenged their interpretation. In the case mentioned above, where a child used toy trains to illustrate his view, the advocate presented this to the FGC in a simple way. A family member commented:

> It was very short and sweet and very to the point. And it was his voice. We all went quiet... We all sat back and thought about what she was saying. We really focused on [the child], and that wouldn't have happened otherwise. If I'd said that, everyone would have carried on talking.
>
> (Family member)

In one case there was a history of domestic violence, and members of the family expressed fear of the children's father. The involvement of the advocate meant that the children could talk through their concerns about putting forward their opinions in a safe setting, and could plan a strategy to deal with this. Families identified the time spent preparing with the child and the work to draw out the child/ren's views as of value.

> I think that it was positive for the advocate to be there and to help the children and to have a meeting before our final meeting [the FGC] to get their thoughts out rather than spontaneously seek at the time what's on their mind, because there may be people in there that may change their

opinions. But if they're unbiased and outside it will actually come out what they actually want rather than just 'I want to stay with mum and dad'.

(Family member)

Concerns about the use of professional advocates focused on three main areas. First, there were some cases where family members perceived the advocacy role to include making an assessment and recommendations for the child, particularly in the case of young children. In one case the mother said she was pleased with the advocate's involvement, as she perceived her report as professional validation of her parenting, to her ex-husband. Another family member consulted through a focus group had been apprehensive when the advocate's involvement was proposed, and after the event remained concerned. She was anxious about what the advocate and children were talking about – she said she gathered that they were asking 'Do you love your mother or father best?'

Linked to this, some family members saw the professional advocates as biased, having assumed that the role of the professional advocate was to be impartial, rather than being there solely for the child. In one case the paternal side of the family felt that the advocate should have visited them too, and perceived them as biased by their contact with the maternal side. This sense that the advocate did not have complete information was echoed in a comment on a feedback form in a different case study:

> An advocate is fine provided they know all the background history. I don't believe they do, which does not give a true picture of how to deal with the child.

(Family member)

A second area of concern was the potential for damage to the child in introducing a new professional, with whom they are expected to develop a trusting relationship. Some children involved in FGCs have had a great deal of contact with services, and may have already experienced a series of adults in whom they had developed trust but who had then left their jobs or completed their work process with the child and ended the relationship, thereby creating uncertainty or confusion in the child.

Third, the involvement of the advocate in family time was seen to be problematic. When we first started the research fieldwork, professional advocates were present for all or some of private family time, although this practice changed midway through the research and they are now only present for approximately ten minutes of this time, by agreement with the family. Adult family members in this study did not in fact report finding it difficult to put forward their views in the presence of professional staff. On the whole these families had already experienced considerable contact with services ('been there, done that, got the t-shirt'). However, as one family member put it, 'of course' the presence of a professional advocate in family time changed the way in which the family would talk to one another.

> During family time, in one case, family members stopped in horror when I came into the room. They clearly started talking about something they didn't want me to know about the minute I was out of the room.
>
> (Professional advocate)

A study in Fife found that FGC coordinators there accepted that the presence of an advocate in family time 'does change the family dynamics'; however, their view was that they 'are also clear that this practice is based on the child's best interests' (Gill 2005).

The opportunity, unique to the FGC, for the extended family to meet and discuss the child/ren's needs together without the influence of a professional presence is removed when professional advocates attend the whole of family time. It is for this reason that the Brighton and Hove FGC Project changed its policy to ensure that advocates remain in the room for only a short time.

Family decision-making, advocacy and power

The inequality of power between adults and children means that it can be easy for families to disregard children's views, especially perhaps where there is conflict between adults and it is through this lens that issues are seen. In a number of the cases in this study, men in the family exerted power through absence, staying away from FGCs and sabotaging the process, thus ensuring that their own position remained unchallenged. There were examples where advocacy clearly helped to strengthen a child's position, and in particular the professional advocates did successfully assist children to have their views heard. Where power was exerted in a very obvious way, through domestic violence for example, an advocate assisted children to plan how to put forward their opinions. In other cases, mothers who felt that their own attempts to advocate for their children were not heard within the wider family welcomed an independent professional taking on this role. Some children actively made use of the FGC process to put forward their point of view, and got their concerns onto the agenda. It was notable that outcomes most valued by children were often changes in behaviour of their parents, for example in maintaining contact more consistently. Other changes that arose from a refocus on children's views and away from adult disputes were contacts with relatives on the 'other' side in divided families.

For some of the families, the behaviour of one or more children was a key issue, and one aspect of this was that the children were perceived to be exerting a considerable amount of power within the family. In such situations, professionals and family members commented that efforts to 'empower' the child within the FGC could be counterproductive. Some respondents felt that the expectation that children are listened to and, in particular, that they attend throughout meant that the adults in the family did not necessarily get any time within the FGC to discuss the issues for the child in their absence. While FGC coordinators' enthusiasm for children's participation is welcome, there was also a need to ensure that family adults were clearly 'given permission' to exclude children from parts of the discussion, where appropriate.

There were several cases where the advocate or family supporter struggled to ascertain the child's view on matters relevant to the FGC. In order to work with these troubled children, they allowed the child to lead their interaction to a great extent. However, in some cases, this meant that children were only able to make a limited contribution to FGC discussions concerning their future. Listening to children's views can be important to finding solutions, but the expectation should not be that children will always identify solutions themselves. Their description of and perspective on their situation – where they are able/willing to share these – could valuably inform adult decisions. Even a reluctance to discuss something about their life gives information. The guiding principle should be to ask their views and listen carefully.

How to support children's effective participation in family group conferences

Our research found that the involvement of a professional advocate was more effective than that of a family supporter in facilitating children's participation in FGC decision-making. Preparation was key, and it was important for professional advocates to build trust before they could gather children's views on very sensitive issues. This resonates with other research which indicates that for young people an effective advocacy relationship requires an optimum of two or three meetings to develop (Dalrymple 2002). Family supporters should be given greater support and guidance in understanding the role being asked of them, and what is involved, so that they can give more effective support.

It was our impression that some of the confusions and issues about the roles of professional advocate and family supporter could be overcome if a more detailed explanation was given before and at the start of the FGC – possibly something written down is needed, as some verbal introduction is already given. This is especially important for those participants who have been less involved in the preparation for the FGC. Family supporters themselves also need greater preparation and guidance in the role they take on, particularly encouragement to prepare with the child. But it also seems likely that some of the misunderstandings reflect inherent difficulties for those who are personally involved with the child and family – and have their own opinions on the issues discussed – in also speaking 'for the child'.

From research undertaken in Wiltshire with Hilary Horan, Dalrymple (2005, Horan and Dalrymple 2003) has argued that advocacy can empower children and young people in relation to their families and to social welfare professionals. The large majority in this study (51 out of 79) accepted an offer of a professional advocate, while 11 chose a family supporter, 6 refused any advocate, and a further 11 aged four or under were not offered any advocacy. The young people emphasised the importance of the independence and confidentiality of the professional advocate's role. They valued a relationship based on trust and listening. Advocates could help young people to work out what to say, and what they need not say, in order to get their point across without hurting or alienating important adults. The advocates in Wiltshire worked in a similar way to those in Brighton and Hove, spending time to build a relationship, often preparing something in writing, and then representing and supporting the young person on the day in a variety of ways.

Advocacy support, particularly from professional advocates, could enable children to have their views represented without needing to be present throughout the FGC. But it was clear from our research that, while advocacy is important, there were also many other elements of the FGC process which could help or hinder children's active involvement in decision-making. Respondents in a number of cases raised concerns about the impact on children of attending an FGC. Children were clear that FGCs were not a pleasant experience for them, even when they preferred to have a say than to be excluded.

When children attended, in order to allow them to participate comfortably in parts but not the entire meeting, another room was required, and a crèche or other age-appropriate provision for older children. The presence of other children could be supportive to children's participation, but there were issues about what other children heard, and they could act as a distraction.

There are resource implications involved in allowing a more flexible approach to children's attendance and involvement in FGCs – more space, crèche/youth workers and professional advocates are all costly. But it is important to have confidence that when children's participation is well supported, it need not harm the child and can benefit their situation. FGCs deal with matters that are complicated and painful to the children and young people concerned. It would be a mistake to look at the power dynamics within them in simple or rigid terms, or to imagine always a clear set of competing interests with defined 'points of view'. Sometimes there are many issues but it is hard to define a clear question. Both adults and children may be uncertain about what the best course of action might be. Nevertheless, FGCs can be effective if everyone works together in the interests of children. Advocacy in this context needs to be given space to assist children in a flexible manner as they find their own way to take part in the FGC process.

With a commitment to learn from experience, there is every chance that the two traditions represented by the practice of FGCs, and the offer of professional advocacy to children, can together produce effective support to children and families in difficulty.

References

Bell. M. and Wilson, K. (2006) 'Children's views of family group conferences.' *British Journal of Social Work 36*, 2–6, 671–81.

Dalrymple, J. (2002) 'Family group conferences and youth advocacy: the participation of children and young people in family decision making.' *European Journal of Social Work 5*, 3, 287–299.

Dalrymple, J. (2005) 'Constructions of child and youth advocacy: emerging issues in advocacy practice.' *Children and Society 19*, 1, 3–15.

Gill, H. (2005) *'Should advocates be part of private family time?'* Together, The FGC Network Newsletter. Family Rights Group, Summer 2005.

Holland, S. and O'Neill, S. (2006) '"We had to be there to make sure it was what we wanted": enabling children's participation in family decision-making through the family group conference.' *Childhood 13*, 1, 91–112.

Horan, H. and Dalrymple, J. (2003) 'Promoting the participation rights of children and young people in family group conferences.' *Practice 15*, 2, 5–14.

Kirby, P., Lanyon, C., Cronin, K. and Sinclair, R. (2003) *Building a Culture of Participation: Involving Children and Young People in Policy, Service Planning, Delivery and Evaluation.* London: Department for Education and Skills.

Laws, S. and Kirby, P. (2007) *Under the Table or at the Table? Advocacy for Children in Family Group Conferences.* Brighton and Hove Children's Fund Partnership and the Brighton and Hove Daybreak FGC Project.

Lupton, C. and Nixon, P. (1999) *Empowering Practice? A Critical Appraisal of the Family Group Conference Approach.* Bristol: Policy Press.

Lupton, C. and Stevens, M. (1997) *Family Outcomes: Following Through on Family Group Conferences.* SSRIU Report No 34. Portsmouth: University of Portsmouth.

Marsh, P. and Crow, G. (1998) *Family Group Conferences in Child Welfare.* Oxford: Blackwell Science.

Marsh, P. and Crow, G. (1999) *Family Group Conferences.* London: National Children's Bureau.

Merkel-Holguin, L. Nixon, P. and Burford, G. (2003) 'Learning with Families: A Synopsis of FGDM Research and Evaluation in Child Welfare.' In L. Merkel-Holguin (ed.) 'Promising Results, Potential New Directions: Potential FGDM Research and Evaluation in Child Welfare.' *Protecting Children 18,* 1–2, 2–11.

Nixon, P (2001) 'Making Kinship Partnerships Work: Examining Family Group Conferences.' In Bob Broad (ed) *Kinship Care: The Placement Choice for Children and Young People.* Dorset: Russell House Publishing.

Nixon, P., Burford, G. and Quinn, A. with Edelbaum, J. A. (2005) *Survey of International Practices: Policy and Research on Family Group Conferencing and Related Practices,* May 2005. Available at www.americanhumane.org/site/DocServer/FGDM_www_survey.pdf?docID=284 (accessed 24 January 2008).

Paterson, K. and Harvey M. (1991) *An Evaluation of the Organisation and Operation of Care and Protection in Family Group Conferences.* Wellington, New Zealand: Evaluation Unit, Department of Social Welfare.

Pennell, J. and Burford, G. (2000) 'Family Group Decision-making and Family Violence.' In G. Burford and J. Hudson (eds) *Family Group Conferencing: New Directions in Community-centered Child and Family Practice.* New York: Aldine de Gruyter.

Rasmussen, B. (2003) 'Vulnerability and energy: the study of the Danish experiment with family group conferencing.' *Protecting Children 18,* 1–2, 124–126.

Ryan, M. (2004) *Harnessing Family and Community Support.* Totnes: Research in Practice.

CHAPTER 6

Challenges and Complexities of Widening Access to Advocacy Services: Lessons from an Evaluation of Voice Advocacy Service

Elaine Chase

He was positive, he told me the possibilities and told me straight… I felt that someone was on my side, he was knowledgeable.

(Alex, age 14)

Introduction

Voice[1] (formerly Voice of the Child in Care (VCC)) was founded in 1975 by Gwen James, following the high profile death of Maria Colwell. Its remit was to allow children and young people in care to have a say in decisions that affect their lives. Over the years the service has gradually evolved from a helpline, to providing a visiting advocacy service to children in secure units, to offering a direct advocacy service for young people in care and in need. At the time of the evaluation Voice had its headquarters in north London and managed four other regional offices covering all local authorities across England. Since 2003 the service has expanded to provide visiting advocacy to ten young offender institutions and since 2004 has developed a range of specialist advocacy services for unaccompanied asylum seeking children, for young people experiencing mental health difficulties and for care leavers. At the time of writing, the service had over 60 permanent staff and a team of

200 freelance advocates and independent visitors around the country. Voice provides a range of independent advocacy services to young people looked after, care leavers and children in need.

In 2004, staff at the Thomas Coram Research Unit (at the Institute of Education, University of London) were invited to conduct an evaluation of the community-based advocacy services provided by Voice. The evaluation, analysis and report writing took place over a period of 26 months between March 2004 and May 2006. It encompassed elements of the advocacy service in central London, Hertfordshire, and, to a lesser extent, Bristol and Nottingham.

The evaluation adopted a case study approach in order to gain detailed insights into young people's experiences of advocacy services, alongside feedback on the service using standardised evaluation forms. In this chapter some of the more detailed findings from the evaluation are presented through a series of illustrative advocacy case studies. These raise a number of issues that are relevant to the current debate surrounding how best to widen young people's access to advocacy services.

The evaluation

The overall aims of the evaluation were: to investigate the extent to which the Voice advocacy service supports the advocacy needs of young people; to explore how or why needs have (or have not) been addressed; and to identify areas for further development within service delivery.

Specific objectives aimed to:

1. Provide an overview of the development of the programme in accordance with the monitoring and evaluation criteria stipulated under the Community Fund Grant.

2. Provide technical support to the ongoing monitoring programme within Voice.

3. Investigate the quality of referral processes and the outcomes of these.

4. Explore in more depth the experiences of a sample of young people who have received face-to-face advocacy support.

5. Elicit the views of a range of advocates, including those within Voice and those who work on a freelance basis with Voice, on their experiences and perceptions of the advocacy programme.

6. Ensure young people's participation throughout the planning and implementation of the evaluation.

The research

In order to fulfil the range of objectives of the study, a varied methodology was employed. In the first instance a steering group which included three young people who had experience of using the Voice advocacy service was established to guide the evaluation. The steering group provided invaluable support to the evaluation throughout the project and also served as part fulfilment of objective six (ensuring young people's participation throughout the planning and implementation of the evaluation).

The main research tool used with young people for the evaluation was a discussion guide. This asked young people about their experiences of how they had learned about the Voice advocacy service; the response they received when they first contacted the service; their understanding of advocacy and the role of the advocate; the types of difficulties they were facing which required the support of an advocate and how the difficulties were addressed or resolved with the help of an advocate; what they felt they had learned from having an advocate; which aspects of the advocacy service had worked well and whether there were aspects of the service that could be improved. Young people were also asked about how they felt at the point when the advocacy service ended and whether they would recommend the service to other young people.

An interview schedule for advocates was designed and covered a range of issues relating to their experiences of providing an advocacy service to young people and how they were supported in this role by Voice as an organisation. A third tool incorporated into the evaluation was feedback from young people who completed a form at the point when they finished working with their advocate. In total 60 forms were returned throughout the course of the evaluation and the findings entered into a spreadsheet from which they were analysed.

A number of factors influenced the course of the evaluation and it is important to consider these before presenting the findings and reflections from the study. Initially, identifying young people to take part in the study proved to be more complicated than was initially envisaged. The aim was only to engage young people in the evaluation who had come to the end of using the advocacy service, i.e. whose case files were 'closed'. Since young people using the service are primarily looked after young people, care leavers or young people in need, it was particularly difficult to access up-to-date contact details for them. This limitation undoubtedly affected the selection of research participants but is by no means unusual in research with young people in and leaving care or those in need (Broad 1996; Wigfall and Cameron 2006). Although every effort was made to sample young people who had used the service from an existing data set in order to ensure that there was a cross-section of experiences by age, gender, ethnicity and geographical location, in practice this was not possible and selection of participants was far more opportunistic than originally planned. Nevertheless, the young people involved in the one-to-one interviews did reflect a high degree of diversity with respect to their age, gender, ethnicity and the issues for which they required an advocacy service.

Furthermore, the process of identifying and involving young people in the research while adhering to codes of confidentiality and data protection meant that there was an unintended demand on Voice project staff time generated by the research. Finally, the data base systems within Voice at the time of the evaluation meant that progress in terms of meeting objective two of the study (providing technical support to the ongoing monitoring programme within Voice) was restricted.

Research participants

In total, 83 young people participated in the evaluation of the Voice advocacy service and a further six young people were involved in their capacity on the advisory group or planning and supporting the development of research tools for the evaluation. Sixty young people completed the evaluation feedback forms at the point when the advocacy service came to an end; the remainder of young people participated in one-to-one interviews, conducted either face to face or over the phone or, in the case of three young people, took part in a focus group discussion. One young person, unable to attend the focus group, sent her views of the service in a letter. Another young person with a hearing impairment felt unable to take part in the evaluation[2] but again shared her views of the service by email.

In total, 17 advocates including duty advocates, freelance and full-time advocates, specialist advocates and the advocacy services manager participated in the evaluation.

Findings

Feedback from the evaluation forms established that young people who used the service and who completed evaluation forms were on the whole very happy with the service they had received both from the duty advocacy service when they first contacted Voice and with the direct service that they had received from an advocate.[3] Opportunities for 'other comments' at the end of the evaluation form generated a range of positive comments about different aspects of the service. When asked to express views on other areas young people liked or disliked about their advocate none of the 60 respondents made negative comments. More than half made additional comments about 'other' things they liked about their advocate and these related overwhelmingly to either human qualities such as being friendly, helpful, caring, funny and trustworthy, or to specific skills such as an ability to listen, being easy to talk to and communicate with, being reliable or efficient.

> She wasn't patronising, actually looked on me as an individual and not a child.

> I had great confidence in X [advocate], he could be trusted, on whatever the subject in hand was.

Similarly, an open question asking young people to identify the most helpful thing about having an advocate identified the fact that the advocate enabled them to do or achieve things that they felt they would have been unable to do without the support of an advocate.

> They [advocate] gave me help with my problem and help me with what I have to say or do in court; I did go through a lot but they help me go through it ok.

> If I felt under pressure about saying something in meetings then my advocate would talk for me.

When asked to make suggestions about any improvements to the advocacy service, the few young people who did comment suggested the need to improve access to advocacy through either the number of advocates available, or their geographical proximity to the young person by making it easier initially to find out about the service.

Detailed interviews provided specific data about young people's experiences of advocacy. The three case studies that follow illuminate key issues in advocacy practice and provide a commentary on the complexities of widening access to advocacy services for young people. The names of young people used in these narratives have been changed and any identifying details have been omitted.

Alex, contacted Voice at the age of 12, when he found that his younger sister (aged 2), for whom he had had a caring responsibility, was being placed for adoption and he was frightened of losing contact with her.

Alex worked with his advocate over a period of about six weeks, meeting four or five times. The advocate initially liaised with Alex's social worker and other professionals working with him to clarify the problem and develop a tactical response. There was a level of urgency in the situation since a date for the adoption hearing could be decided at any time. The advocate first convened a meeting between Alex and his social worker as Alex did not feel that his concerns were being heard. The situation required a degree of legal knowledge, so the advocate also sought legal advice from a specialist legal advisor at the Voice London office. The advocate then contacted the guardian ad litem appointed to Alex's sister who subsequently visited him to explain the court proceedings regarding his sister and to hear what he wanted to say to the court about the proposed adoption. Alex described how this enabled him to have a 'visual idea of what was happening in the court' and the effect of adoption on his sister. Alex met with his advocate before each meeting with the guardian to plan what he wanted to say.

In view of Alex's concern about his sister's adoption the advocate suggested that an independent assessment of the parenting abilities of Alex's mother would be helpful. The advocate identified the need to be persistent in his approach with the social services department in order to secure this assessment. Although he was eventually successful in obtaining this, the advocate also recognised the necessity for Alex to understand that ultimately he might not be able to prevent the court making a decision in favour of placing his sister for adoption. Nevertheless Alex also needed to be reassured that he had done everything possible to prevent this happening.

Alex's situation illustrates a number of key characteristics which appear to be at the heart of successful case advocacy. The quality of the relationship between the advocate and Alex and his foster carers was clearly valued by all concerned. A combination of personal attributes such as honesty, respect,

While the long-term situation of the placement of his sister was at the time of the research still unresolved, the decision had been made for Alex to see his sister three times a year where previously contact with her had been denied. Asked why he thought things had gone well, Alex commented that the advocate had 'stuck up for me and said what I wanted him to say'. He also appreciated the fact that the advocate had talked to him honestly and directly about what was happening. Alex stated that the advocate had helped him gain confidence, 'stand up to people', 'speak up for myself' and given him knowledge about accessing help and support from an advocate should he require this again. At the point when he stopped working with the advocate, Alex stated that he had the result that he wanted and that it was an appropriate time for the advocate to stop working with him.

From the perspective of Alex's foster carers, the advocate had been able to mediate the situation between Alex and the social services department when they themselves had been told very clearly not to interfere on Alex's behalf. The carers felt that the advocate's support changed the outcome for his sister substantially. Arranging for the guardian appointed to Alex's sister to come and talk to Alex meant that his views on the adoption were presented in court. The personal qualities of the advocate, 'very professional, very efficient, willing to listen to the child and us', were highly valued by the carers.

Throughout the process the advocate's aim was to remain realistic about what could be achieved and to not raise Alex's expectations. The advocacy process benefitted from Alex's ability to remain focused and articulate about what he wanted from the situation and by being well supported by his foster carers. Working with the foster carers in this case was an important part of the advocate's role since they were the main source of support to Alex. The advocate described this as 'managing the whole advocacy process'. In Alex's case, the context was a legal one and this put limitations on what the advocate could do alone but did not undermine the role that he could take in supporting Alex. He commented,

> 'My response is that it is about jobs, whose job is it? The advocate's job is to help the young person represent themselves, the solicitor has a job, the guardian ad litem has a job – it's about managing that process...the clout [of advocacy] comes from having someone else looking in and seeing what is happening.'

loyalty and an ability to listen and other skills such as professionalism and efficiency were alluded to as key tenets to this relationship.

The clarity of the role of the advocate evidently encompasses a further determinant of success. In Alex's case, this required the advocate to know exactly where his role sat with that of the other professionals he came into contact with, and to have an understanding of the limitations of that role and an ability to facilitate a process whereby the role of the advocate and those of other professionals were synergised to work to Alex's best interests – the solicitor, the guardian ad litem, the foster carers, the social services department and the court were all being key players in this situation.

Further dimensions illustrated by Alex's situation are the task-orientated and time-limited principles to advocacy, consistency in working from directions given primarily by the young person and maintaining a strong sense of reality of what can be achieved through the advocacy process. In Alex's case, the combination of these elements of the advocacy process appeared to create a situation which afforded him a degree of control over what was happening with his sister, increased his confidence in being able to articulate his views and expectations, and knowledge that there are legitimate means of having his voice heard and having a say in decisions made by others that personally affected him.

Beth was interviewed for the study when she was 14 years old. At the age of 12 her foster carers, with whom Beth and her sister Helen had been living for about four years, decided to move to another part of the UK. Beth and her older sister were happy to move and wanted to stay with their 'parents' (foster carers). However, the responsible social services department refused to allow them to go and said they would have to stay within the local authority, where an alternative placement would be found for them.

After speaking to a duty advocate at Voice they were appointed an advocate who visited them within two weeks of the referral. Once he had established their reasons for wanting to move with their foster carers, the advocate wrote a letter on their behalf to the social services department. When the social services department refused to reverse their decision, the foster carers appointed a solicitor and went to court to request a residence order for Beth and her sister. At this point the advocate was not required to do any more on their behalf in relation to the court process. However, he did liaise throughout the case with the solicitor to ensure that the views of Beth and Helen were put to the court. The court decided in favour of the girls remaining with their foster parents and moving with them to their new home.

Through Beth's description of their relationship with the advocate, it was clear that specific things were very important to them. These included the following:

- the advocate always checked that he had written down things that they wanted to say accurately and in enough detail

- he was precise about appointments and time-keeping

- he spoke to their foster parents as well as to themselves

- he was able to relate to them about everyday things like their pets and hobbies and not just about the advocacy situation.

In terms of the success of the advocacy situation, Beth was convinced the successful outcome was a direct result of having advocacy support.

Beth also highlighted additional outcomes that improved her mental well-being. These included the knowledge that there were people available who would listen to her, who would also stick up for what she wanted, which enabled her to gain the confidence that she never had before to say what she wanted. Her only regret about the advocacy process was that the social services department had not been willing to admit any fault and offered no apology for the distress that she felt they had caused.

The foster carer described how a previously very good relationship between the family and social services had gone 'horribly wrong' with the appointment of a new social worker who 'threatened to remove the girls' when it was revealed that the family planned to move. As a result of having an advocate, the girls were appointed a new social worker who was 'very supportive'. For the foster carer, it was the value of having a neutral person to counter the 'power' of social workers and social services department that had really helped the girls. In the foster carer's view, for Beth and Helen, this had come from the combined work of the advocate and the solicitor.

Initially, the role of the advocate was to explore with Beth and Helen their understanding of the situation and what they wanted to happen. The next step was to liaise with the social work team to ascertain the rationale for refusing to allow the girls to move with the foster carers and whether they had listened to the views of the young people.

> 'It was all towards the agenda of the professionals involved...what they thought was in the best interests of the child, without actually talking with the child about what they think are their best interests.'

The skills of the advocate involved careful negotiation with other professionals and the complexities surrounding these discussions. Some social work professionals had expressed concerns about the care provided to Beth and Helen, despite a lack of clear evidence concerning poor quality or inadequate care. A further complication was that information shared by Beth's sister (Helen) in a confidential counselling session (and not directly related to child protection concerns) was disclosed to the social services department and used as evidence as to why the sisters should not remain with their foster carers. Part of the advocate's role was therefore to find out from the counsellor how the decision had been made to breach confidentiality.

The advocate worked with Beth and Helen for over a year, during which time the foster carers engaged the services of the solicitor. During this time, there was a change in the link worker for the family placement team and a change, at the request of Beth and her sister, in the social worker. These changes made liaising and mediating between the different teams and the young people and their carers complicated. The situation is also illustrative of the common situation where young people request advocacy support in the first instance for a specific issue but once the advocate begins to work with them other issues arise and need to be worked through. Although he felt that contractually and from a managerial position it would be easier to look at these matters – in this case the placement move and the change of social worker – as separate areas of work, in practice this was not always possible and it went against the ethos of providing an holistic service to young people.

> The advocate felt that a lot of the difficulty had arisen from a break-down in the relationship between the young people and the professionals involved in making plans for them. Part of his role therefore was in attempting to rebuild these relationships. He felt that he had made a difference because his presence had made other professionals really 'take stock of' what the young people were saying.

The aspects of advocacy illustrated in Beth and Helen's situation are similar to those exemplified by Alex's experiences of advocacy. Central to the success of the advocacy process were again the positive relationships that the advocate was able to nurture and the trust that he built with both Beth and Helen and with their foster carers. The skills of liaison and negotiation between different professional positionings are also evident. Arguably, where the advocacy process differs from the work with Alex is in how far it can be said to be task-specific and time-limited. While initially the advocacy was to ensure that Beth and Helen were actively involved in the decisions being made about the placement, once this work had commenced the advocate began to address other concerns such as their wish for a different social worker and the breach of confidentiality by their counsellor. Given the drawn out and complex legal process involved for the foster carers to secure a residence order, the advocate worked with Beth and her sister for more than a year – possibly then providing the opportunity for other issues to be raised and addressed. This example therefore raises significant questions about the extent to which it is possible to remain task-focused and apply the time-limited principle in practice. Inevitably, the provision of personalised and individual support to young people requiring an advocate is unpredictable in terms of its complexity, the time it takes and whether or not young people's lives are prone to other shifting circumstances that affect the pattern of the advocacy process. Such unknown elements have a direct impact on both access to and availability of advocacy services more broadly.

> Arben was 19 years old at the time of interview, having arrived in the UK at the age of 13 from Kosovo as an unaccompanied young asylum seeker. He had been placed in foster care by the local authority responsible for him and had remained there for about five years. As his 18th

birthday approached, Arben was told that he would have to leave the placement, and that the social services department would stop financial support, and would not provide alternative accommodation.[4] Arben's social worker put him in contact with Voice and he was allocated an advocate the following day. Arben felt that this problem had arisen because his discretionary[5] leave to remain in the UK as a child had come to an end, his legal status was uncertain and he was waiting for a decision from the Home Office.

When the advocate met Arben, two priorities were identified:

- to clarify his asylum status

- to work out where he would be living when he turned 18.

As the advocate did not have the necessary specialist knowledge to support Arben, she advised him to engage the services of a solicitor and Arben was able to find one within the same legal practice representing him with the Home Office concerning his immigration status.

The social worker believed that the local authority's decision to withdraw all support from Arben was wrong. He was particularly concerned about the absence of any planning meeting prior to this decision and that Arben had not been warned about the possibility of being homeless at the age of 18. The social worker therefore supported Arben's complaint to the social services department. Additional support came from Arben's solicitor, who had been involved in the Hillingdon Judgement[6] earlier that year (2003) and had a wealth of knowledge about the statutory responsibilities of local authorities to support unaccompanied asylum seeking young people during their transition from care.

While the solicitor took on the legal aspects of Arben's situation, the advocate's role was to ensure that Arben's care was sustained by the local authority between reaching the age of 18 and receiving a final decision from the Home Office. The main concern for the advocate was to ensure that Arben's immediate needs were met and to prevent him becoming homeless. Arben and his advocate agreed to request that his placement with his foster carers was extended since they were happy for this to happen. The advocate was also concerned that Arben should have been supported to apply for an extension of his leave to remain in the UK on the run up to his 18th birthday. However, this application had not been followed up by the local authority responsible for his care and, as a minor, it was not something that Arben could have done himself – but he was being penalised as a result.

The advocate worked with Arben by contacting the social services department and reminding them that the Children (Leaving Care) Act 2000 would apply. This ensures that support continues after a young person reaches the age of 18, including the provision of accommodation in the local authority area. She also noted that Arben had the right of legal redress should they refuse to accommodate him.

Arben valued the fact that his advocate was easy to understand ('could speak in simple English'), was helpful and was able to inform him about his entitlements and the statutory obligations that the social services department had to him. Without the advocate, Arben was certain that he would have been 'on the streets' and that having someone to speak up for him had made social services realise that he understood his rights. Ultimately the advocate and the solicitor together were able to support Arben so that his rights were not violated. The social services department agreed that Arben could continue to live with his foster carers and receive support from the social services department until he received a definitive response from the Home Office about his immigration status.

Arben's case presents an evolving dimension to advocacy practice: that of specific specialist advocacy areas. In addition to the elements of advocacy discussed in the earlier two case studies, Arben's situation also illustrates the need for specialist knowledge in some instances. In this case the advocate had a clear role in brokering the legal technical knowledge and skills required to support Arben in relation to immigration and social care law. At the time of writing Voice had developed a number of such specialist services in response to the increasing demands from young people for particular areas of advocacy expertise. These are discussed briefly further on in this chapter. Within the broader debates surrounding the widening of access to advocacy services, the area of specialist services is one that is receiving increasing attention and has implications for how services are planned and configured.

Discussion

The three case studies identify the level of professionalism and experience required of advocates to enable them to provide an effective service to young people in complex situations. In the current climate where there has been increasing debate on the importance of providing independent advocacy support to young people, it is this level of expertise that is in danger of being overlooked. Consultation on the *Care Matters* Green Paper (DfES 2006) identified the need to ensure that all young people in the care system have access to an independent advocate. While in principle this suggestion should be applauded, the proposition in the Green Paper that this role be assumed by teams of *independent visitors* has understandably raised concerns among those more attuned to the advocate's role.

The distinctions between the roles of advocate and independent visitor are frequently confused, not only in terms of their distinct skills and expertise but also in terms of the fundamental reasons for the existence of the two roles. Independent visitors play a critical role in providing a level of continuity of emotional and practical support to looked after children who have limited or no contact with their families as they move through the care system – as such their relationship with the child is one characterised by building friendship and a rapport with young people over a period of time. The role of advocate, however, is fundamentally task-limited and provides independent support to young people for specific difficulties that they are faced with and which require the neutral support of an advocate to enable them to have a say, be listened to and exercise their rights.

The studies also illustrate the unique role of the advocate vis-à-vis other professionals in primarily voicing the concerns, views and perspectives of the child or young person in decisions that affect them. As such, unlike other professionals, they do not assume a role of defining or working to 'the best interests of the child' as perceived by others but as perceived by the young people themselves. This positioning of the advocate in relation to the young person was referred to by both young people and advocates to represent the distinctive role of the advocate.

> Well, I guess the best of their abilities is to not only listen to what I was telling her but to put that into action...the advocate is the only voice that the child has that is going to be listened to.
>
> (Young woman, age 15)

...to put people's views in and keep young people's view in the work or problems that family and social services have or between the family and social services.

(Boy, age 12)

Despite the need to clearly separate the role of advocate from that of the independent visitor (and other professionals such as personal advisors, key workers and social workers involved in the care or support of looked after young people), the task-focused nature of an advocacy service can be problematic. The circumstances of children and young people in care or/and in need are often characterised by fluidity, instability and upheaval. As such, although a young person may initially engage the support of an advocate for a specific issue such as to contest a placement change, maintain contact with family or to exercise a complaint against a local authority, other issues requiring advocacy support may arise. As the advocate working with Beth and Helen indicates, this can complicate the role of the advocate. In theory, each issue faced by a young person requires a specific advocacy service for which contractual arrangements with the local authority are negotiated. In practice, advocates are working with young people who have complex lives and needs and strive to maintain a degree of 'holism' in terms of the way they work with young people. There are undoubtedly therefore residual issues in terms of how best to maintain the balance between task-focused and holistic support while working within the resource limitations faced by all advocacy services.

A further issue emerging from the evaluation of the Voice advocacy service was the degree of neutrality and independence of the advocacy service offered to young people. The perceived independence of the Voice advocacy service was highly valued by both young people and advocates. One advocacy manager commented:

I think there have been a few young people who have refused to work with children's rights officers (CROs) in local authorities because I think they are very compromised as they can't challenge practice in similar ways if they are based within the local authorities. It is definitely an advantage having that level of independence... We are starting from a different place I think.

Having said this, Chapters 2, 8, and 9 note from their research that the reliance of advocacy services on contracts from local authorities can undermine their ability to see themselves as independent in any meaningful way.

Since 2004, Voice has been developing more specialist advocacy services designed to meet the specific needs of certain groups of young people. The areas of specialism include services for unaccompanied young people seeking asylum in the UK, young people using mental health services and young people who are 16 years and over and consequently more likely to be experiencing the transition from leaving public care. In addition, Voice has undertaken extensive work in developing services to meet the advocacy needs of disabled children and young people. It was evident from the evaluation that the expert advocates were generating new demands on the service – which perhaps indicates both young people's needs and the success of advocates in meeting these needs. One of the key recommendations of the evaluation was that adequate resources were made available not only for specialist advocates to work directly with young people but also for the necessary research and development required for each of these services.

The significance of a specific role of duty advocacy – the front line service provided to young people when they first contact the Voice advocacy service – was also highlighted in the evaluation. There was an overall sense that, despite certain 'peaks and troughs' in the demand for advocacy support, the overall trend was an upward demand for services alongside a rise in the level of complexity of the issues confronting young people. Since advocacy issues were frequently resolved by the duty advocacy team and never required referral to a case advocate, the need to adequately resource this element of the service became apparent. Unfortunately, despite the pivotal role of duty advocacy – described as the 'front door' of the service – current contractual arrangements with local authorities did not cover the costs of this element of the service, which was instead resourced through other charity-based funds. As a result, a recommendation from the evaluation was to consider how the duty advocacy costs might more easily be absorbed into local authority contracts. This would benefit the duty advocacy service by allowing scope for further review and development.

One of the obstacles to accessing advocacy services identified by young people was the lack of knowledge of services and knowing how to access them. At the time of the evaluation, Voice had re-branded its service – changing its name to Voice for the Child in Care – and gone through an extensive publicity initiative. A further recommendation of the evaluation was to monitor the extent to which young people in care or in need are aware of advocacy services provided by Voice and what impact the re-branding and publicity initiative has had on young people's knowledge of the advocacy service. Furthermore, the provision of advocacy services to children and young people in need is a relatively new area of work for Voice. The evaluation suggested special consideration of how the service can best be promoted within services likely to be accessed by young people in need. The implications in terms of the capacity of the service to fulfil the likely large demand on services from children and young people in need will also require special con-sideration and planning.

The issues raised through the evaluation of the Voice advocacy service are likely to be relevant to the provision of advocacy services more widely. The in-creasing profile of advocacy on the landscape of programmes and policies pro-moting the care and well-being of marginalised young people will inevitably mean a continued rise in the demand for advocacy services that are able to be responsive to ever changing advocacy requirements. The major questions facing advocacy services appear to be ones of both quality and quantity. Advocacy services will need to continue to offer a growing number of young people the support of well-trained and expert advocates, while at the same time develop specialist services for specific groups of young people.

References

Broad, B. (1996) 'Young people leaving care: moving towards "joined up" solutions?' *Children and Society 13*, 81–93.

DfES (2006) *Care Matters: Transforming the Lives of Children and Young People In Care.* London: DfES.

Wigfall, V. and Cameron, C. (2006) 'Promoting Young People's Participation in Research.' In E. Chase, A. Simon and S. Jackson (eds) *In Care and After: A Positive Perspective.* London: Routledge.

Endnotes

1   While 'Voice' is predominantly used as the name of the organisation throughout the report, 'VCC' is also used, particularly when quoting directly from research participants.

2   Although provision was in place to facilitate this young person's participation in the evalua-tion, she felt unable to take part in an interview due to other factors and not as a result of her hearing impairment.

3   For a full report of the evaluation findings visit www.voiceyp.org.uk (accessed 14 February 2008).

4   Unaccompanied asylum seeking children may be entitled to services provided under Schedule 2 to the Children Act. Often they are 'looked after' by the local authority and provided with accommodation under Section 20 of the Children Act 1989.

5   Discretionary leave is normally granted for a period of three years but may be less. People who have discretionary leave have full access to employment and are normally eligible to apply for indefinite leave to remain after six years.

6   The *Berbe* v. *London Borough of Hillingdon* judgement (August 2003) helped clarify the respon-sibilities of local authorities in providing support to unaccompanied young people. It said that minors under the age of 18 years arriving in the UK, who had no one with parental responsibility for them, should usually be accommodated under Section 20 of the Children Act 1989 and subsequently therefore be eligible for support when they reach 18 years under the Children (Leaving Care) Act 2000.

CHAPTER 7

Providing Advocacy for Disabled Children, Including Children Without Speech

Abigail Knight and Christine M. Oliver

Introduction

It is well documented that children and young people have traditionally been excluded from participating in decisions affecting their everyday lives. For several reasons, disabled children and young people are even more likely to be excluded in this way. First, they are growing up in a society that tends to value passivity in children and views disabled children as particularly vulnerable and in need of protection. Second, disabled children are more likely to be the subject of abuse and neglect (Marchant and Page 1993). Third, they are more likely to enter the care system, where some are still at risk of abuse (Russell 1995). So that the well-being and rights of disabled children are safeguarded, it is crucial, therefore, that disabled children and young people have the opportunity to access independent advocacy (Sherwood 2004).

The need for disabled children and young people to be able to access advocacy has been recognised by government policy. The Social Services Inspectorate report of 1994, *Services to Disabled Children and their Families*, made the recommendation that social services departments should provide advocacy schemes for disabled children to enable them to express their wishes. More recently, the Strategy Unit report (2004), *Improving the Life Chances of Disabled People*, states that disabled young people will need increased opportunities to access advocacy in the future.

Advocacy for disabled children is indeed important. Yet, how does it differ from advocacy provided for non-disabled young people? What are the potential benefits for this group and what might be the particular challenges when advocating for disabled children? Of course, disabled children do not constitute a homogenous group. For many disabled children, the practice of advocacy does not differ at all. However, for young people who experience severe learning disabilities and/or do not communicate using speech, providing advocacy may present greater challenges and dilemmas.

Drawing on the findings from a research study carried out at the Thomas Coram Research Unit (Oliver, Knight and Candappa 2006), this chapter will discuss some of the possible benefits of advocacy to disabled children and some of the difficulties facing advocates working with this group. The study involved a telephone survey of advocacy schemes in England between October and December 2003, followed by qualitative face-to-face interviews with advocates, young people, parents and professionals within ten advocacy services across England in 2004.

This chapter makes reference to the findings that emerged from both the survey and the qualitative interviews of the study that relate to disabled children. Most of the examples of disabled young people presented here are drawn from research carried out in a specialist advocacy service working with disabled children in the north of England, although some reference is also made to other disabled young people from other advocacy services included in the research. Data was obtained from 12 disabled young people using advocacy services, as well as interviews with a small number of advocates, parents and professionals working with disabled children. Further information on the research can be found in a published summary of the findings (Oliver *et al.* 2006).

Communicating effectively

Having the skills and knowledge to communicate effectively with young people who are severely learning disabled and/or do not use speech is one of the main challenges facing advocates working with disabled children. It is important to set out with the belief that all people can express themselves through some form, whether this is through body language, gestures, signs, noises and other behaviours. As the *Children Act 1989 Guidance and Regulations* state:

Even children with severe learning disabilities or very limited expressive language can communicate preference if they are asked in the right way by people who understand their needs and have the relevant skills to listen.

(Department of Health 1991, p.14)

The *National Standards for the Provision of Children's Advocacy Services* (Department of Health 2002), similarly points out that no young person should be prevented from accessing services because of their communication difficulties.

Yet, communicating effectively with young people with specific communication needs requires relevant knowledge, training and the commitment of time. There is now a significant body of guidance and research detailing the approaches available to consult and communicate with young people with learning disabilities and the ethics that need to be taken into account (Beresford 1997; Marchant *et al.*, 1999, Morris 2002; Ward 1997). Some methods are more specialist and include augmentative and alternative communication methods, a term referring to the variety of techniques used by people with communication impairments to enhance communication, such as symbols (Murphy and Scott 1995; Scott and Larcher 2002) and Talking Mats (Brewster 2004; Germain 2004; Murphy 1998).[1]

So how did the advocates in our study communicate with their disabled clients? For those with some speech, a variety of methods was used, such as using simple words, using techniques such as sad and happy faces, drawing and games. Advocates reported needing to use an 'experimental approach' by being creative and flexible and by finding an activity which interested the child and then engaging them in this while talking about a particular problem that concerned him or her. Some used more specialist communication methods, such as Makaton. As one social worker explained, it is important to make communication meaningful to the young person:

If a child has a learning disability, it affects how much they can make an informed decision. It's about trying to involve them in decisions they can make an informed choice about, it's about making a real decision. A lot of the young people we work with have very complex needs and communicating with them is very hard, so it's about trying to make communication and decisions meaningful.

(Kim, social worker, children with disabilities)

Not surprisingly, the need to explore the wishes of young people who do not use speech to communicate was also one of the greatest challenges for advocates. Advocates commonly used a multitude of methods, such as becoming familiar with a young person's likes and dislikes, their moods and general personality over a period of time, by observing the young person's gestures and other non-verbal signs. This knowledge was then backed up by exploring the views of key individuals in the young person's network of carers, family and friends. Yet the difficulty in *really* knowing what the young person with communication impairments wants is one of the main dilemmas facing advocates working with severely disabled children and young people.

Advocacy: theory and practice

Advocates were asked to define advocacy for the study, as part of both the survey and the qualitative part of the research. The vast majority of advocates surveyed defined advocacy in terms of 'speaking up' on behalf of children and young people, enabling them to 'have a voice' or 'put their views across' by themselves. An important part of the role, according to advocates, was enabling young people to express their views, even if the advocate did not agree with them. A defining characteristic of advocacy was that advocates eschewed involvement in assessing the child's 'best interests'.

> Pure advocacy is putting forward the child's view, regardless of their best interests.
>
> (Advocate)

> The aim of advocacy is to help the young person voice their opinion and pursue what *they* consider to be in their best interests, which you or other professionals may not necessarily agree with.
>
> (Advocate)

Yet, advocates working with children and young people with specific communication needs expressed anxiety about the dilemma they faced between representing a child's views when they are able to verbally articulate them ('pure advocacy'), and interpreting a child's non-verbal communication. Advocates working with children without speech are often engaged in a process of getting to know a young person, developing a picture of their likes and dislikes and, on the basis of this information, attempting to ascertain their wishes (defined here as non-directed or non-instructive advocacy). Often, advocates consulted people in the young disabled person's family and social network. This complex process produced anxiety in some advocates and a concern not to take advantage of their role. One advocate expressed the dilemma like this:

It's a thin line: are you saying what you think, or what they want?

(Volunteer advocate)

Two case studies are given below to illustrate the kinds of situations encountered in advocacy with children with communication impairments:

Alan, age 19 at the time of the research, was a wheelchair user with profound physical and learning disabilities and complex healthcare needs. He communicated mainly through high-pitched crying and rolling his head. When he did not want something, he hit things out of the way. Alan was being looked after by social services when he was referred to the advocate. The main role of the advocate was to support his move from the children's unit to appropriate adult care and to bridge Alan's transition to adult services. Because the advocate knew Alan well, her role was also to ensure that the staff at the new unit knew Alan's likes and dislikes so that they could be more effective in meeting his needs.

Martin, age 15, and his sister, Isabel, age 17, suffered from a severe physical disability, which also affected their communication skills. Their home life was complex; there were some incidents of domestic violence and the parents found the management of Martin's and Isabel's disabilities difficult. The family situation restricted the children's access to leisure opportunities so, in order to improve their social life, the advocate arranged after-school activities for them.

In both these examples, the young people had not instructed the advocate to do these tasks; therefore it may be argued that this is not 'pure' advocacy. Yet, when working with young people who cannot instruct an advocate in a formal way, it is surely better that someone, like an advocate in this case, is taking an active interest in the welfare of the disabled young person. As one of the professionals we interviewed explained:

[Advocates are] doing the best they can in the circumstances, including in circumstances where they're not absolutely certain what the child's views are. But it's far better than doing nothing.

(Principal Officer, Children and Families)

When working with Alan (the disabled young person described above), his advocate explained:

You've got to acknowledge that the disability will influence the way you work with the young person. He doesn't communicate verbally; I can tell he likes certain things and not others from experience, but even knowing his dislikes and likes and then being able to say to him 'where would you like to live?' is implausible. There's absolutely no way that I can do that. What I can do is to look at what does work for him, what doesn't, making judgements after seeing him, talking to staff who know him, talking to parents, talking to anyone who knows him really. But at the end of the day, I still don't know whether he really thinks 'I don't want to move there, I don't like the plans you are making for me.' I really wouldn't be able to say.

(Advocate)

In this context, the advocate reported that she felt able to advocate on the young man's behalf after getting to know him well, by observing him and by seeing him as a 'typical' 18-year-old young man:

I can only base it on my experience of him: what would an average 18-year-old wish and what kind of things would this sort of young man be looking for? For example, he likes his music on loud so he would need to be housed with people who wouldn't object to him having his music loud.

(Advocate)

Taking a 'rights' approach

Some advocates, particularly those working with disabled young people, attempted to resolve the complexities of advocacy practice with children without speech by adopting a clearly articulated rights-based model of advocacy. This approach emphasises the rights of the child under legislation such as the Children Act 1989 and the UN Convention on the Rights of the Child 1989. For some advocates, it was one way of helping them to be clear about their role when there were difficulties in obtaining a young person's views due to communication difficulties. The rights model was also seen as particularly valuable in situations where advocates were expected to advocate for children who were not present at meetings. As these advocates explained:

For children with disabilities, we work on more of a rights model. Children have a right to education, family life, services and resources to sustain them in their family home. Then we ask other professionals and other people to give us an assessment and ask why this hadn't happened.

(Advocate)

I come from a children's rights model and use legal documentation to provide a mandate to get people to provide services. I have used Article 12 of the UN Convention and Section 17 of the Children Act to argue that a disabled child is a child in need and is therefore entitled to a service that the social worker is saying they shouldn't have.

(Advocate)

Advocacy and participation of disabled young people in decision-making

Findings from the research highlighted some key factors that functioned to inhibit or facilitate the participation of children with communication impairments in decision-making. Inadequate resources in regard to skills, staffing and funding, particularly in relation to generic advocacy projects, were cited as the main obstacles to working effectively with disabled children. However, opportunities for maximising disabled children's participation were identified, despite these limitations. For example, it was felt that professionals could demonstrate more willingness and sensitivity to involving disabled children in meetings by slowing the pace of discussions and taking more time and a range of communication methods to ensure that children understood, as far as possible, what was being discussed.

It has already been stated that one of the reasons why advocacy is particularly important for disabled young people is that they are traditionally perceived by society as passive, vulnerable and in need of protection. It is also this perception that makes providing advocacy for disabled children especially challenging. Many advocates in our study reported how difficult it was to work with a group who were not used to being asked for their views or given opportunities to participate in decision-making. According to one advocate:

The other dilemma is working with people who are so unused to making choices and decisions and they are always going to say 'yes' to everything.

(Advocate)

One young disabled woman was described as having difficulty getting her coat in her residential unit, which was placed on a high hanger in a wardrobe. Yet, as the advocate said:

She was mortified at the thought that I would ask social services to change it, challenge the service. After some time and work, she asked the manager herself.

(Advocate)

Group work

One specific way of encouraging and empowering disabled young people to participate more in decision-making, highlighted by some advocacy services, was the use of group work with disabled young people, in both schools and residential units:

> We run small groups in a special school on decision-making and making choices and we support young people to put their views across.
>
> (Advocate)

Group work functioned as an important and preliminary step in building children's confidence to participate in decision-making. Advocacy group work was also identified by some parents as improving their disabled children's confidence and independence by providing them with opportunities for socialising and gaining the support of their peers.

Establishing a positive relationship

One of the key factors identified in the study to maximise the opportunity for disabled young people to participate in decision-making was the importance of giving time and commitment to establishing a close and positive relationship between advocate and young person. In fact, for young people who were profoundly disabled, the need for a positive relationship was seen as crucial:

> Three years ago, a young man, with no other sources of support – it was not clear what he wanted. [The advocate] attended meetings, struggles, because he was not verbalising. [The advocate] knew him previously and managed to ascertain that he didn't want the residential unit they wanted to put him into. It ended with him getting a better package of care.
>
> (Social worker)

The importance of an advocate spending time with a disabled young person in order to get to know them well and establish a positive relationship was also recognised by some of the parents and carers we spoke to for the study. One parent, for example, reported that the advocate spent more than a year developing a relationship with her disabled daughter. The advocate visited and observed her daughter in different settings and contexts, such as at home and school, allowing the advocate to find out about the young woman's life, her likes and dislikes. This approach helped to gain the trust of the parent as well as give the young woman obvious pleasure at the advocate's visits. In meetings, the parent felt that the advocate was able to show that 'she really knew' her daughter.

However, the desirability of consulting family members and professionals in a young disabled person's life also produced tensions. A key dilemma for advocacy practice concerned the sometimes difficult process of separating the views of disabled children from their parents and carers. A second theme concerns the tendency for the confidentiality needs of disabled children to be compromised or limited by adult concerns for their protection.

Who is the client: disabled child or parent?

According to the advocates who participated in the study, an area of confusion that sometimes emerged in advocacy practice with disabled children concerned the question of who actually is the client: the young person or the parent? On the whole, advocates were very clear that the disabled child was their overriding concern. However, there was also a tendency for advocates to feel pressure from parents of disabled children who perceived the advocate to be their ally in fighting for services for their child. One parent, for example, described the advocate as someone who would:

> ... listen to your needs, to support and guide you in the right direction, to help with your problem.

> (Mavis, parent)

Some advocates felt that parents often adopted a 'best interests' approach to their disabled children and, as a result, may not always inform their son or daughter of all the options. One volunteer advocate reported that she found this conflict of interests a challenging aspect of advocacy practice. She described the case of a young disabled woman who was in residential care and who was in the process of moving on to supported living. She said that the parent repeatedly contacted the advocate to 'find out what was going on':

> And the young person's parent had different needs and wants for the child, rather than what the child wanted. [The parent] was saying, 'What is happening? Why hasn't that happened?' And I am saying 'Are you sure she wants that? Or are you just speaking as a parent, wanting the best for your child?' ...You have to say, 'Look, I'm an advocate for your child, not for you. I can only deal with what she wants to tell me, not what you want to tell me. I can take your views into consideration, but I'm only here for her'.

> (Citra, volunteer advocate)

Indeed, some social care professionals we spoke to were rather critical of advocacy for disabled children, which they perceived to be carer-led rather than child-led. As one social worker said:

> We have a respite care service downstairs and most of the time the young people don't want to come and it's about the parents' needs. I think this is what the advocate could get involved in as it's about negotiation and try and work out a compromise and be more child-led.

> (Kim, social worker, disabled children)

However, for some foster carers, it was *because* the advocate was child-led, and prioritised the wishes and views of children and young people, that they felt supported. One foster carer of a severely disabled child said:

> [The advocate] made it quite clear that she couldn't support me in the way I needed, because she was there for Peter. But I felt that if she was helping Peter, she was helping me. When she walked away, I felt supported without being supported.

> (Cynthia, foster carer)

Confidentiality

A further theme that emerged from interviews with disabled young people concerned the importance of talking to someone in confidence. One 15-year-old young woman, for example, described advocacy as:

> Someone you can talk to… It stays in this room and [she] won't tell other people. When you tell, it matters she'll do something about it… Just because you're disabled or fostered doesn't matter, she treats us as special.

> (Sally, age 15)

However, our interviews with social care staff, parents and advocates revealed the issue of confidentiality as very contentious when working with disabled young people, particularly those with complex communication needs and severe disabilities. Many adult interviewees expressed doubts about the significance of confidentiality as a result of what they perceived to be a lack of understanding on the part of the young person or a perceived need for enhanced protection of the disabled child. One social worker, for example, expressed her doubts in the following way:

> I think there needs to be a sharing of information in the best interests of the child or young person. It would hinder if they didn't address the concerns

with you, it could become a problem if you're not working for the same thing and if you don't know there's a problem for the young person, you can't do anything about it.

(Lynne, social worker, children with disabilities team)

The need for parents and professionals to share information about a young person, thereby limiting confidentiality, was also expressed by these two parents of severely disabled young people:

[I'm] very comfortable [with confidentiality]…but this is not applicable to Michael. You have to rely on people caring for him understanding his needs.

(Rose, parent)

I think it's difficult because everyone is entitled to say what they want to say without fear of other people picking on them but with Sara, it is really diffi-cult, because if you don't have a hint that something is wrong, it is difficult to put it right. There needs to be professional boundaries here, but often professionals should only offer limited confidentiality. Sara wouldn't un-derstand what that meant anyway.

(Anthea, parent)

It would seem, therefore, that among adult carers and professionals disabled children's need for confidentiality is accepted in principle but that, in practice, the more severe the communication impairment, the less relevant confidentiality is perceived to be – either because children are less able to articulate their views and feelings, or because they are perceived as lacking a capacity to understand the meaning of the word. Yet, the dependency of disabled children on others for care can mean that children without speech are more vulnerable to abuse, and to the loss of rights to be consulted about matters of concern to them. This is a situation which underlines, rather than limits, disabled children's need for independent advocacy. Those disabled children who were able to articulate their views placed a high value on the confidentiality offered by advocates.

How do disabled children and young people experience advocacy?

While this chapter, so far, has attempted to discuss the different perspectives of those engaged in advocacy with disabled children, a further issue of central importance concerns disabled children's satisfaction with advocacy.

Do they understand the advocacy role? How do they experience having an advocate?

Disabled children did not always draw a rigid distinction between the role of the advocate and other social care professionals in their lives. For example, Molly, who was aged ten at the time of the study, and living in foster care, made a distinction between her social worker and her advocate when she said that the social worker was someone who 'takes her out and stuff' whereas the advocate 'sees how you are'. She went on to say that she thought the advocate was 'fun' to be with and that she would feel able to speak to her about her placement if she was unhappy there. When asked if she knew what 'advocacy' meant she defined it as follows:

It means people who look after me.

(Molly, age 10)

Another young person, age 14, described the advocate in this way:

The advocate is like a second mum.

(Tina, age 14)

In this respect, it is notable that disabled children tended to emphasise the caring and relational aspects of the advocacy role, as well as its informality.

Generally the disabled children and young people who could express their views verbally for the study were very positive about having an advocate. Overall they said having an advocate helped them feel nurtured and that they valued being listed to and taken seriously. One learning disabled young person felt that she was able to express herself more in meetings as a result of feeling listened to by her advocate:

RESEARCHER: 'Did people listen before Sarah [the advocate] came along?'

YOUNG PERSON: 'I don't think so.'

RESEARCHER: 'Why do you think Sarah was able to make them listen to you?'

YOUNG PERSON: 'Because she said that they have to listen.'

RESEARCHER: 'Did you feel able to speak up in meetings?'

YOUNG PERSON: 'I didn't before, but now I can.'

Being represented in meetings such as planning and review meetings with education and/or social care professionals was an important part of having an advocate, according to the disabled young people and advocates in our study. One young man, for example, who had learning disabilities and mental health difficulties, had been prevented from attending his review by his social worker because she argued it would have been too stressful for him. To ensure that the young man felt more valued and included in this process and received accurate feedback from the review meeting, the advocate arranged for key professionals, including the Independent Reviewing Officer, to see the young person straight after the review meeting.

A common role undertaken by advocates working with disabled children and young people was liaising with social care staff in residential units about issues of personal care. In this context, the role of advocates in helping to protect children's personal privacy was highly valued. For example, Jonathan, age 16 at the time of the study, had learning disabilities and presented with some challenging behaviour. He had lived in a residential unit for disabled children and young people for two years. The advocate used to visit the unit and hold group meetings with the young people there on a monthly basis. At one meeting, Jonathan told the advocate that he did not like having a bath and that he preferred to have a shower because he could put a curtain around him. When the advocate asked him why he could not lock the bathroom door, Jonathan told her that he was not 'allowed' to as the laundry basket was kept in there. As a result, the advocate spoke to the staff about issues of privacy and, by asking staff to move the laundry basket to another place, young people at the residential unit were given more respect and privacy when having a bath or shower. These may be viewed as minor advocacy interventions, but they might also be attributed with having a major impact on the quality of disabled children's everyday lives.

The emotional and practical support offered by advocates who were closely involved in life-changing situations for disabled young people was also affirmed. For example, Sunna was age 17 at the time of the study. An Asian young woman, who had a learning disability, she had become pregnant as a result of sexual abuse and was as a result placed with a foster family. Social services were planning to remove the baby from Sunna's care but this was against the young woman's wishes. As a result of the advocate's intervention, Sunna was enabled to keep her baby with her and to stay in long-term foster care:

> [The advocate told social services that] Sunna doesn't want to be split up from her baby and she doesn't want to go back to her family...and they said I can't care about him [the baby], but I can. My aunty [foster carer] helps me... They said I have to go to court to see what the judge says. And then

we went to court and the judge said that the mother and baby should stay together. The judge said, 'Take a residence order for the baby, and they can stay in foster care long term.'

(Sunna, age 17)

In these circumstances, it is unlikely that Sunna would have been able to achieve her goal of keeping her child without the advocate's willingness to challenge the local authority and to pursue the case in the courts.

Conclusions

Some young people with severe disabilities are not able to directly 'instruct' their advocates, or to speak on their own behalf. As a result, some advocates respond by taking a rights-based approach, advocating for disabled children's rights to education, care, play and other central tenets set out in the UN Convention of the Rights of the Child. Additionally, some advocates take the view that their legitimate role is to insist that disabled children should be entitled to the same level of support and service provision offered to any young child of a similar age. In this context, advocacy is not strictly about 'having a voice'. Indeed, this conceptualisation places children without speech at a disadvantage. It is, however, about ensuring that disabled children, particularly those with specific communication needs, have an adult champion who is able to explore their likes and dislikes, feelings and views about matters of concern to them.

The study showed how advocacy is helping disabled children and young people, not only in their everyday lives, but also by increasing their participation in decision-making and thereby promoting their social inclusion. Many of the examples of advocacy practice with disabled children highlighted in this chapter emphasise the importance of spending enough time over many weeks or months to establish a positive relationship with the young person. By observing the young person in different settings and contexts, by getting to know their behaviours, likes and dislikes, and by obtaining information from other adults in the young person's social network, a close and positive relationship may be established. Although this process is resource-intensive, in terms of time, patience and, possibly, specialist training, it is only by getting to know the disabled young person well that advocacy will be truly effective. This means that, if disabled children's rights to participation are to be made a reality, advocacy work with disabled children needs to be sufficiently well-resourced.

The central role of the advocacy relationship in shaping the effectiveness of advocacy for children with specific communication needs produces a number of dilemmas and tensions. Historically, the parents of disabled children have had a key role to play in challenging service providers and 'advocating', albeit in an informal way, on their children's behalf. It is not, therefore, uncommon for the parents and carers of disabled children to see themselves as their child's best advocate. Professional advocates stressed the importance of working closely with other adults who are significant in the young person's life, such as social care professionals and parents, in order to build up a comprehensive picture of the young person's life. However, advocates also have to be careful not to lose sight of their central role in advocacy for the child, and not the parent. Indeed, some social care professionals working with disabled children felt that, on occasion, advocates needed to be more rigorously child- rather than parent-led. At the same time, advocates participate in a young disabled person's life for only a limited period of time. While advocates were generally clear about their role and communicated this to the parents and carers of disabled children, they also highlighted the need for tact and skill to reduce the risk of advocacy disrupting a young disabled person's existing network of support.

Children's right to confidentiality represents a key debate in advocacy for all children and young people. However, in relation to severely disabled children, particularly children without speech, the issues are intensified, drawing in issues of the sexual and personal autonomy of disabled children, as well as child protection concerns. Where they were able to articulate their views, disabled children highlighted the high value they placed on the confidentiality of advocacy and their frustration when information about them was shared inappropriately and without their consent. Children without speech, who are dependent on others for care, are arguably most vulnerable to abuse and therefore in need of independent advocacy as a source of protection as well as a means of supporting their rights to participation.

References

Beresford, B. (1997) *Personal Accounts. Involving Disabled Children in Research.* York: Social Policy Research Unit, University of York.

Brewster, S. (2004) 'Puttng words into their mouths? Interviewing people with learning disabilities and little/no speech.' *British Journal of Learning Disabilities 32*, 4, 166–9.

Department of Health (1991) *The Children Act 1989 Guidance and Regulations: Volume 6. Children with Disabilities.* London: HMSO.

Department of Health (2002) *National Standards for the Provision of Children's Advocacy Services.* London: Department of Health Publications.

Germain, R. (2004) 'An exploratory study using cameras and Talking Mats to access the views of young people with learning disabilities on their out-of-school activities.' *British Journal of Learning Disabilities 32,* 170–174.

Knight, A., Clark, A., Statham, J. and Petrie, P. (2006) 'The views of children and young people with learning disabilities about the support they receive from social services: a review of consultations and methods.' Thomas Coram Research Unit, Institute of Education. London: Report for the Department for Education and Skills.

Marchant, R., Jones, M., Julyan, A. and Giles, A. (1999) *Listening on All Channels: Consulting with Disabled Children and Young People.* Brighton: Triangle.

Marchant, R. and Page, M. (1993) *Bridging the Gap: Child Protection Work with Children with Multiple Disabilities.* London: NSPCC.

Morris, J. (2002) *A Lot to Say.* London: Scope.

Murphy, J. (1998) 'Talking Mats: speech and language in practice.' *Speech Language Therapy in Practice,* Autumn, 11–14.

Murphy, J. and Scott, J. (1995) *Attitudes and Strategies towards AAC: A Training Package for AAC Users and Carers.* Stirling: University of Stirling.

Oliver, C., Knight, A. and Candappa, M. (2006) *Advocacy for Looked After Children and Children in Need.* Thomas Coram Research Unit, Institute of Education. Report for the Department for Education and Skills. Available at www.dfes.gov.uk/research (accessed 24 January 2008).

Russell, P. (1995) *Positive Choices – Services for Children with Disabilities Away from Home.* London: National Children's Bureau.

Scott, J. and Larcher, J. (2002) 'Advocacy for People with Communication Difficulties.' In B. Gray and R. Jackson: *Advocacy and Learning Disability.* London and Philadelphia: Jessica Kingsley Publishers.

Sherwood, S. (2004) 'Advocacy: the challenges of providing advocacy for children and young people with communication impairments.' *ChildRight* (November) 17–18.

Social Services Inspectorate (1994) *Services to Disabled Children and their Families. Report to the National Inspection of Services to Disabled Children and their Families.* London: Department of Health.

Strategy Unit (2005) *Improving the Life Chances of Disabled People.* London: Cabinet Office.

Ward, L. (1997) *Seen and Heard. Involving Disabled Children and Young People in Research and Development Projects.* York: Joseph Rowntree Foundation.

Endnote

1 A summary and review of some of these methods can be found in Knight *et al.* (2006).

CHAPTER 8

Complaints and Children's Advocacy in Wales – Getting Behind the Rhetoric

Andy Pithouse and Anne Crowley

The vast majority of complaints are received from adults who are complaining about services the child receives rather than necessarily representing the child's wishes...

Introduction

The above quote from a local authority children's complaints officer stems from interview data gathered as part of a major survey of complaints and advocacy services across Wales funded by the Children First Branch of Welsh Assembly Government (Pithouse *et al.* 2005a). It reveals something of the uncertain and contested realm of children's complaints to local authority social services and alerts us to the need for some careful reflection about their number, nature, and background organisational context. Accordingly, the chapter will illustrate key challenges to the effective delivery of support to children that will promote their participation and rights in having their concerns addressed. The comments that follow are based upon survey returns and secondary data from local authorities and advocacy providers and interviews with relevant professionals. Children's perspectives on complaints and advocacy in Wales that we gathered in the course of our research are addressed in Chapter 9 and hence we do not quote their views here.

Essentially, there are two modes of advocacy – case-based and cause-based, the former more engaged with matters raised by individuals, the latter seeking to generate systemic change but often informed by case-based issues (Dalrymple 2003, 2004a; Dalrymple and Hough 1995; Henderson and Pochin 2001). It has been demonstrated (Pithouse and Parry 2005) that, across Wales, advocacy is purchased as a service level agreement by the 22 unitary local authorities from five national voluntary sector providers who deliver mainly case-based support to: children looked after, children in the child protection system and children with disabilities.

Key investigations that shaped the policy terrain in which complaints and advocacy now operate in Wales (Carlile 2002; Clarke 2003; Jones 1999; Waterhouse 2000) have helped inform changes to the Children Act 1989, introduced in the Adoption and Children Act 2002, that provide children in need and care leavers with a statutory right to advocacy when intending to make a complaint (Welsh Assembly Government 2003a). National Standards for advocacy (Welsh Assembly Government 2003b) define the aims and expectations of provision for children and young people (including those leaving care) up to the age of 21. The Standards recognise that children are not 'adults in training' but people able to form and express opinions, participate in decision-making processes and influence solutions. They set a basic level that children and young people can expect from professionals providing advocacy services. While all advocacy providers in Wales endorse the Standards and seek to inform their services accordingly, the critical issue is whether children and young people can access these. As we shall see, relatively few children's complaints that we examined involved professional advocacy.

The study

The methods used to identify (a) the number and characteristics of children's complaints involving advocacy and (b) the role and characteristics of advocacy services included the following:

- A pre-tested survey instrument sent to all 22 local authorities in Wales about the characteristics of complaints in the financial year 2003–4 involving children and local professional advocacy provision for children. All 22 responded to the survey and were able to provide data on involvement of advocacy service, number of complaints, type of complaint, care status, age and gender of child and other categories around disability, ethnicity and language. Not all were able to indicate if children's peers had acted as advocates. One authority was unable to indicate if a complaint was child-led or adult-led. The survey instrument for reasons of economy was not designed to capture child-specific categories such as living in an area of poverty, immigration status, religion, ethnic sub-group – variables often associated with disadvantage and erosion of rights (Children's Rights Development Unit 1994). Information on language, disability, and membership of Black or minority ethnic community was requested.

- Audio-taped interviews with senior staff from all children's advocacy services; audio-taped interviews with all children's complaints officers (or staff designated) in the 22 authorities. Secondary data on advocacy such as monitoring data, quarterly management reports, annual reports, service level agreements, gathered from advocacy providers and/or local authorities.

Ethical approval was sought through the University of Wales and informed consent was obtained from all participating authorities, organisations and individuals regarding the publishing of material. Anonymity was assured for all respondents.

All local authorities in Wales were requested to complete a survey instrument in relation to activity during the financial year 2003–4 at complaints stages 1, 2, and 3. These stages (as contained in *The Children Act 1989 Guidance and Regulations, Volume 3 – Family Placement and Volume 4 – Residential Care* (Department of Health 1991) were defined for the purposes of the survey as: stage 1 (problem-solving or local resolution and formally noted as such); stage 2 (formal complaint involving investigation by named individual with reporting requirements); stage 3 (panel meeting involving independent members with reporting requirements). The Children Act 1989 and associated guidance also requires local authorities to produce annual reports on complaints activity involving children. We commence with a summary of survey returns regarding the number and key characteristics of complaints.

Stages of complaint

Stage 1

Survey returns indicated a total of 611 stage 1 complaints involving children and young people during the financial year 2003–4. Of these, 20 complaints were included in returns but without any details of whether these were adult- or child-led. A majority of stage 1 complaints involving children are led by adults, mainly kin (n=390 or 64%), almost double those led by children and young people (n=201 or 33%). Looked after children feature prominently in complaints (Padbury 2002); within the 611 stage 1 complaints a sizeable minority (43%, n=264) concerned children being looked after. Of these 264 complaints, some 38 per cent (n=101) involved children fostered in the local authority area; 44 per cent (n=116) involved children in residential care in the local authority area; 9 per cent (n=23) involved children fostered or in residential settings placed out of the local authority area; and another 9 per cent (n=24) where children were defined as looked after but were living independently or with kin or friends. Here, we might note that 70 per cent of the 4,315 children looked after children in Wales at 31 March 2004 were in foster placements and only 6 per cent placed in residential care (Welsh Assembley Government 2004). This does suggest a disproportionate number of complaints from those in residential care in the year in question. This is likely to be due, in part, to the high number of complaints (59) in one large urban authority where most children in residential care were known to have demonstrated their shared disapproval of local authority policy changes by making a complaint. Other reasons might include the possibility (albeit our study did not seek evidence for this) that advocacy providers find something of an accessible 'captive population' in residential care as opposed to a widely dispersed clientele in foster care. Thus those in residential care may be better informed and supported in bringing grievances or concerns to notice via complaints systems.

Most stage 1 complaints featured older age groups, approximately 3 to 1 for those aged 10+ compared with those aged 0 to 9. Around a quarter of the 611 complaints involved children who were not looked after (n=144, 24%) but living at home with kin, mainly parents, other carers or friends in the area. Very few complaints (n=4, 0.6%) involve local children living with kin or friends based outside their local authority area.

If we are to assume that children find the complaints process challenging (Wallis and Frost 1998) then we might expect to see more use of professional advocacy funded by local government in Wales. Yet, when looking at involvement with some type of local authority funded professional advocacy in relation to these 611 complaints, the returns indicate some 63 (10 %) complaints involved such a service. Of these 63 complaints, 40 involved children leading their own complaint with professional advocacy support. In addition, there was a small cluster of nine (2%) complaints involving children and young people who led their complaint but were supported by other professionals (such as teacher, health professional, drugs and alcohol voluntary worker) acting as an advocate.

Some 138 (23%) complaints (of which 113 involved children looked after) were led by the child or young person *without* support from *any* adult. Whether this proportion of child-led complaints without support is somehow indicative of a facilitative complaints system that makes advocacy unnecessary or whether it reflects a lack of accessibility to advocacy by children and professionals (Aiers and Kettle 1998) is not something we can determine from the survey returns alone. Survey returns provided no information on any peer support children and young people may have received in leading a complaint.

Overall, one Welsh speaker was identified across all the survey returns. Less than 5 per cent (n=26) of complaints were known to involve children registered as disabled according to returns. Less than 3 per cent (n=15) of complaints were identified as linked to Black and minority ethnic communities (not dissimilar to proportions in the wider population). The diversity of need in relation to advocacy has long been recognised (Herbert and Mould 1992) but in respect of complaints the main social divisions seem to collect around white Welsh children who are looked after or are children living at home with kin.

Stage 2

As complaints became more formalised at stage 2 they reduced in number (n=57): on average around two to three per authority for the year in question. They were much less likely to be led by children and much more likely to be led by adult kin (70%, n=40). Overall, four out of five complaints were led by kin and/or professional advocates. Most children involved were in 10+ age groups. Unlike stage 1 complaints, there were more complaints involving children living in the local area with kin or friends (n=47, 81%). There were eight complaints in regard to children in foster care, one in residential care (out of local area) and one in independent living (out of local area); thus ten in all who were looked after (19% compared with 43% at stage 1). There were, proportionately, slightly more complaints involving children registered as disabled at stage 2 (n=5, 9%) than in stage 1 (n=26, 5%), but the numbers overall are small and comparison may be unwise. One Welsh speaker was identified. No children from minority ethnic communities were noted in survey returns for stage 2.

Proportionately, more cases at stage 2 (25%, n=14) compared with stage 1 (10%, n=63) involved support from local authority-funded advocacy services. There were, proportionately, more children who led in complaints and got support from local authority funded advocacy providers at this stage

(19%, n=11 compared with 7%, n=42 at stage 1). Very few children advocated for themselves alone at this stage (n=3, 5% compared with 23% at stage 1). Thus we can note that at stage 2 it is typically the case that adult kin have taken the complaint forward involving a child that is living in the local area with them or other kin or friends. We were unable to identify the likely causes of this pattern of complaints at stage 2, particularly the *decrease* in the involvement of looked after children at this stage compared with stage 1. Whether this means that children looked after are less likely to find their complaints heard at stage 2 because they have no adult kin to motivate a complaint compared with children living at home and whether this implies some disadvantage for children in foster or residential care remains a topic for future enquiry.

Stage 3

At stage 3, in which panels convened to examine complaints, we see very few cases and these were all led on behalf of children, mostly living at home, by adult kin. Survey data for stage 3 revealed ten complaints in 2003–4 across the whole of Wales. Most authorities reported nil cases. None reported more than one case. Of the ten cases, two were linked to a local authority funded advocacy service. The small numbers allow no useful comparison apart from noting the low incidence of complaints at this stage and the prominent role of adult kin.

Across all complaints and stages (n=678) we can note the apparent low use of a professional advocacy service, as reported by local authorities (around 12%, n=79) and greater involvement of adult kin and self-advocacy. Authorities, of course, may not always know about or accurately record advocacy activity. As has long been noted (Harris 1993), adult kin are more likely to lead complaints involving children and this was so in our study throughout all complaints stages. This adult-led patterning to complaints could be the outcome of complex processes that may include adult/professional views of children as 'recipients' of services, 'self-evidently' lacking competence (Mayall 2002) and needing an adult voice in order to be represented. It may also reflect a lack of knowledge by children about advocacy as well as a reluctance to complain (Aiers and Kettle 1998). There are likely to be organisational influences too whereby advocacy is not recommended to children by professionals or agencies reluctant to become the object of any critical attention (Boylan and Wyllie 1999; Dalrymple 2004b). Also, advocacy services may not always be sufficiently proactive in 'selling' their service (Pithouse *et al.* 2005a). We will explore some of these possibilities soon but first we outline the reasons for the above complaints.

Themes within complaints involving children

Our analysis of complaints rarely allowed for coding into discrete and generalisable categories. Complaints were typically multi-issue and complex in their causes and resolution. A weave of primary and secondary issues arising back and forth across time and place lay behind many presenting concerns. In short, most complaints have no linear career or simple bounded sequences such as 'event' leading to 'complaint' leading to determination of 'evidence' leading to 'judgement'. Instead, a more equivocal and negotiable process typifies the way many complaints arise and run their course. An unknown number are dealt with outside of formal procedures altogether and most are resolved at stage 1 without determinations of guilt or blame attaching to parties in some strict administrative or juridical sense. Hence, we avoided a 'league table' analysis of complaints that might denote some overly 'realist' perspective that complaints activity can become a proxy measure for 'poor' or 'good' performance by local authorities and thereby allow comparison. Instead, we asked local authorities to complete an open-ended question within the survey instrument that asked them to identify primary and secondary reasons for each complaint and to cluster these where appropriate as child- or adult-led. In respect of child-led complaints we noted four distinct domains:

- concerns in relation to foster care arrangements, leaving care and placements appeared more often led by children and were areas where most child-led complaints were located

- concerns in relation to contact between children looked after and their parents, kin or significant others also appeared prominently represented in child-led complaints

- concerns (albeit few, fewer than five) in survey returns from looked after children being subjected to bullying by other children, or about the behaviour of other service users, were led by children

- concerns in relation to ineffective communication between local authority and service users over decisions was a notable cluster and seemed to be as often raised by children as adults.

Children were more likely to complain in relation to matters of personal care, contact with kin and effective communication with staff – seemingly more to do with the emotional and relational side of care and well-being. Children's complaints, perhaps predictably, seemed to connect to some unhappiness about how or where they were being cared for and their relationship with significant others. By contrast adult-led complaints involving children collected more around the appropriateness or quality of provision, decision-making, the perceived attitude/conduct of staff and the accuracy or tone of records/minutes of meetings. Adults were more likely than children to challenge allegations by social services about abuse or neglect. Disability-related matters were also likely to be led by adults.

Advocacy – the social organisation of ambivalence

While our study did not address the reasons for what appears to be a relatively small number of complaints involving independent children's advocacy, we do in this chapter discuss key organisational and professional issues that we believe bear upon the ability of advocacy services to engage more extensively in complaints and other fields of related activity. Advocacy is clearly valued within policy and the official rhetoric of local authorities but it seems less regarded and sometimes marginalised through a combination of factors to do with service capacity, independence, market competition and attitudes of local authority staff. We now selectively present professional viewpoints and secondary material that point to advocacy as a sometimes unwelcome and often awkward visitor to the world of work in children's services.

Service capacity

First we note the obvious point that support for complaints was but one part of what advocacy services offered children. Additional activities included: promoting the advocacy service with targeted groups of children (looked after, child protection, disability); promoting children's participation in various policy and practice development forums; providing independent visiting to children looked after; offering advice and support often via multi-media techniques. The targeted population was in reality a geographical and conceptual diaspora of children and needs, most in foster care or with kin and sometimes in far-flung places. Relatively few were easily grouped as in residential care. Engaging with this dispersed population was a challenge for many projects that typically had one to three full-time advocacy staff, some of whom combined a management role with that of advocate. Variation across advocacy agencies in relation to staff tenure (full time, paid sessional, unpaid volunteer), their physical location, their training and qualifications tended to mark out key differences. Of interest was that children's views were typically very positive across the board and not associated with some schemes and staffing structures rather than others (Pithouse et al. 2005a, pp.11–12).

When we examined involvement in complaints by professional advocacy funded by local authorities we noted they supported 79 (12%) of the 678 complaints and, of these 79 complaints, over two thirds (n=48) involved children looked after. Thus of the 274 complaints involving looked after children some 18 per cent had the support of a professional advocate funded by the local authority. Whether this relatively small involvement is a function of looked after children not wishing to seek advocacy or not knowing about the service (Boylan and Boylan 1998) is not known. Advocates would thus seem less involved in the task of complaints than in advising and helping children more generally to voice their rights and wishes with service providers about case-based issues. Activity around complaints can of course be time-consuming and complicated and may require additional technical/legal expertise; thus the number of such cases involving advocacy tells us little about actual staff time and other related costs such as specialist advice.

In brief, there are no agreed unit costs for advocacy that might allow comparison across projects in relation to supporting complaints led by children, achieving regular contact with target groups of children: providing phone lines, a website, leaflets, newsletters and promotion events; supporting participation by children and young people in various policy and practice development forums. These sorts of activities were attempted to varying degrees by most advocacy providers in Wales but typically as a case-based process with limited opportunities to promote or campaign for systemic change from this work, which might be a more ideal combination (Willow 2002).

Most providers claimed that their funding offered little margin to respond to an expanding demand for advocacy. The idea of going 'the extra mile' that is expected in many commercial relationships was unlikely according to some respondents in small projects (as were most), because neither their grant income nor their scale of resource allowed such flexibility. As social services' patterns of activity shifted in Wales during the period of study (e.g. more children being looked after for shorter periods, more reliance on foster care, more children out of area; see Welsh Assembly Goverment 2004) so the challenges and costs for advocacy inflated. In such circumstances, advocacy providers tended to re-target their narrow resource to where risk and visibility combined to shape an agenda around looked after children and child protection, which 'made sense' to local authorities but as a consequence other priorities identified in service level agreements such as children with a disability and other children in need, tended to get displaced.

Data returned by advocacy providers indicated a total of some 695 children (over 79% of these were looked after) seen by a professional advocate across 20 of the 22 authorities in Wales in 2003–4. The total funding that supported advocacy activities was approximately £966,000 according to figures supplied by advocacy providers (around £300,000 of this came as contributions from their own coffers, the rest from local government). Funding per project ranged from around £25,000 to around £150,000 (Wales average £48,500). The numbers of children seen by an advocate per authority during 2003–4 varied between five in one authority to over 80 in another (Wales average 35). There was no necessary connection between numbers seen and size of project funding. It was notable that some authorities with some of the lowest numbers of children seen in the year by an advocate (e.g. authorities with between 5 and 15 children seen) were authorities where there had been a change in advocacy provider, or where the authority had introduced a service level agreement for the first time at the beginning of 2003–4. That said, the below-average numbers of children seen by some above-average funded projects do raise 'value for money' and capacity questions. Of course, low referrals may also be caused by advocacy 'rejection' by professionals, resulting in less access to children and young people and less influence by advocacy in relation to potential changes to the way social work services are provided to children.

Independence and market competition

Our interviews with senior staff from all children's advocacy providers indicated a shared perception that they do not see themselves as independent in any meaningful sense given their reliance on contracts from local authorities. All would prefer a more distanced and neutral mechanism for funding advocacy and for arbitrating over disputes or concerns that either party to a contract might have about their respective activities. As with other advocacy providers (Boylan and Wyllie 1999; Dalrymple 2004b; Wise 2004), several respondents spoke of friction with local authorities when seeking to empower young people in their criticism of services and in a few instances there were fundamental differences over the very purpose of advocacy. Several respondents were concerned that they should remain 'outsiders' and not become incorporated into what Dalrymple (2004b) terms the 'protectionist discourse' of welfare services, whereby advocates would be expected to routinely attend the reviews of looked after children or to attend child protection conferences to help listen, engage with and represent children, when arguably much of that work should be part of the social work task. This tension between what was an appropriate social work advocacy role and what was the task of the professional advocate continues to engender some differences of view and confusion within children's services, both in the UK and in the US (Dalrymple 2003; Litzelfelner and Petr 1997, p.398; Padbury 2002). Being there to assist at reviews and conferences only when a child had a dispute over some significant matter (and when the child explicitly consents to advocacy support) was for several respondents the appropriate means by which a child-led and rights-led service should be activated. By contrast, some authorities wanted their advocacy providers to be much more proactive in meeting with and helping children to navigate more smoothly the child care system.

The marketisation of their services was seen by most advocacy respondents to undercut independence and to generate unhealthy competition that potentially might influence the way advocacy providers approached their task. The claim that service integrity can be compromised by the desire to win contracts is scarcely news (Clarke 2003; Henderson and Pochin 2001). What was notable in this instance was a distinct air of distrust between some advocacy providers who stated they were wary about publicly sharing good ideas about best practice in case this might lend some commercial advantage to 'the competition'.

Respondents thought three-year contracts that underwrote many service level agreements were too short a period and promoted uncertainty over project planning, insecurity for staff, and fractured relations with children if contracts were not renewed (five authorities changed advocacy providers during 2004–5). None of our respondents (advocacy providers and local authority staff) described the transition from one advocacy agency to another when contracts changed hands as in any sense 'straightforward'. On the contrary, most spoke of the lengthy implementation period (several months) to get a new provider up to full speed. Feedback from service users illustrated how a change in advocacy service provider could lead to young people feeling let down, confused and, in some cases, very angry and upset. They would have to take time to get to know and invest trust in a whole new set of individual workers. Advocacy is not some 'plug in and play' service. It takes time for the recipient of a new contract to recruit and induct professional advocates and managers, to vet and train new sessional and volunteer workers, to engage with a number of local stakeholders to gain their interest and trust and to make contact with targeted children, most of whom will be dispersed in foster care and some will be out of the local area. It would not be hard to imagine that such circumstances could impede the way concerns and complaints come to the notice of advocacy services.

Professional attitudes

Measures of advocacy impact resist simple definition. For example, were we to take the number of children supported by an advocate as an indicator then much depends upon the willingness of social workers and other key staff to refer children to the service. Yet, it seemed evident that in some authorities there was a reluctance by social work teams to meet with advocates and make referrals. This stemmed from a culture of mistrust and a belief that advocacy 'creates complaints' and undermined practitioner attempts to control risks and pursue organisational and protectionist agendas (Goldson 2001; Payne 2000; Wattam and Parton 1999). However, as with other social workers (Noon 2000) many social work teams endorsed strongly the work of advocates. Indeed, some social workers were thought by advocacy staff to refer too enthusiastically: by assuming advocacy to be a ready source of generic support to children in need, rather than a selective and problem-focused service, commissioned mainly to assist children in the looked after system or those involved in child protection matters.

All local authorities were sent a questionnaire directed at senior staff with involvement in purchasing and overseeing the delivery of children's advocacy (Pithouse et al. 2005b). In brief, they were asked to describe the advantages and disadvantages of advocacy and to outline what they perceived to be the key challenges for children's advocacy in their authority. The questionnaires were returned by 20 authorities, mainly completed by middle managers from a range of operational, strategic and commissioning backgrounds. Key challenges were the limited ability by a majority of authorities to fund effective advocacy in relation to children with a disability living in or out of area, particularly children who might receive respite services (social services and health) on a regular if short-term basis. While there is no shortage of good advice on the advocacy skills needed to support children with serious disabilities (Cavet and Sloper 2004), this was one area where nearly all authorities spoke in terms of aspiration rather than achievement in regard to providing such children with effective advocates.

A majority of authorities (12) referred to advocacy providers joining with complaints officers and other staff appointed to help promote children's rights, in 'reaching out' to children looked after, via a mix of visits, participation forums, newsletters, flyers and care reviews. Time and costs were noted by many as precluding their keeping in touch in any meaningful and regular way with a wide scatter of fostered children and a minority in residential care, in and out of the local area. Regular mailshots and occasional forums were the more typical way of keeping in touch. As with other services (Dalrymple 1998), most provision was task-centred and reactive but with some proactive work in relation to key trigger points (becoming looked after, looked-after review, child protection conference) that generated contact with the child from a complaints officer and/or advocacy worker and/or leaflets being sent and materials made available to the child or young person offering support.

The importance of evaluation in order to enhance advocacy for children looked after is well made by Dalrymple (2004b, p.6). However, very few authorities evaluated the advocacy service beyond quarterly meetings to monitor activity and discuss issues. When asked about the benefits of advocacy, five authorities cited clear benefits to the child and young person. Five returns claimed no particular benefits associated with the service at all. Other returns spoke instead of challenges such as: extending the service to other vulnerable children not looked after; lack of choice over advocate due to single-advocate service; getting social services managers and staff to understand and value advocacy. Few mentioned any direct benefits to the local authority or the services they provided.

Views from local authority complaints officers

The questionnaire returns helped inform subsequent audio-taped and structured interviews with staff from all 22 authorities whose remit included responsibility for dealing with children's complaints. These respondents, typically designated as children's complaints officers, were frequently in contact with advocacy providers on a day-to-day basis and often charged with a developmental role in relation to promoting advocacy with operational staff and looked after children in their authority. Having accessible complaints procedures does not mean they will be used by children looked after (Dickson 2004), hence the importance of complaints officers in mediating the complaints system to children cannot be underestimated (Ball and

Connolly 2004; Connolly 2000). Complaints officers were based in a wide range of non-operational and operational settings and some were line managed by staff with operational responsibilities. Consequently, conflicts of interest were not unlikely in several authorities. Several complaints officers carried responsibilities for adults and some stated that this impeded a more dedicated focus on children and young people who were looked after, particularly those hard to reach out of area or dispersed widely in foster care throughout the authority.

Complaints officers were typically located at basic social worker or administrative grades. Several spoke of status-related difficulties in lacking the seniority to challenge operational staff and/or promote system change. Complaints officers spoke of the 'culture' within their organisation in respect of the way complaints were understood and dealt with. It seemed evident that some authorities were notably open and supportive in respect of children's complaints. Others were less receptive, particularly in respect of foster care, which was seen as a scarce and precious resource that could be undermined by complaints and needed to be protected from same. Much depended upon key figures in senior and middle management who set the 'tone' over whether complaints were understood as a likely adversarial threat with potential disciplinary implications or an opportunity to reflect on the way services were provided.

There were also frequent reports from complaints officers about the challenge for some managers and social workers to integrate a 'children's rights' approach to case management (Dalrymple 2004b, pp.10–11). Thus, while social services staff could appreciate there could be tension between their view of a child's best interests and the child's wishes and rights, they could not always appreciate that the advocate was there to help voice the child's wishes rather than moderate these wishes or mediate between parties. The lack of understanding or sympathy for a rights-led advocate role was considered to be more problematic in relation to 'front-line' staff than in relation to those more senior management who had 'signed up' to advocacy in a commissioning capacity but rarely had any day-to-day contact with either children or advocates. The need for more training in children's rights was noted by respondents, as it has been more generally for child care professionals who have responsibilities for children looked after (Boylan and Lebacq 2000).

The diversity of need in relation to advocacy has long been recognised (Herbert and Mould 1992). Respondents too recognised this and most referred to attempts by themselves and advocacy providers to jointly seek out 'hard to reach' groups about their needs for support. The gaps in this aspect of provision, notably in relation to children with a disability, children placed out of area, those in short-term respite care, and children dispersed in foster care, were commented upon by many respondents. The financial, logistical and time costs in engaging individually with a large and/or dispersed population of children looked after were noted by several respondents as a major challenge in meeting and promoting children's interests and wishes.

Conclusions

Advocacy services in Wales are typically focused around children looked after, child protection and children with disabilities, and are typically case-based. Advocacy needs to be part of a wider participation strategy that can include children whose voices are not much heard (DeVernon 2001). Various levels and forms of advocacy can be complementary in meeting different types of need. Our study revealed that while innovative services and committed staff typified much of children's advocacy there were issues around limited capacity, independence and some rejection by a minority of local authority front-line staff and team managers. Of some concern was that several local authorities saw little added value through advocacy in relation to its developmental potential for raising service quality and saw it as of relevance to the child or young person only. A minority of local authorities believed advocacy to offer a range of benefits to both child and the authority. A few authorities reported a history of quite strained relations with advocacy providers that had led to another supplier being awarded the contract.

The above complex organisational and professional terrain lay beneath the bare statistics about the type and number of complaints and indeed all other activities that advocacy providers undertook. It made the interpretation of complaints activity an unwise venture and instead compelled us to not consider what might be some optimal level of complaints (whatever that might be) but instead to recommend to Assembly Government the need for more far-reaching change to the way we support children and young people more generally. At the time of writing, Welsh Assembly Government are consulting on a major step change that seeks to deliver at local and regional level a matrix of children's rights, advocacy and participation across public services (Welsh Assembly Government 2007). While not yet formulated as government policy, the Assembly are considering the feasibility of advocacy commissioned at regional level by consortia of local authorities, health trusts and their partners. A more comprehensive tiered model is envisioned that offers users a 'one stop' service that is inter-connected and mainstreamed within local public services. Tier 1 would offer specialist support to children and young people making complaints against any public service; tier 2 would also be a specialist service that seeks to reach vulnerable groups whose voices are not well heard; tier 3 would comprise a more generalist role of promoting children's rights and capacity-building to support children's participation within public services. A qualifications framework for practitioners operating within these tiers is also expected to be part of future consultations.

This vision of a new advocacy service involving all local public services and administered by appropriately qualified professionals and funded through multi-agency commissioning can only be sketched here. There will be much future debate by interested parties as to whether this vision is feasible; for example would it best be delivered by the independent sector or by dedicated units drawn from public services themselves, or a mix of these, in order to embed advocacy as a normative aspect of mainstream provision. Indeed, all the issues raised here and in other chapters will hopefully inform the policy consultation that is yet to enter the public domain in Wales. Whether the vision outlined above survives to become an official policy proposal and whether this proposal survives the scrutiny of public debate is yet to be seen, but what is clear is that advocacy and children's rights are prominently on the policy agenda in Wales at the moment and significant change of some kind seems inescapable.

References

Aiers, A. and Kettle, J. (1998) *When Things Go Wrong: Young People's Experience of Getting Access to the Complaints Procedure in Residential Care.* London: National Institute for Social Work.

Ball, C. and Connolly, J. (2004) 'Something to complain about.' *Community Care 1505* (15 January), 38–39.

Boylan, J. and Boylan, P. (1998) 'Promoting young people's empowerment: advocacy in North Wales.' *Representing Children 11* 1, 42–48.

Boylan, J. and Lebacq, M. (2000) 'Rights for wronged children: training child welfare professionals in advocacy and children's rights.' *Child Abuse Review 9*, 6, 444–447.

Boylan, J. and Wyllie, J. (1999) 'Advocacy and Child Protection' In N. Parton and C. Wattam (eds) *Child Sexual Abuse: Responding to the Experiences of Children.* Chichester: Wiley.

Carlile, Lord A. (2002) *Too Serious A Thing: Review of Safeguards for Children and Young People Treated and Cared For by the NHS in Wales.* Cardiff: NafW.

Cavet, J. and Sloper, P. (2004) 'Participation of disabled children in individual decisions about their lives and in public decisions about service development.' *Children and Society 18*, 278–290.

Children's Rights Development Unit (1994) *UK Agenda for Children.* London: CRDM.

Clarke, P. (2003) *Telling Concerns: Report of the Children's Commissioner for Wales' Review of the Operation of Complaints and Representations and Whistle-blowing Procedures and Arrangements for the Provision of Children's Advocacy Services.* Swansea: Children's Commissioner for Wales.

Dalrymple, J. (1998) *Making Advocacy Accessible: An Evaluation of the Advocacy Centre.* Bristol: University of the West of England.

Dalrymple, J. (2003) 'Professional advocacy as a force for resistance in child welfare.' *British Journal of Social Work 33*, 5, 1043–1062.

Dalrymple, J. (2004a) 'Developing the concept of professional advocacy: an examination of the role of child and youth advocates in England and Wales.' *Journal of Social Work 4*, 2, 181–199

Dalrymple, J. (2000b) 'Constructions of child and youth advocacy: emerging issues in advocacy practice.' *Children and Society 19*, 3–15.

Dalrymple, J. and Hough, J. (eds) (1995) *Having a Voice: An Exploration of Children's Rights and Advocacy.* Birmingham: Venture Press.

Department of Health (1991) *The Children Act 1989 Guidance and Regulations, vol. 3: Family Placement.* London: Department of Health.

Department of Health (1991) *The Children Act 1989 Guidance and Regulations, vol. 4: Residential Care.* London: Department of Health.

DeVernon, N. (2001) *Advocacy for Children and Young People in Milton Keynes.* Buckingham: Milton Keynes Council and Barnardo's.

Dickson, D. (2004) 'I'll complain the way I want.' *Community Care 1509* (12 February), 34–35.

Goldson, B. (2001) 'The Demonisation of Children.' In P. Foley, J. Roche and S. Tucker (eds) *Children in Society: Contemporary Theory, Policy and Practice.* Basingstoke: Palgrave.

Harris, N. (1993) 'Complaints about social and education services for children.' *Family Law 399* (23 October), 587–590.

Henderson, R. and Pochin, M. (2001) *A Right Result? Advocacy Justice and Empowerment.* Bristol: Policy Press.

Herbert, M. and Mould, J. (1992) 'The advocacy role in public child welfare.' *Child Welfare 71*, 114–130.

Jones, A. (1998) *Report of the Examination Team on Child Care Procedures and Practice in North Wales.* London: HMSO.

Litzelfelner, P. and Petr, C. (1997) 'Case advocacy in child welfare.' *Social Work (US) 42*, 4, 392–402.

Mayall, B. (2002) *Towards a Sociology of Childhood: Thinking from Children's Lives.* Buckingham: Open University Press.

Noon, A. (2000) *Having a Say: The Participation of Children and Young People at Child Protection Meetings and the Role of Advocacy.* London; The Children's Society.

Padbury, P. (2002) 'A problem shared.' *Community Care 1309* (5 September) 36–37.

Payne, M. (2000) *Anti Bureaucratic Social Work.* Birmingham: Venture.

Pithouse, A., Crowley, A., Parry, O., Payne, H., Dalrymple, J., Batchelor, C., Anglim, C., Holland, S. and Renold, E. (2005a) *A Study of Advocacy Services for Children and Young People in Wales: A Key Messages Report.* Cardiff: Cardiff University School of Social Sciences; Social Inclusion Research Unit University of North East Wales, Department of Child Health; Wales College of Medicine.

Pithouse, A., Crowley, A., Parry, O., Payne, H. and Dalrymple, J. (2005b) *A Study of Advocacy Services for Children and Young People in Wales: Data Analysis Report.* Cardiff: Cardiff University School of Social Sciences; Social Inclusion Research Unit University of North East Wales; Department of Child Health; Wales College of Medicine.

Pithouse, A. and Parry, O. (2005) 'Children's advocacy in Wales – organisational challenges for those who commission and deliver advocacy for children who are looked after.' *Journal of Adoption and Fostering 29,* 4, 45–56.

Wallis, L. and Frost, N. (1998) *Cause for Complaint: The Complaints Procedure for Young People in Care.* London: The Children's Society.

Waterhouse, R. (2000) *Lost in Care: Report of the Tribunal on Inquiry into Abuse of Children in Care in the Former County Council Areas of Gwynedd and Clwydd.* London: HMSO.

Wattam, C. and Parton, N. (1999) 'Impediments to Implementing a Child Centred Approach.' In N. Parton and C. Wattam *Child Sexual Abuse: Responding to the Experiences of Children.* Chichester: Wiley.

Welsh Assembly Government (2003a) *Providing Effective Advocacy Services for Children Making a Complaint.* Welsh Assembly Government (October). Cardiff: WAG.

Welsh Assembly Government (2003b) *National Standards for the Provision of Children's Advocacy Services.* Welsh Assembly Government (February). Cardiff: WAG.

Welsh Assembly Government (2004) *Personal Social Services Statistics Wales 2003–4.* Cardiff: Local Government Data Unit.

Willow, C. (2002) *Participation in Practice: Children and Young People as Partners in Change.* London: The Children's Society.

Wise, K. (2004) 'Two-way stretch.' *Community Care 1514* (18 March), 32–33.

CHAPTER 9

Advocacy and Complaints Procedures: The Perspectives of Young People

Anne Crowley and Andy Pithouse

The best advocates will listen. They will have satellite ears, a big brain and they will use their head. They will have open and fiery eyes but they are not angry. They will get people's attention. They will be familiar and be someone you can relate to.

(Tania, age 14)

Introduction

This chapter examines the views of young people gathered in the course of a review of advocacy provision commissioned by the Welsh Assembly Government. The shape of the review was largely determined by the concerns raised by the Children's Commissioner for Wales about the inadequacy of both complaints procedures and the advocacy services available for children wishing to raise concerns or make complaints about health, social care or education services (Children's Commissioner for Wales 2003).

Young peoples' perspectives on advocacy and the making of complaints were sought and their responses, as we shall see, challenge the perceived wisdom that complaints procedures and advocacy support services of themselves are sufficient to safeguard our most vulnerable children from abuse within or by those services that aim to promote their well-being. The findings suggest that until we tackle the 'power dynamics' of adult–child relations and embrace a wider vision of children and young people's participation and children's rights, radically altering the attitude and behaviour of those working directly with children and young people in our public and independent services, complaints systems and independent advocacy are likely to remain fairly blunt instruments of protection and empowerment.

Our study (Pithouse *et al.* 2005) engaged with over 100 young people who had either used independent advocacy and/or complaints procedures, or who were considered (by the Welsh Assembly Government) as potential beneficiaries or users. Respondents included:

- young people who had not necessarily had any exposure to independent advocacy or complaints procedures in the public welfare services but who were deemed to be potential beneficiaries of independent advocacy services because of their vulnerability and reliance on public welfare services

- young people who had used independent advocacy services across Wales including some young people who had received advocacy support to make a complaint to social services, the local education authority and/or the NHS

- young people who had made a complaint to social services or the NHS, some of whom had accessed independent advocacy support to help them pursue their complaint.

Ethical approval was sought through the University of Wales. Young people were invited to participate in the study via support and advocacy projects, local authority complaints officers and, in one case, a school teacher. Informed consent was obtained prior to the interview or participation in a focus group and anonymity was assured. Researchers prepared young people-friendly information on the findings and outcomes of the study and fed this back to the young people through the gate-keepers.

A reference group was established at the start of the project comprising young people who were, or had been, users of advocacy services. The group informed the development of the research methodology and provided a valuable source of advice for the research team.

The chapter also draws on a follow-up consultation exercise commissioned again by the Welsh Assembly Government which collated the views of nearly 1,500 children and young people (aged 6–20) on the handling of complaints in the NHS, by social services, within schools or by the local education authority. As part of this exercise, in a series of consultation events and surveys up and down the whole of Wales, children and young people were asked what sort of support they would like to be able to access if they wanted to raise a concern or make a complaint about any of these services. The young people's views and experiences of seeking help and support to get their voice heard in decisions, or raise concerns and/or make complaints about public services have considerable implications for both the strategic direction and the operational management of advocacy service provision in the UK.

Policy context

Over 20 years ago children receiving social services were given the right to make representation about services they received. Section 26(3) of the Children Act 1989 required local authorities to establish procedures to deal with representations, including complaints about 'the discharge by the local authorities of any of their functions in respect of services for children in need'. As Chief Inspector of Social Services, Sir William Utting, the architect of the Children Act of 1989, regarded children's complaints procedures under the Act as an integral part of the system of safeguards for looked after children (Ball and Connolly 2005).

More recently in Wales, following the publication of the Carlile Report on safeguarding children in the NHS (Carlile 2002) and the Clywch Inquiry report (Children's Commissioner for Wales 2004) there have been small but significant steps taken in policy, if not yet in practice, in recognition of the importance of complaints initiated by children and young people as a crucial process in safeguarding children's interests in education and health service settings (Children's Commissioner for Wales 2005). The requirements under Section 29 of the Education Act 2002 that all governing bodies of all maintained schools in Wales establish procedures for dealing with complaints including those from pupils, and the subsequent, accompanying guidance for School Governing Bodies on Procedures for Complaints Involving Pupils (Welsh Assembly Government 2006) represent a first step in the right direction.

The availability of advocacy services for children and young people in schools and educational settings in Wales is still very limited (Crowley 2006). The Welsh Assembly Government in its guidance (2003), *Providing Effective Advocacy Services for Children and Young People Making a Representation or Complaint under the Children Act 1989*, noted that it is committed to making advocacy services available to all children and young people in social care, education and health settings.

Key standards within the National Service Framework for Children, Young People and Maternity Services in Wales require that independent advocacy is freely available to all children and young people and complaints systems are child-friendly and accessible and acknowledge complimentary letters (Welsh Assembly Government 2005). The Assembly Government is planning a major development programme.

More of this later; for now, part way through the first decade of the 21st century, our Welsh study is the latest in a long list of studies to reveal shockingly low levels of complaints brought by children and young people (Aiers and Kettle 1998; Wallis and Frost 1998). Sir William Utting's report, *People Like Us: The Report of the Review of the Safeguards for Children Living Away from Home* (1997), highlighted the effort that local authorities had put into establishing complaints procedures but also raised serious doubts about the faith children had in the complaints process. He commented on the very small proportion of complaints that emanate from children and the lack of confidence children had in the process. Our survey of the 22 local authorities in Wales indicated that in the year 2003–4 local authorities received just 201 stage 1 complaints led by children or young people with a minimal numbers of complaints led by young people at stage 2 or stage 3 (see Chapter 8 for more information on the nature of these complaints). Stage 1 is the first 'problem-solving' stage, stage 2 involves a more formal investigation by a named individual and at stage 3 a panel involving independent members considers the complaint. On 31 March 2004 there were estimated to be 4,315 children looked after in Wales. The total number of children in need was not collated that year but was based on returns from individual local authorities we can estimate there were well over 10,000 children receiving social services, all of whom would be eligible to make a complaint under Section 26.

To counter the low level of usage, over the last decade there has been an increasing emphasis on making complaints procedures more child-friendly and on providing independent advocates to support children and young people in making a complaint. This culminated in the provision under the Adoption and Children Act 2002 placing a duty on local authorities to ensure that children looked after and care leavers have access to independent advocacy.

The Welsh survey also highlighted how few children or young people utilised the professional advocacy services that were available in all 22 local authorities. Local authorities reported that only 12 per cent of complainants accessed professional advocacy services with a greater involvement of adult kin and self-advocacy. Overall, adult kin were more likely to lead complaints involving children throughout all stages.

More than 15 years after the Children Act of 1989 required local authorities to establish complaints procedures that could be used by children and young people themselves, and ten years after most local authorities in Wales started commissioning independent advocacy services, we have to continue questioning why so few children and young people do use the procedures or access the available independent advocacy services to support them in that process.

Uniquely, both the Wales study and the subsequent consultation exercise gathered the views of children and young people positioned at varying angles to advocacy and complaints systems, including young people who had never used advocacy services or made a complaint or had anything to do with social care. Their testimony should inform our understanding of children and young people's help-seeking behaviour and shape the development of more accessible, integrated and user-friendly complaints procedures and advocacy services across health, education and social care.

Review of advocacy services: the Welsh study

Advocacy and complaints – the view from afar?

As indicated, young people with different relationships to, and understandings of, advocacy provision took part in the Welsh study. A number of focus groups took place with the young people who were deemed to be in potential need of independent advocacy services because of their vulnerability. The groups specified included: young people looked after; young people in need; young people living in disadvantaged communities; gay and lesbian young people; young people from Black and minority ethnic communities; and young refugees and asylum seekers.

Six focus groups involving over 60 young people aged between 9 and 21 were held around Wales to explore young people's understanding of their rights and in particular their right to complain about public services; their understanding of advocacy; their views and experiences of advocacy services that are available for children or young people; and the sort of advocacy services they like to be able to make use of if they did want to raise a concern or make a complaint about a public service.

There are a number of common themes in the responses from young people. For those young people who have never used advocacy services, the concept of 'advocacy' is difficult to understand and in some cases off-putting.

> Advocacy is a bit confusing, but maybe an advocate could be useful or help when you're not happy or in a difficult situation and don't know what to do and you don't know anyone to talk to, when you don't know what's going on or when you're getting shunted around.

> (Amiai, age 16)

Young people feel they are ill-formed about their rights. Promoting the use of advocacy support requires young people (and the significant adults around them) to be much better informed about their rights – what young people can and can't expect, how to complain and what will happen if and when they raise concerns. Young people are reliant on key, supportive adults around them (people they know and trust) to help them access advocacy services – teachers, group workers, foster carers and parents/friends seem to be particularly significant in this regard. These people also often act as advocates for young people. This is viewed positively by young people (they would rather have an advocate they know) but advocacy services are seen as really helpful in more formal situations or when there is a conflict of interest.

> X [group worker] really helped us get our voices heard. To get across the difficulties we have to deal with like getting on buses and getting into buildings that aren't accessible.
>
> (Jane, age 17)

Children's views of the complaints process

In the Wales study we interviewed 25 young people who had made a complaint to social services. Finding children or young people who had made a complaint to social services or the NHS proved to be problematic. Initially, we attempted to identify young people for interview via the local authority complaints officers. Complaints officers in each of the 22 local authorities in Wales were asked to identify one young person who had made a complaint within the previous 12 months and to approach them to see if they would be willing interviewed by the researcher. At least seven local authorities reported that they could not comply with our request because they had received no complaints from children or young people in the preceding 12 months or indeed the recent past.

The young people's description of making a complaint to social services indicated that they needed support from the adults around them (mainly social services staff or foster carers) and/or a proactive, local advocacy service to actually find out about and access the complaints procedures. Many of them described seeing information (typically, posters or leaflets) about the complaints procedure but most said this literature did not tell them enough about the procedure and the different stages, or explain *how* to complain, what they should expect to happen as a result or how they would be involved and kept informed (Aiers and Kettle 1998).

> The information is not enough on its own. You need an explanation as well, not just a leaflet.
>
> (Michael, age 15)

> My social worker wasn't quite clear – I didn't understand the part about when you make a complaint it will go to X [social services Children's Rights Officer]. I didn't know who or what X was!
>
> (Jack, age 17)

The experiences of these 25 young people also suggest that 'informal complaints' (stage 1) are not always acknowledged as such at the outset by some authorities:

> They didn't treat it as I was complaining. I never filled out or was offered a complaints form.
>
> (Kelly, age 13)

In a minority of cases this led to lengthy periods of dealing with concerns as well as evident confusion for young people over the status of the matters they had raised:

> I thought it was going to be quick and simple; it took me ages, no one came, things got lost in the post…
>
> (Tara, age 19)

Initial delays of six weeks or more in responding in writing to complaints were reported by half of our interviewees.

Many young people remained unclear about the process they and their complaint had gone through even after they had completed the process.

Complaints, like other organisational processes in social work, reflect a view of childhood and children that can appear ambivalent; thus 'children's' complaints procedures are essentially adult designed and can be daunting to young service users (see Wallis and Frost 1998). It may not be surprising to note that, overall, the views of respondents suggest a lack of clarity about roles and the rights of young people to progress the full complaints process.

The most common reason young people gave for deciding to complain to social services was not being listened to or taken seriously. All the young people interviewed stated they had tried repeatedly to get their concerns dealt with by social services and felt that staff had not given due weight to the issues they raised.

I had had a gutsful. It was going on too long. I tried all sorts of other things to get it sorted. My social worker was useless.

(Tanya, age 16)

Young people claimed they often struggled to get answers from social services to apparently simple questions about what help or support they were entitled to.

My social worker was not listening and neither were the staff. If you're a young kid you can't get your voice heard over adults – can you? I had to do something; staff said they couldn't do anything to stop me being moved.

(Sara, age 14)

These responses are similar to the relatively few studies into why children complain to social services and that point to the way some professionals construct children as having marginal status and limited capacity to be self-determining and whose views are thereby less significant (Dalrymple 2005; Dalrymple and Hough 1995).

Despite the difficulties that many of the young people reported in getting their complaint acknowledged and taken seriously by social services, once in the 'system' over half of those interviewed were satisfied with the complaints process. Approximately a third were dissatisfied and the remainder were neither satisfied nor dissatisfied. Half of the young people interviewed (13) received decisions on their complaints within the time framework recommended by legislation. For three of these young people the decision reached was made up of an explanation for events and a promise to make improvements or some other kind of resolution to the complaint.

I thought it would be a load of people coming in and telling me what to do, but it was really good.

(Teodora, age 16)

Overall, nearly three quarters (18) of the young people we interviewed thought it had been worthwhile making a complaint to the local authority; four young people had mixed feelings and three said using the complaints procedure had not been worthwhile.

I felt like I was the only one doing this. They didn't have a clue how to deal with me.

(Joanna, age 19)

While it is encouraging to note these positive responses it is still the case, as with earlier studies (Aiers and Kettle 1998; Wallis and Frost 1998), that young people feel it is hard to raise concerns and make a complaint. While key reports (Children's Commissioner for Wales 2003; Waterhouse 2000) urge authorities to give clear messages that those who make complaints should not fear repercussions, it was nonetheless the view of several respondents that such fears were part of what makes it hard for some young people to raise concerns.

> Complaining gets you labelled as 'awkward'. There are notes on my file that say that.

> (Hayley, age 17)

Advocacy and complaints

The Welsh study included interviews with a third set of young people: those who had used professional, independent advocacy services. Twenty-three young people aged between 10 and 24 years of age were interviewed to determine satisfaction with the services received: compliance (from the young person's perspective) with National Standards and young people's suggestions for improving advocacy services across health, social services and education. The young people were selected from anonymous lists provided by five advocacy service providers. The advocacy services were chosen to represent the different models and providers operating in Wales at that time. We cannot claim that the sample was representative of all children who enlist professional advocacy support, but it was inclusive of a range of service users and circumstances.

Accessing advocacy support proved difficult for some of our respondents. Guidance on where to find support and advocacy was not always offered to our respondents when they first decided on making a complaint. Most young people didn't contact the advocacy service 'cold'. Children's complaints officers, social workers and other care professionals were proactive in helping a third of respondents gain support from advocacy.

> Before I made the complaint I was offered an advocate. I didn't know who or what they were. I just knew that they helped young people to make a complaint

> (Teodora, age 16)

The qualities that children and young people enjoy in relation to advocacy support are well documented (Noon 2000). Trust, respect and confidentiality were raised by our respondents as being crucial elements of a positive advocacy relationship.

Independence and distance from the local authority were also seen as important by most of the young people. Some respondents recognised that their social workers and others (such as complaints officers) were not independent and as employees of the local authority, they could be compromised in the role of advocate (Barford and Wattam 1991; Dalrymple 2004). Yet, interestingly, where local authority complaints officers were committed to making the process child-friendly and had skills in relating to young people, independent support was not always seen as essential or preferred.

> I phoned the complaints officer and he came to see me. He offered to go and speak to the staff [in the children's home] and try and sort it out or he said he could give me some telephone numbers to take it further. I didn't really feel that I needed any more support.
>
> (Mohammed, age 16)

Some respondents saw the advocacy service as lacking independence because it was commissioned by the local authority and there was a financial relationship.

> They are funded by social services which makes them biased…they are all pally pally, work close together. It's disappointing and it lets people down.
>
> (Tracy, age 18)

Other elements of the advocacy relationship that respondents valued included the practical and emotional help they received in negotiating the complaints procedure and the fact that the advocate stayed with them throughout the process (Noon 2000).

> It's a big procedure. Advocacy helped me a lot. They kept using big words and advocacy explained them all to me. They were really rude to me in my house – tapping their heels and stuff. Having advocacy around made me feel more confident and able to say what I thought. I felt the advocate was on my side. She was great.
>
> (Joanna, age 19)

The sense of close involvement by an advocate in helping progress the complaint was a key determinant in young people's overall satisfaction with the process of making a complaint. Respondents tended to view the relationship as almost one of 'friendship' built on a more equal and, in their view, respectful basis wherein time and a willingness to listen was not in short supply (see also Dalrymple 2005, p.7).

> She [the advocate] was straight about things – she treated me like an equal.
>
> (Rhian, age 17)

> They listened. They were on my side. They helped me know what to do. I trusted them.
>
> (Michael, age 16)

Children and young people appreciated practical help in getting their voice heard but without their views being moderated or transformed in some way by an advocate (see Templeton and Kemmis 1998).

> She gave me names and addresses. I needed someone to give me the info – like the direct line to so and so's office.
>
> (Cerys, age 15)

> They helped me in lots of practical ways like photocopying letters, making phone calls, speaking to people, getting meetings sorted – always pushing it further.
>
> (Rhian, age 16)

The interviews with young people who had made complaints to social services give some sense of the barriers that young people face. Despite much time and effort being expended by local authorities across Wales to make social services complaints procedures child- and young person-friendly, young people generally perceived themselves and then their advocates to be pushing the local authority to take their complaint seriously. Of those respondents who did not use advocacy support when making their complaint (n=5), four of them stated they struggled to get their complaint acknowledged and it was evident that they had little idea about the purpose and working of the complaints process compared with others.

A number of respondents gave positive feedback on their interaction with the local authority complaints officer. From our small sample we can note that complaints were more likely to be treated as such and kept to time and purpose and young people's rights respected were when a proactive, interested, (usually children's) complaints officer was involved.

Vulnerable young people need a professional to act on their behalf with vigour and determination (Cleaver 1996, p.24) but only a few young people spoke positively about the role their social worker had played in encouraging them to make a complaint. In general, young people were critical of their social worker (or the lack of a social worker) in their lives.

> I never saw my social worker and I didn't understand what was going on. I had no support and you know I really needed it. I was at risk. I wanted to know what I was entitled to as a care leaver and no one would tell me.
>
> (Joanna, age 19)

For over a fifth of respondents it was their social worker and the service they received that was the basis of their complaint. Most respondents recalled that they had tried to get their concerns resolved through other less formal channels. The role of the social worker as an advocate for their client was largely absent from the young people's perspective.

Children and young people's views on the new arrangements for handling complaints

In 2005, following on from the all-Wales study of advocacy and complaints, the Assembly Government commissioned 18 of the 22 local strategic children and young people's partnerships in Wales to consult with children and young people on proposed changes to the arrangements for handling complaints across the NHS, socials services and education. A list of questions was agreed with a template for collating responses. Fourteen hundred and fifty-nine children and young people aged 6–20 participated in a series of consultation events across Wales. There are a number of key themes arising of children and young people's responses in relation to help-seeking behaviour.

Overall, children and young people want to be able to talk to someone they know and can trust about their concerns. That person needs to know about how to make a complaint and be able to give advice and support to the child or young person. This person needs to be skilled in communicating with children and young people; be approachable, non-judgemental and im-partial; stick up for children and young people; and be able to keep children's confidences – to be and to be, seen to be, trustworthy.

> You need to be able to talk to someone you can trust – someone that isn't going to go and tell everybody else and won't laugh at you or think you're silly.
>
> (Gemma, age 11)

The most important thing for children and young people is to be listened to, to be believed and to have their concerns taken seriously by adults. Many children and young people feel they are not respected by the adult professionals in schools, the NHS or social services and consequently have limited confidence in adult systems designed to help them raise concerns or make a complaint. Teachers, youth workers, peers, friends, and family as well as complaints officers and workers from external, independent organisations have a particularly key role in helping children and young people to feel able to raise a concern or make a complaint.

> I'd rather talk to someone like a trained complaints officer. They all stick together here.
>
> (Marcus, age 16)

> If I had a problem, it would depend what it was about… I'd probably speak to my auntie and if I was too embarrassed, I'd speak to my friend.
>
> (Jess, age 13)

Children and young people need reassurance that they will be listened to and taken seriously and that their concerns will be handled in confidence – with the actions of the responsible adults not making things worse. The spectre of bullying from other children and young people (and indeed from adults) arising from the stigma attached to 'seeking help' or 'having a problem' looms large for many children and young people. This all suggests that a genuine commitment to implementing user-friendly complaints procedures for children and young people (that will help to protect them as well as to empower them) demands that the implementation of procedures for handling complaints from children or young people is placed firmly in the context of a wider approach that actively demonstrates to children and young people that they are valued and respected. The responses indicate that the adults working with children and young people in schools, the NHS and social services have a lot of work to do if they are to successfully assure children and young people that they will be listened to and have their concerns taken seriously.

These findings echo similar conclusions of studies of vulnerable groups. Cashmore, in her review of research literature from the UK, North America, Australia and New Zealand (2002) highlights how young people in care do not know to whom to complain or are not confident that their concerns and complaints will be taken seriously. Often they prefer to ask a trusted adult to act as their advocate on their behalf rather than use formal complaints procedures. Without the support and encouragement of someone they knew and trusted few young people were willing to use formal complaints mechanisms even if they knew about them. The main reasons were that they were scared that they would not be listened to or believed, and feared repercussions for speaking out.

Summary of key messages

In this chapter we have sought to illuminate barriers and highlight facilitators to enhancing children's participation from the perspective of the child or young person. Children and young people's views and experiences of complaints, advocacy and getting help to support them in resolving a problem have significant implications for current public policy and practice.

Most children and young people will be unfamiliar with the concept of advocacy, of what an advocate might be or do. They know little (and understand less) about complaints procedures and rely on key adults in their lives (the people they know and trust) to advise them of how to complain, and what support might be available. Having their rights supported and swift access to support if their rights are threatened should be something children and young people grow up expecting. We still need a sizeable shift in attitudes towards the rights of children and young people and their role in helping shape our public services.

While children and young people who have experience of advocacy speak positively about the service they also think it needs to be more accessible and visible. The myriad of posters and leaflets and current dissemination strategies do not seem to be working as intended. Our respondents suggested that advertising in the mainstream media and in places that children and young people frequent would be more effective. But service providers and commissioners alike should note, as Butler and Williamson (1994) have observed, that children make careful judgements about whom to trust with their problems and often choose confidantes from their local network or primary group and can be fairly circumspect about approaching adults and adult-run services. Any marketing strategy is likely to have limited impact without some insight into the ways in which children understand their local environment and seek sources of support. The dearth of naturalistic observations into children's everyday worlds, particularly how they seek help, remains an area not much researched (see also Tudge and Hogan 2005, p.106).

Children's skills, concepts and knowledge, wrought daily through collaboration with their peers in largely urbanised landscapes, remain something of a mystery. There are of course many different childhoods in time and place and children's behaviour will differ accordingly but, until we understand better the day-to-day ecology of children through relevant research and practice skills that are only now beginning to be assembled (Greene and Hogan 2005), we shall be at some disadvantage in knowing how to get children and advocacy on a more mutually aware footing. In the meantime standards about bringing advocacy to the notice of children and our varied attempts to do so may well remain more aspirational than achieved.

The majority of advocacy service users interviewed in the Wales study had requested support with raising concerns and/or making representation on more than one issue in their lives. A generic service, available for all children and young people, is required to support young people making representation and/or complaints to schools, social care and health. There needs to be more active promotion with 'hard to reach' groups, for example Black and minority ethnic young people, young people placed in specialist residential provision long distances from their home community, and children with a disability.

Young people were appreciative of advocacy support when making a complaint. Confidentiality and the independence of advocacy services were highly valued. The majority of young people had suggestions for how their experience of making a complaint could have been improved upon. This included key adults (social care staff and foster carers) taking a more proactive support role; raising awareness through child/young people-friendly information and explanations; better access to independent support; and speeding up the length of time to get a decision. Young people suggested that a commitment to education, information, support, and an effective and positive approach to listening to and resolving complaints need to be put in place if children and young people are to be encouraged rather than put off by the complaints process.

Our study highlighted the key role of the specialist children's complaints officer in terms of both helping young people to understand the procedures and experience them as meaningful and responsive and to introduce sources of independent support and in some cases mediate and facilitate a satisfactory resolution. Often, complaints officers have insufficient status or authority to influence solutions at case and at service level.

Most children and young people seeking to complain about a health service do not have access to an independent advocacy service. Community Health Councils in Wales provide some advocacy services for users of health services but few are able to offer specialist skills and capacity in regard to children. A small number of children's advocacy pilot projects have been commissioned by NHS trusts and local health boards in partnership with local authorities. Very few complaints to health services in Wales are led by children or young people; most are led by adults (parents/carers).

Children's advocacy services in Wales are typically case-based and need to be part of a wider participation strategy. Various levels and forms of advocacy can be complementary in meeting different types of need. Innovative services, highly committed staff and strong approval from users typify much of local authority commissioned children's advocacy services. At the same time there are problems around independence, capacity, consistency, competition, value for money, and lack of strategic overview across advocacy provision in Wales. Staffing structures can be fragile and impair continuity of service and relationships. Several local authorities saw little added value through advocacy in relation to its impact upon service delivery or quality and saw it as of relevance to the child or young person only. Other local authorities believed advocacy to offer a range of benefits to both child and the authority. A few authorities reported a history of quite strained relations with advocacy providers leading to a change of contract and supplier.

All respondents in both the focus groups and the individual interviews touched on the emotional and behavioural component of the advocacy role. Respondents wanted time and opportunity to 'know' the person, to be able to trust them and disclose their problems. The 'ideal advocate' was approachable, child-friendly, would listen, understand, and would speak out for young people. Thus, it was important to the young people that advocates were confident, informed and able to help young people voice concerns, take action and defend and promote their rights. Trust, respect, confidentiality and action were identified as core elements of a positive advocacy relationship.

The emotional work involved in care, trust and openness that are the building blocks to effective intervention mean that, as in some traditional welfare relationships of an earlier age (Pithouse 1996; Pithouse and Atkinson 1988), there is a running together of *being* an advocate and *doing* advocacy. This intertwined role and identity that service users clearly perceive is likely to make for a more intense engagement between advocate and child. In short, there seems to be a moral order underlying advocacy where expectations over commitment and affect are set much higher than say between teacher and pupil, social worker and client or doctor and patient. Sustaining this relationship (albeit intensity may differ depending upon type of need) can be testing, particularly if there are unrealistic wants from a child or unreasonable requirements of the child from unsympathetic service providers or family. Dealing with such contrary and conflicting demands calls for knowledge, skills and values that find scant exposition in national standards and which warrant much more analytical attention to delineate the key components of the effective advocate and the sort of service likely to meet children's often multiple and diverse needs.

Conclusion

Children and young people's views and experiences of complaints, advocacy and getting help to support them in resolving a problem have significant implications for current public policy and practice. There is need for root and branch reform to move advocacy into the mainstream and rescue it from its marginalised position on the edge of the lives of most children and young people. We have key targets in the National Service Framework for Children, Young People and Maternity Services in Wales for independent advocacy to be freely available to all children and young people and complaints systems to be child-friendly and accessible (Welsh Assembly Government 2005).

The need to find ways to make independent advocacy more accessible to children is urgent if advocacy services are to fulfil their very important function of supporting vulnerable children to raise concerns or make a complaint. In response to abuse within the care system successive governments placed emphasis upon complaints procedures and the provision of independent advocacy support as a means of protecting children from abuse and mistreatment (Kahan and Levy 1990; Utting 1997). The Welsh study of advocacy and complaints suggests that until we do much more to place advocacy and complaints in the wider context of children's rights, with adults listening to children and young people and taking them seriously, reliance on advocacy services or complaints procedures as a means of protecting and safeguarding children is misplaced.

References

Aiers, A. and Kettle, J. (1998) *When Things Go Wrong: Young People's Experience of Getting Access to the Complaints Procedure in Residential Care.* London: National Institute for Social Work.

Ball, C. and Connolly, J. (2005) 'Children need someone to listen.' *Community Care*, (6 May).

Barford, R. and Wattam, C. (1991) 'Children's participation in decision-making.' *Practice 5*, 93–101.

Butler, I. and Williamson, H. (1994) *Children Speak: Children, Trauma and Social Work.* Harlow: Longman.

Carlile, Lord A. (2002) *Too Serious A Thing: Review of Safeguards for Children and Young People Treated and Cared For by the NHS in Wales.* Cardiff: NafW.

Cashmore, J. (2002) 'Promoting the participation of children in care.' *Child Abuse and Neglect 26*, 837–847.

Children's Commissioner for Wales (2003) *Telling Concerns: Report of the Children's Commissioner for Wales' Review of the Operation of Complaints and Representations and Whistleblowing Procedures and Arrangements for the Provision of Children's Advocacy Services.* Swansea: Office of the Children's Commissioner for Wales.

Children's Commissioner for Wales (2004) *Clwych Report of the Examination of the Children's Commissioner for Wales into Allegations of Child Sexual Abuse in a School Setting.* Swansea: Office of the Children's Commissioner for Wales.

Children's Commissioner for Wales (2005) *Children don't complain... The Children's Commissioner for Wales' Review of the Operation of Complaints and Representations and Whistleblowing Procedures, and Arrangements for the Provision of Children's Advocacy Services in Local Education Authorities in Wales.* Swansea: Office of the Children's Commissioner for Wales.

Cleaver, H. (1996) *Focus on Teenagers: Research into Practice.* London: The Stationery Office.

Crowley, A. (2006) *Scoping Paper on Pupil Participation* (for the Welsh Assembly Government: unpublished).

Dalrymple, J. (2004) 'Developing the concept of professional advocacy: an examination of the role of child and youth advocates in England and Wales'. *Journal of Social Work 4*, 2, 181–199.

Dalrymple, J. (2005) 'Constructions of child and youth advocacy: emerging issues in advocacy practice'. *Children and Society 19*, 3–15.

Dalrymple, J. and Hough, J. (eds) (1995) *Having a Voice: An Exploration of Children's Rights and Advocacy.* Birmingham: Venture Press.

Greene, S. and Hogan, D. (eds) (2005) *Researching Children's Experience: Approaches and Methods.* London: Sage.

Kahan, B. and Levy, A. (1990) *The Pindown Experiences and the Protection of Children: A Report of the Staffordshire Child Care Inquiry.* Stafford: Staffordshire County Council.

Noon, A. (2000) *Having a Say: The Participation of Children and Young People at Child Protection Meetings and the Role of Advocacy.* London: The Children's Society.

Pithouse, A. (1996) 'Managing Emotion: Dilemmas in the Social Work Relationship.' In K. Carter and S. Delamont (eds) *Qualitative Research: The Emotional Dimension.* Avebury: Aldershot.

Pithouse, A. and Atkinson, P. (1988) 'Telling the Case: Occupational Narrative in a Social Work Office.' In N. Coupland (ed) *Styles of Discourse.* London: Croom Helm.

Pithouse, A., Crowley, A., Parry, O., Payne, H. and Dalrymple, J. (2005) *A Study of Advocacy Services for Children and Young People in Wales: A Key Messages Report.* Cardiff: Cardiff University School of Social Sciences; Social Inclusion Research Unit University of North East Wales; Department of Child Health; Wales College of Medicine.

Templeton, J. and Kemmis, J. (1998) *How Do Young People and Children Get Their Voices Heard?* London: Voice for the Child in Care.

Tudge, J. and Hogan, D. (2005) 'An Ecological Approach to Observation of Children's Everyday Lives.' In S. Greene and D. Hough (eds) *Researching Children's Experience: Approaches and Methods.* London: Sage.

Utting, W. (1997) *People Like Us: The Report of the Review of the Safeguards for Children Living Away from Home.* London: The Stationery Office.

Wallis, L. and Frost, N. (1998) *Cause for Complaint: The Complaints Procedure for Young People in Care.* London: The Children's Society.

Waterhouse, R. (2000) *Lost in Care: Report of the Tribunal on Inquiry into Abuse of Children in Care in the Former County Council Areas of Gwynedd and Clwydd.* London: The Stationery Office.

Welsh Assembly Government (2003) *Providing Effective Advocacy Services for Children and Young People Making a Representation or Complaint under the Children Act 1989.* Cardiff: WAG.

Welsh Assembly Government (2005) *National Service Framework for Children, Young People and Maternity Services in Wales.* Cardiff: WAG.

Welsh Assembly Government (2006) *Guidance for School Governing Bodies on Procedures for Complaints Involving Pupils.* Cardiff: WAG.

CHAPTER 10

The Family Court Process: Young People, Care Proceedings and Advocacy

Maureen Winn Oakley

Introduction

This chapter explores the understandings and experiences of children subject to care proceedings concerning the advocacy role of solicitors within court processes, and the role of children's guardians. It considers two questions. What did children and young people think about the legal process and those professionals who represented their views? What understanding, if any, did they have about their own participation in the court process? Findings highlight the importance of enabling young people to become more aware of the legal aspects of care proceedings and to make informed decisions about their participation in court processes. The study has important implications for the ways in which non-legal advocates might support children in court processes and other decision-making fora.

The Children Act 1989 emphasises that the welfare of the child is paramount and in care proceedings two specific representatives for the child, the social-work trained children's guardian and the legally qualified specialist children's solicitor, are both appointed to ensure that the views of the child are heard when the court is considering decisions based upon the best interests of the child. Part of the role of the children's guardian is to specifically ascertain the wishes and feelings of the child, or young person, subject to the legal proceedings, and some guardians do refer to this as an advocacy role. However, the overriding remit for guardians is to make recommendations to the court based upon what is in the best interests of the child or young person and such recommendations may clash with the views of the child or young person. Overall, then, the role of the children's guardian is not as an advocate. The distinctiveness of the advocacy role is that advocates support a child or young person to say what they choose and help them to promote their wishes and feelings irrespective of whether the advocate agrees with their views (Kelley 2002). Advocates respond to a request to promote the views of the child or young person usually when they do not feel that they are being heard.

The solicitor for the child, however, retains the traditional advocacy role. The solicitor is appointed as legal advocate in the proceedings and the child or young person is named as the client with legally aided assistance provided on this basis. The child or young person is acknowledged as being a 'party' to the proceedings. When the client is a baby or young child – and is therefore deemed to be too young to give instructions – the solicitor will work more closely with the guardian, but the solicitor remains the child's advocate and is not the appointed solicitor for the children's guardian. Guardians and solicitors liaise and work 'in tandem' but solicitors can, and do, take direct instructions from children and young people if they are deemed to be competent and if their wishes conflict with the recommendations being made to the court by the guardian. Overall, the role of the solicitor is to speak *for* a child or young person with a duty to protect their legal interests (Kelley 2002).

Background

Between 1995 and 2004 the NSPCC (the National Society for the Prevention of Cruelty to Children) funded research at the University of Warwick focused on socio-legal dimensions of representing children. There has been an increasing awareness that policy makers and service providers lacked knowledge of children's perceptions of health, education, social services and the legal system. In particular, at the time of the research, little was known about children and young people's perceptions of public law proceedings. Previous research in this area had concentrated upon the views of adults, such as professionals (Hunt and Macleod 1997), and parents and carers (Freeman 1994) involved in care proceedings. Obtaining knowledge about representation that is derived from focusing on children and young people's views and experiences would add a further dimension.

There has also been increasing recognition that children and young people were invisible and their voices unheard in this field of socio-legal research. Existing child research had tended to be *about* children rather than research *with* them and so maintained an adult focus. Indeed, the need to focus upon children's own perceptions was highlighted in a study funded by the NSPCC which found that professionals sometimes made assumptions about the views of children and young people which were subsequently proven to be incorrect. The message from this research was that adults must learn to listen to children and young people more closely (Butler and Williamson 1994).

Finally, a number of barriers to the development of child-friendly and child-centred legal services have been identified. First, there are gaps in provision – for example, in family law there is no provision for children and young people to attend family law courts. Second, in criminal trials young defendants, who may be as young as ten years old, are entitled to a defence lawyer but there is no automatic provision for a court welfare officer, advocate or lay supporter. A third problem is that CAFCASS (Children and Family Court Advisory and Support Service), set up to develop joined up child-centred services, has been criticised for failing to promote the welfare of children (Kelley 2002).[1]

The study

The research, which was undertaken between 1996 and 1998, was conducted in two stages. First, a pilot study was set up with a group of older young people involved with the work of the NSPCC who had heard about the research project on the NSPCC grapevine and contacted the researcher. They had each been subject to public law proceedings (that had now concluded) and some of them had also been witnesses in criminal proceedings where carers were prosecuted. None of these young people had been present at any of the civil public law hearings. They had been unaware that as 'parties' to the proceedings they could have been more involved in the court process. Such involvement would obviously have depended upon their age and maturity, but the young people said that they felt angry about being excluded and felt that they had not been fully informed about their possible involvement in the process. While some had understood they had been put 'under' care orders, others did not understand this status even though they had been sent written information.

These young people made contact in order to help pilot the research project. They made an invaluable contribution to the research process. There were two elements driving their willingness to become involved:

- their input could be helpful to other children and young people who become subject to such proceedings in the future

- their involvement in the project might be therapeutic for them and help dispel the anger they harboured.

In the second stage, a small-scale investigation was conducted, involving just young people between 8 and 17 years who had active cases. All the children and young people approached were happy to be included in the research and were given information about the project before their consent was sought. The researcher then attended meetings that children and young people had with their representatives: the children's guardian (at the time known as the guardian ad litem), and their solicitor. The researcher only attended court hearings if the young person also went. The researcher then observed what information was imparted to the child or young person, verbally or other-wise, in order to ascertain their understanding of the process. All three – the guardian, the solicitor and the young person – were also interviewed sepa-rately once the proceedings had concluded in order to ascertain their views on the case and process.[2]

Findings

Professional perspectives

A number of legal professionals and other adults were unhappy with the notion that children and young people should be asked their views about their experience of care proceedings. Consequently, a number of cases failed to be included in the research project. One could argue that these adults leaned towards a protectionist or paternalistic view without being aware that such a perspective may deny children and young people a voice. They ex-pressed concern that children would be upset by such intervention. There is a body of evidence from the legal professionals, particularly those involved in the higher courts, that children and young people should not participate in legal proceedings, particularly proceedings concerning their care (see, for example, remarks *per* Waite in the case of *re C* [1993][3], and also remarks by the Official Solicitor in the case *Re W* [1994]).[4] It is evident that some profes-sionals believe that all young people subject to such proceedings are best served by being shielded from this process and that attempts both to inform them more fully and to include them are abusive. It has also been argued that numerous perspectives can be identified as existing within child care policy covering the rights of the child, the rights of the family, and the rights of the state, such as that supporting state paternalism and child protectionism (Fox Harding 1991).

Young people's access to information on court processes

The study found that not all children and young people are made aware that there is to be an application at court about their care. The involvement of children in decisions that affect them is, of course, subject to age and maturity but we found that even older young people were not aware of the details surrounding the child protection concerns. They did not know about the application at court or why it had been made. Two young people were told by their social workers that the court need to make decisions about their care. It may be the role of the social worker to discuss with children and young people any child protection concerns and inform them about the possible involvement of the court, and some social workers do endeavour to undertake this role. Discussing legal issues with their young clients may however be difficult. The social worker is not independent and is not necessarily able to advocate for the child or young people since their role is clearly to act in the best interests of the child or young person. There may well be a conflict between the wishes of the child or young person and the evidence of the social worker to support the local authority's court application about concerns of significant harm. Once proceedings commence the local authority will be the applicant, the parents will be the respondents and the child or young person will be a party to the proceedings with their own legal advocate, the solicitor for the child. For some children and young people, the first they knew of the court's involvement was when they met with the children's guardian or solicitor for the child. Any information they received about the process came directly from these legal professionals, appointed once the court process had begun.[5]

However, the research did find that children and young people trusted their representatives, in particular the children's guardian. Most young people were fairly clear about the role of their guardian but many were confused about the difference in the role of the solicitor. Some had engaged well with their solicitor; others were unaware that they had had a solicitor. There was a lack of understanding about the legal process and particularly about the young person's possible participation in it. Very few young people attended court or realised that this could have been an option. Only a few had received any written information about the proceedings.

Few solicitors who represented children and young people in such public law proceedings produced information leaflets about the process. Only some solicitors wrote letters to their young clients. Solicitors argued that children and young people would not understand the contents, although all solicitors confirmed that they did write informative letters to parents, when acting for parents in such proceedings, irrespective of their level of understanding. There were some solicitors, however, who were most adamant that they would always write to their young clients, particularly once proceedings had been concluded at court, in order to inform them of the decisions made. Some solicitors visited young people on their own, but other young people had no visits. Some solicitors chose to visit with the guardian although there were solicitors who appeared to remain in the background and let the guardian take the lead.

At the time of the research, there were over 50 different panels of guardians throughout England and Wales. A significant number produced written information leaflets, some having involved local school children in drawing illustrations. However, there was no duty upon guardians to use the individual leaflets that existed. Therefore, while some children had access to these leaflets and some received them, others did not receive any at all. Furthermore, there was no national consensus on the contents of leaflets. Further analysis of existing leaflets found considerable variety in the information given. While all mentioned the role of the guardian, some mentioned the role of the solicitor briefly, and one did not refer to the solicitor at all. There were also a number of major contradictions. For example, on the issue of young people going to court, one leaflet stated that 'children did not usually go to court', another that 'you may have to go to court, but not for long', while a third stated that 'children and young people have a choice about going to court'. In fact, ultimately, it is up to the court to decide about such attendance. Clearly, children and young people receiving these leaflets were getting some very different messages about their participation in the process.

While Article 12 of the United Nations Convention on the Rights of the Child (UNCRC) states the importance of ensuring that children and young people have a voice concerning issues that affect them, it is equally important to ensure that young people receive accurate information about processes, that affect them and their possible participation in those processes to enable them to then give informed opinions. The right to receive information is enshrined in Article 13 (UNCRC) and an element of advocacy is about helping children and young people to achieve understanding. Other studies also highlight children and young people's lack of understanding about processes and the importance of giving them information about how they might participate in the process (McCausland 1999; Reugger 2000; Sinclair and Clark 1999).

The issue of young people actually attending court to see and hear what is being said is a contentious one. Not all the young people in the study wanted to attend court or to engage more than they were currently doing. However, other young people said that they *did* want more understanding and involvement in the court process. First and foremost, they need information about this possible participation and then, having decided to get more involved, they wanted their wishes advocated and debated. The young people did not expect to get everything they wanted but they did want their representatives to advocate their wishes to the court. Some solicitors and guardians were proactive in this but others commented upon the fact that they knew some judges who were very opposed to such requests and would be irritated by any professionals seeking to raise these issues. Yet, professionals readily stated that attending part of a hearing or a full hearing such as the discharge of a care order could be a very positive experience for a young person.

One apparently competent teenager in the study was offered a visit to an empty court when he pushed to attend and hear what was being said. He told the researcher that he had replied that 'he wasn't interested in the architecture of the building' and he did feel let down that he had not had the chance to be more involved. Although he felt aggrieved, no one raised the issue of him making a complaint about this; indeed, no discussions about the right to make a complaint were raised with any of the young people. Recent debates about opening up family courts to public scrutiny seem rather premature given practices that continue to exclude young people from the court. Arguments that children subject to care proceedings may lose their right to privacy seem somewhat ironic.

Dissemination of the research

Knowledge as power: development of an information pack

By 1999 the NSPCC had agreed to fund more work to set up an advisory group to look into the possibility of producing an information pack for children subject to care proceedings. It was decided at the outset that any advisory group must have young people as members with full status equal to the other older members and that such an advisory group should have young people with direct experience of public law proceedings. Contact was made with a group of looked after young people, the Birmingham-based Rights of Children (ROC) group, which was facilitated by independent (non-legal) advocates working sessionally for the in-house Birmingham Children's Rights Service. The group was asked if they would be interested in having representatives on an advisory group, and in having input into the information pack. ROC were very clear that they would be interested in having input on the basis that 'we want to be in from the start, we are not seen as "token young people" and that our views are listened to and are taken seriously'. The professionals agreed with these demands. Three young people, all with personal experience of public law proceedings and still under care orders, were chosen by ROC members to sit on the advisory group.

Young people on the advisory group wanted the packs to be called *Power Pack*. The adults had reservations about this as it conjured up negative connotations of fists and violence or that of 'a battery', as one adult member had said cynically. The young people argued eloquently however against these negative perceptions. They reminded the professionals that the adults are the power-holders and as such have difficulty acknowledging power in relation to younger people. The young people also acknowledged that they had not initially identified Power Pack in terms of being a battery, however they could now see a positive potential here rather than the negative image portrayed. Power Pack was indeed a battery: it was positive energy. Power Pack completed the existing expert system. Young people's views were that when you bought a toy or item and the box stated 'batteries not included' the item did not work; no matter how well it was designed the item was powerless. Power Pack completed the legal circuit by linking the energies of the guardian, the solicitor, the magistrate/judge, the court process and the young person: the all-inclusive Power Pack. There were no arguments against this and Power Pack was born.

The three young people spoke freely about their own experiences and the professionals found the young people's views to be refreshing and invaluable. Overall, some 35 young people assisted in the process over the 18-month period.

As a result of this process two packs were developed: one for children and one for older young people.[6] The packs are 'wordy', particularly the packs for young people, because the extra text considers issues such as the independence of the guardian, confidentiality with representatives, issues over care plans, and disagreements with guardian's recommendations that may lead to the young person giving separate instructions to their solicitor. Questions about the young person attending court are also discussed.

Ammanda Walsh, now an independent advocate with the Birmingham Children's Rights Service, wrote of her involvement at the time.

I am a young person who has been involved in the development of Power Pack from the start. As I have been through court proceedings myself, I feel that my input to this project has been very valued. This project has been an excellent opportunity for me to turn my bad experiences into something positive. It has also given me a fresher and more positive outlook on the people that make big decisions in your life, particularly judges and solicitors. I realise that they are only human and that they don't just see the work they do as a job. My involvement in the Power Pack project has opened a lot of closed doors for me, because I understand totally how painful and upsetting it can be to be going through court proceedings. It is even harder when you know court proceedings are going on but nobody ever really tells you what is really going on. The positive thing I have salvaged out of working on Power Pack is now I understand why some things happened the way they did. Hopefully, Power Pack will inform young people on what is going on and why people like guardians are making big decisions in their life and hopefully they can play an active role too.

This project has helped me to understand why things have happened in my life. It has also been an opportunity to help young people know what is important for them to know. Even if it was a little late for me, it doesn't have to be for others, and I want to thank the people that have helped me see and feel this way.

Each pack is enclosed in anonymous, coloured A5 binders that are deliberately blank. Whereas the adults liked the idea of having logos over the front cover that would reflect the professionals and organisations supporting the pack, and this would include the ROC logo too, the young people from ROC were adamant that the binders should remain anonymous: if they fell out of a school bag they stayed inconspicuous. The packs are not seen as a substitute for the expertise of the children's guardian or the solicitor for the child. On the contrary, the researcher supports the existence and continuation of the 'tandem' system. The packs encourage children and young people to become involved with their representatives and to engage with them. The packs are written to inform children and young people of the process and so are seen as a complement to the present system of representation. Whilst the packs aim to empower children and young people, they also make it clear that children and young people will not necessarily get what they want.

Views of legal professionals

The findings of the research provoked a range of responses. Lawyers at a conference in Durham in 1999 had been particularly angry about suggestions that solicitors did not speak with their young clients to ascertain their views. Obviously these lawyers were very proactive about meeting with their young clients and taking their instructions. One such lawyer met the researcher some years later and admitted that, as a judge, he was now aware that practices between solicitors varied tremendously and that this did need addressing.

A number of judges expressed concern that the Power Pack made references to the possibility of young people attending court, and were unhappy about such a development. One judge met the researcher and asked for this reference to be removed. It was felt that attendance at court was not acceptable and possibly abusive to young people. It was also pointed out that judges or magistrates had little contact with such young people and so would have to change their practices and language. Other members of the judiciary have, however, welcomed debate on such a development and believe it to be a more inclusive approach. A number of judges currently meet with young people if asked to do so. Such practices are common in European courts where regular appointments are made for young people to meet the judge.

Power Pack was a joint enterprise and a number of presentations and articles have also been done jointly with young people from ROC (see, for example, Oakley with Walsh 2001). Conference presentations have included the 2001 Annual Conference of the Association of Directors of Social Services and an invitation by Dame Butler-Schloss to present at her 'Voice of the Child' judicial conference in 2003.[7]

Developing Power Packs for disabled children and young people

During 2002 the original Power Pack advisory group turned their attention to developing a resource for disabled children and young people. It had become clear that additional formats were needed for those children who could not access the hard copy printed versions. These were children of all ages with a wide range of sensory and communication impairments. There were also other issues relevant to disabled children such as access to documents and accessing court premises. As a result, the original advisory group was broadened to include professionals and young people from relevant charities and organisations. Members of Birmingham's Rights of Children Group remained involved but specific contact was now made with their newly formed Saturday Disabled Rights of Children Group and the advocates who supported them. Contact was also made with the Young Disabled People's Forum at the Greater Manchester Coalition of Disabled People.

Three sub-groups researched and examined the specific needs of deaf children, children with a visual impairment and those with learning difficulties. It was concluded that a DVD version would best meet the needs of the majority of disabled children including those with sight impairment and would also be of help to non-disabled older children with limited literacy skills. For children with learning disabilities, an easy read version was developed with more accessible text and illustrations with supporting notes for professionals and carers to use with children.

The launch was in London in July 2006 and young people involved in developing the Power Packs gave presentations. The young people from the Greater Manchester Young Disabled People's Forum promoted the need to inform and engage with deaf and disabled young people. Their overall message was the significance of advocating that children with disabilities are given the opportunities to participate in processes that affect them.

Conclusion and implications for non-legal advocacy

The research clearly highlighted that children and young people subject to care proceedings may not be aware that there is to be an application at court about their care. They may not have had prior warning and or know the reason for the application. It could be argued that the social worker is the professional who should be talking to the child or young person about this, and certainly social workers endeavour to undertake this role. However, social workers are not independent; they are agents of the local authority and their role is ultimately to act in the best interests of their young clients which is inevitably likely to make it difficult, if not impossible, to advocate their wishes and feelings. For this reason social workers are not always able to support the views of the child or young person.

It would therefore seem appropriate that children and young people should, wherever possible, have the support of an independent non-legal advocate, from an advocacy service, long before an actual application is made at the court.[8] Non-legal advocates work outside of legal proceedings and can be appointed at any time and for any issue that necessitates supporting children and young people involved with social care services. Local authorities are under a duty to ensure that all looked after children already in the care system have access to advocacy. However, advocacy is not always considered for those children subject to child protection investigations, for example, even though current *Working Together to Safeguard Children* guidance on attending child protection conferences states 'The child, subject to consideration about age and understanding, should be invited to attend and to bring an advocate, friend or supporter if s/he wishes' (Department of Health 2006, p.125). Where care proceedings are taken as a result of a conference the independent advocate has to be clear about their role: 'Advocates need to have an understanding of both the care system and the basic principles underlying the advocacy role so that they can distinguish between advocating for the child and promoting the child's best interests' (Winn Oakley and Masson 2000, p.32). It is unlikely that an independent advocate will be allowed to be party to any court proceedings but they may well have a role in explaining the process to the child or young person concerned.

While a number of local authorities commission independent advocates to support children and young people in child protection conferences, they are less likely to commission advocacy services for child protection investigations and so children and young people are unaware of this possible support. Such advocacy provision would ensure these children and young people not only have their views promoted but that they were better informed of the processes and so could then give informed opinions. Advocates work exclusively for the child or young person and in so doing ensure that their views are promoted at a time when their care is in question. Such advocacy would then ensure children's views about where and with whom they live would be raised and debated at child protection conferences, before extreme measures such as court proceedings became necessary.

Many children and young people responded to the *Every Child Matters, Care Matters* consultation Green Paper (Department for Education and Skills, 2003)[9] and one particular issue for them was that alternative carers such as extended family and other kin were not fully investigated before seeking to place them into care with strangers. Arguably then, an added bonus of this advocacy intervention could be to prevent unnecessary processes being invoked. Such support could fall within a prevention remit and so contribute to the preventative strategies that local authorities are now keen to promote. Referrals can be made by children and young people themselves or by carers or professionals working with or on behalf of them. Increasingly, professionals such as social workers and independent reviewing officers now make referrals to advocates for looked after children and young people. These developments highlight the fact that professionals recognise the positive input of such advocacy.

Non-legal advocacy could also be made available to those children and young people brought into contact with the local authority through the use of Police Protection and Emergency Protection Orders. Masson *et al.* (2007) highlighted the fact that children and young people subject to the power of Police Protection often saw themselves as having done something wrong and particularly so when taken to the local police station. Police officers found it difficult to explain the process to the children and young people concerned because most had not been trained in the use of this power. It is usual for only child protection police to receive this training. Ensuring advocates were available to support such young people would help them to voice their concerns and get answers to their queries.

To return to the court scenario, once a final hearing has taken place at court the role of both the solicitor for the child and the children's guardian comes to an end. Some judges are now increasingly involving advocacy services by requesting referrals are made for support. Recently, the designated care centre judge in Birmingham asked at the final hearing that the appointed children's guardian should make a referral to the local Children's Rights and Advocacy Service to ensure an advocate could continue to promote the voice of the child now that the legal professionals had completed their role. Other local judges have also suggested that non-legal advocates attend hearings and facilitate the attendance of the young people involved. This has been controversial, although some legal professionals welcome the input as they feel they are not always able to be more supportive because of resource and contract issues.

Kelley (2002) points out that children and young people cannot access sources of legal advice and assistance in the same way as an adult when their rights are violated. Invariably, there is no advocate or lawyer to support them or, if there are services available, it is unlikely that children and young people will know about them. She puts forward a number of recommendations from her research, including the need for advocacy and legal services to work in partnership with the Lord Chancellor's Department to increase public awareness of the role they both play in supporting children and young people to seek redress and claim their rights. She argues for a spectrum of advocacy and legal support which are clearly accessible so that children and young people can choose a child-friendly advocate or lawyer who cares about them as well as the 'outcome' of any court proceedings.

This chapter has outlined one specific child-focused research project and the practical developments that followed as a result. Sometimes in our quest to present such work as academics, we risk losing the very essence of the issues for the children and young people involved. Such 'bias' can dilute or even negate the contributions of children and young people. On the surface it may appear to some that mere 'trivia' is being included, yet it is often the smaller details that assist in our understanding of the bigger picture and so enable us to develop the significance of advocating the views of our children and young people.

References

Butler, I. and Williamson, H. (1994) *Children Speak.* Harlow: Longman.

Department for Education and Skills (2003) *Every Child Matters, Care Matters.* London: DfES.

Department of Health (2006) *Working Together to Safeguard Children. A Guide to Inter-agency Working to Safeguard and Promote the Welfare of Children.* London: The Stationery Office.

Freeman, P. (1994) *Parents' Perceptions of Care Proceedings.* Bristol: Socio-legal Centre for Family Studies, University of Bristol.

Fox Harding, L. (1991) *Perspectives in Child Care Policy.* London: Longman.

Hunt, J. and Macleod, A. (1997) *The Last Resort.* Bristol: Centre for Socio-Legal Studies, Bristol University.

Kelley, N. (2002) *Minor Problems? The Future of Advocacy and Legal Services for Children and Young People.* London: Office of the Children's Rights Commissioner for London.

Masson, J., McGorem, D., Pick, K. and Winn Oakley, M. (2007) *Protecting Pavors.* Chichester: Wiley/NSPCC.

Masson, J. and Winn Oakley, M. (1999) *Out of Hearing: Representing Children in Care Proceedings.* Chichester: Wiley

McCausland, J. (1999) *Guarding Children's Interests.* London: The Children's Society.

Reugger, M. (2000) *Hearing The Voice of the Child.* Lyme Regis: Russell House Publishing.

Sinclair, R. and Clark, A. (1999) *The Child in Focus.* London: National Children's Bureau.

Winn Oakley, M. and Masson, J. (2000) *Official Friends and Friendly Officials. Support, Advice and Advocacy for Children and Young People in Public Care.* London: NSPCC.

Winn Oakley, M. with Walsh, A. (2001) 'Knowledge is power.' *Family Law Journal 9,* September, 6–8.

Endnotes

1   CAFCASS was set up under the Criminal Justice and Court Services Act 2001 to replace three court welfare services – the Family Court Welfare Service, Guardian ad litem and Reporting Officer Service and the Children's Division of the Official Solicitor Service.

2   A full account of the research can be found in Masson and Winn Oakley (1999).

3   Re C (a minor) (child's wishes) [1993] 1 Family Law Reports 832.

4   Re W (secure accommodation order: attendance at court) [1994] 2 Family Law Reports 1092.

5   These professionals are only appointed once an application is made at the court and their involvement is expected to end once a final hearing is concluded at the court.

6   Packs are available from both the NSPCC and CAFCASS and text can be downloaded from www.nspcc.org.uk/inform (accessed 23 January 2008).

7   In 2004, CAFCASS produced its own 'new' leaflets for children and young people. Divided into three age ranges, they are specific to private or public law proceedings. Information is limited as the leaflets amount to a few pages in total. It is interesting to note that the public law leaflets for children and young people fail to make any reference to the possibility that young people may be able to engage with the court process. Attending court is not mentioned. The consequence of this is that young people will not necessarily be informed at all. Any information on this will be at the discretion of the professional concerned.

8   Emergency cases would clearly limit the length of such involvement.

9   Consultation responses can be downloaded from www.dfes.gov.uk now called www.dcsf.gov.uk, accessed 24 January 2008, or from www.rights4me.org (accessed 24 January 2008).

CHAPTER 11

The Impact of Advocacy

Christine M. Oliver

Introduction

Research on advocacy for children and young people has grown apace in recent years. Nevertheless, evidence for the impact of advocacy on the individual lives of children and on strategic developments in children's services has received limited attention. It has been argued that, to be effective, advocacy needs to operate at two levels: the emotional and the instrumental (Lee-Foster and Moorhead 1996). In practice, this might mean that a child achieves a desired and tangible objective, such as a placement of their choice, but also other benefits, such as enhanced self-esteem and confidence. Advocacy might also be evaluated according to the outcomes of individual casework (or micro-level) advocacy, and its impact on strategic or policy developments (or macro-level) advocacy (Dalrymple 2001). Yet, a review of the literature identified promising but limited evidence for positive gains at the level of the child or service level, or for the relationship between the two (Oliver 2003). Ideally, advocacy might be expected to produce positive gains for individual children, while also functioning as a valuable form of internal audit, highlighting those areas of service delivery that could be improved for the benefit of *all* children in similar circumstances.

Drawing on the findings of a recent investigation of advocacy for looked after children and children in need in England (Oliver, Knight and Candappa 2006), this chapter explores advocacy outcomes from a range of stakeholder perspectives, namely advocates, children, health and social care professionals and, where appropriate, parents or carers. In this way, it seeks to explore the impact of advocacy in-the-round, highlighting key themes but also identifying points of convergence and divergence in perspective. At the same time, and consistent with the underpinning values of advocacy, it gives centre stage to the views and voices of young users of advocacy services, including their reasons for contacting an advocate and their satisfaction with the advocacy support they received.

Background

At the level of the individual child, Willow (1996) distinguishes between the 'soft' (or emotional) and 'hard' (or practical) outcomes of advocacy and argues that advocacy can contribute towards improved decision-making skills, and a lower level of psychological problems among looked after children. Excluding looked after children from decisions about their care might be expected to exacerbate feelings of frustration and powerlessness. Yet, there is little documented evidence that advocacy can produce positive gains in terms of young people's mental health and well-being. Nevertheless, it is claimed that the process of advocacy can have a positive impact, even if desired outcomes are not achieved. Simons (1995), for example, found that of 23 people who had used advocacy schemes (age unspecified), all were positive about the experience, even though they did not always get what they wanted. Moreover, none of those benefiting from the support of an advocate abandoned their complaint before the end of the procedure. It seems possible that advocacy may assist children in achieving 'staying power' in disputes with providers of children's services. A more nuanced picture is offered in research conducted by Winn Oakley and Masson (2000), who found that advocacy services were valued by children who had access to them, but that the availability of support did not necessarily give young people the confidence to raise concerns or make complaints. This poses the question of whether self-confidence represents a pre-condition or an outcome of advocacy.

Henderson and Pochin (2001) claim that:

> at its best, professional casework advocacy combines a values-driven focus on relationships, empathy and solidarity with a high level of expertise in and knowledge of local service systems, and how to effect change on behalf of individuals within those systems. (p.9)

However, at a service level, evidence for the impact of advocacy on strategic developments in children's services is limited. A review of 21 local authorities providing independent advocacy services found that 19 had identified senior management teams as a vehicle for influencing the development and delivery of children's services. Of these, seven local authorities had designated a member of staff to undertake this task (Children's Commissioner for Wales 2003). The extent to which such institutional arrangements contributed to positive change in services for children and young people is unclear. It has also been argued that the radical potential of advocacy to challenge adult-oriented decision-making systems may be thwarted by a process of organisational assimilation. Boylan and Wyllie (1999), for example, argue that advocacy in child protection arenas has contributed to its 'proceduralisation'. These debates and gaps in knowledge informed the development of our study, which sought to explore evidence for the impact of advocacy from the perspectives of a range of stakeholder groups.

About the study

Findings on the outcomes of advocacy presented here form part of a wider investigation into the principles and practices of advocacy for looked after children and children considered 'in need'. The study, which was funded by the Department of Health as part of its evaluation of the Quality Protects initiative, aimed to develop a taxonomy of advocacy provision across England,[1] as well as an in-depth investigation of understandings of advocacy, and their translation into practice, from a range of stakeholder perspectives.

The study was conducted in three related stages. Following an initial review of the literature (Oliver 2003), an empirical study, which comprised a telephone survey of advocacy services across England (n=75), was followed by a qualitative investigation of a ten advocacy services, selected for their variety of location and target population. Interviews were undertaken with 48 children and young people of varying ages, disabilities and ethnic origin; 18 advocates, 40 health and social care professionals; and 13 parents and carers of children and young people considered 'in need'. Informants were selected on the basis of their experience of one of the selected advocacy services included in the sample. The fieldwork was completed in 2004–5.[2]

Findings

In the initial telephone survey of advocacy services, advocates' views concerning the perceived impact of advocacy were explored.

Impact on individual children and young people

The most common view held by advocates who participated in the tele-phone survey was that children valued being listened to and having an opportunity to express their views (36%), even if they did not achieve their desired outcome. The main benefits to young people in this respect were identified as being psychological: that, as a result of being listened to by the advocate and other adults in their lives, young people were perceived as gaining in self-confidence and self-esteem. In a small number of cases, the view was expressed that, by allowing a young person to know why a decision had been taken, advocacy had enabled young people to compre-hend their situation more fully, and to move forward with their lives.

> Children and young people consistently say that having an advocate at a meeting makes a difference. They say their reviews have never been like that before and it's because you were there. Often children and young people ask us to attend a review because it makes a difference to how others behave.
>
> (Sheila, advocacy service manager)

Advocacy was also identified as having more quantifiable and practical outcomes, which might be expected to have a considerable impact on young people's well-being. Over a third of advocates reported that they had achieved decisions in young people's favour (35%). Of these, placement issues were the most commonly mentioned. Advocates reported that they had been able to prevent the indiscriminate use of temporary agency place-ments, preventing placement moves against the young person's wishes, and ensuring that a child was removed to a place of safety.

> A lot of young people are in temporary agency placement. We have been able to speak up for them and to stop this to ensure their stability over and above the allocation of local authority resources.
>
> (Carol, advocacy service manager)

> We got compensation for one young person who had had 24 placements in two years.
>
> (Carol, advocacy service manager)

Changes to a young person's care plan, improving young people's access to needed services, such as psychiatric care or a place on a play scheme, and achieving access to accommodation for care leavers were also reported. In some cases, these achievements were described as 'small victories' but, in one case, the intervention of advocacy was reported as literally life-saving:

> We saved a young person's life by going to the High Court of Justice when a medical team wanted to end a young person's life. We reported on the young person's quality of life and right to life.

> (Janice, advocacy service manager)

Impact on the strategic development of children's services

A majority of advocates (56%) identified specific policy changes which they attributed to the intervention of the advocacy service. Of these, the most common achievements cited concerned improvements to policies on review meetings, financial support and accommodation for care leavers, complaints procedures, overnight stays, and anti-bullying initiatives in residential care. Improvements to children's participation in child protection processes were also highlighted.

However, just over a fifth of advocates (21%) were more mixed in their views about the impact of individual advocacy on the strategic development of children's services. Of these, some reported that it was too difficult to assess the impact of advocacy, or too early to judge or that, as far as they were concerned, advocacy had had no obvious impact at a strategic level.

> No, I don't like to make excuses but I know we need to start influencing policy, but there's only me and I have a manager who doesn't understand my job. I can't change this organisation on my own. It takes time and I'm not sure if there's commitment at the highest level to want to change.

> (Anne, advocate)

Frustration was expressed about the apparent failure of some local authorities to learn from advocacy casework, and the negative impact this was perceived as having on looked after children, year after year:

> We end up fighting the same issues repeatedly because the policy doesn't change. We try different ways, but we are still at their mercy. We are building consultation to try to raise young people's voices, for example, through the Young People's Panel.

> (Catherine, advocacy service manager)

A further group of respondents (9%) were more optimistic about the potential impact of advocacy on policy development, but acknowledged that local authorities were sometimes slow to change. Of these, a small number felt that individual advocacy had had an impact on individual social work practice, but not on the wider organisational culture or on the development of strategic policies. Some advocates reported that, to achieve strategic change, individual advocacy needed to work alongside broader participation work.

> We struggle to be honest. We've had some impact on the way asylum seekers are treated, but it's not as strong as we would have liked. There needs to be two of me so we can also do the strategic stuff. Advocacy has had a patchy effect on the culture of social services.

> (Pat, advocate)

Stakeholder perspectives

Later, data obtained from the telephone survey of advocates was compared with more in-depth information obtained from face-to-face interviews with advocates, health and social care professionals, parents and carers, and children to identify differences and similarities in perspective.

Impact on the individual child

Although many advocates were modest about the perceived achievements of advocacy, an impressive range of personal and practical benefits were identified as resulting from their interventions. Reflecting on the findings of the telephone survey, advocates highlighted their role in achieving reversals to unwanted placement moves or, alternatively, helping children to stay in the placement of their choice. Advocacy may therefore have a positive role to play in achieving stability of care for some children, and of improving children's satisfaction with their care. The evidence also suggests that advocacy may have a role to play in protecting young people from care placements that could put them at further risk. One case that might be cited as illustrative here was that of a young woman who had been looked after for three years. It was reported that her mother was about to be released from prison and that the care plan was for the young woman to be returned to the care of her mother:

> The mum was planning to go abroad and take the child with her, where she was involved with drug trafficking. As the advocate, we highlighted to

social services the impact this would have on the child, the sort of impact it would have on her life chances. So they reversed that decision. The girl is settled in a placement, got friends, is doing GCSEs and wants to stay here.

(Shaheen, advocacy service manager)

In this context, advocacy may be described as offering an important check on inadequate social work practice. This theme was reflected in interviews with some social care professionals. Advocacy interventions were variously described as 'making us think', 'putting us on notice' and as preventing professionals from 'glossing over issues'. Social care professionals also tended to agree with advocates that casework advocacy had enhanced young people's involvement in reviews, and increased their confidence and communication skills. It was acknowledged that some care plans had been changed as a result of advocacy interventions:

It most clearly has pushed young people's views and been able to change plans and the approaches we take. It might be about a decision about money, but it's also around changing a placement.

(Christopher, social work manager)

However, a minority of social care professionals expressed the view that advocacy had had a negative impact on the lives of individual children. It was reported that, as a result of advocacy, some children were 'overly heard' and that, as a result, decisions were made that were not perceived to be in the child's 'best interest', or which exposed them to an unacceptably high risk of harm.

The advocate spoke to [the children] wrote letters, spoke to the family and carers – and became overly involved. The worst possible outcome for these children was reached. They could have left the care system and returned to their birth family. I feel that the children were overly heard – sometimes children need to know that responsible adults make decisions and why...

(Nigel, social work manager)

Parents and carers were interviewed on the basis of their child's contact with one of the selected advocacy services, either because their child was involved in child protection processes, or because their child was disabled or very young. Parents and carers were generally satisfied with advocacy, citing the achievement of their own goals regarding the care of their birth or foster child, or of overturning a decision concerning their child's healthcare. Others did not necessarily perceive advocacy as achieving their child's goals, but felt that the involvement of the advocate had led to a more positive attitude toward themselves as carers on the part of social care professionals. Only one parent, whose child was supported by an advocate in child protection arenas, criticised advocacy for being, in her view, ineffective:

> From what I've seen, I know they listen to what people have to say, but it's not enough...for the information they gather, no preparation beforehand; I can't see the point. Because I've found myself at every meeting...having to express Peter's true feelings.
>
> (Jackie, parent)

Some parents and carers perceived their children as gaining in confidence as a result of advocacy, sometimes becoming more 'outspoken' in the process. Group work organised by advocacy services was identified as having particular benefits for children with disabilities in terms of improving their opportunities for socialising, and gaining the support of their peers:

> She's given him a lot of opportunities and he's meeting lots of different people. Now they're talking about going on a weekend, like an adventure weekend. So he's had a lot of opportunities which have made him feel quite grown up. It's good that he can go on his own as we'd normally take him.
>
> (Mavis, parent)

Although advocates tended not to emphasise their role in facilitating children's access to services, they offered accounts of their work that suggested they play an important role in this respect. Examples were cited of advocacy having helped children and young people obtain better healthcare (such as support for dealing with self-harm, access to GP services, drug rehabilitation services and sexual health advice); access to education and training (by helping young people to attend schools and further education colleges of their choice); access to services for single parents (such as child care, Sure Start programmes and playgroup facilities); and access to leisure facilities (by putting young people in touch with football and other sports trainers, obtaining free swimming passes, and making referrals to youth clubs, for example). Advocates felt that this dimension of advocacy work, though practically oriented, demonstrated to children and young people that they cared enough about them to act:

> It makes a difference to them on the practical day-to-day stuff, but also someone who cares enough to do something for them, and they feel important enough that you did something, even when you couldn't get what they wanted.
>
> (Bea, advocate)

Echoing the findings of the telephone survey, advocates commonly believed that assisting young people to get their views heard by service providers was 'empowering' of children and young people, whatever the outcome. Paying genuine attention to involving children and young people in the decision-making process had, it was thought, played an important part in restoring children's faith in the care system.

Strategic impact of advocacy

Most social care professionals concurred with advocates that a range of policy initiatives could be partly or wholly attributable to advocacy, including: improved financial support for care leavers; changes to incentive schemes for children in secure units; more relaxed procedures on overnight stays; and the development of guidelines for supporting looked after young people admitted to hospital. The introduction of training for foster carers to raise awareness of the effects of treating looked after children differently from the carer's own children; the suspension of leaving care reviews when young people sat their GCSEs, and the raising of the leaving care age from 16 to 18 years, was also mentioned. These initiatives were particularly evident in local authorities that reported using casework advocacy as a form of internal audit:

> We've moved from being an organisation that met our needs to one that met young people's needs.

> (Gilly, manager, children's services)

Advocacy was also often perceived by both social care professionals and advocates as driving greater cultural acceptance of young people's participation. Some local authorities, for example, were described as beginning to listen to younger children, such as 7–12-year-olds, at conferences and other fora for looked after children. Finally, some social care professionals emphasised the importance of the combined impact of individual and collective advocacy as contributing towards the development of children's services. One secure unit, for example, emphasised the value of listening to the ideas of one young person because other young people might also benefit:

> Because trends change, fashions change, and the kids keep us up to speed with everything… Being in their Council – it's like being in a boxing ring, because they all come with their thoughts and ideas, and sometimes I feel I have to call time and say, hang on a minute. But that's great. That's how it should be.

> (Marion, deputy manager, secure unit)

However, a minority of advocates and social care professionals believed that their work had no, or little, impact on the development of care policies and practices at a strategic level. In these circumstances, organisational cultures that resisted listening to children and young people were identified as a major barrier in this respect, despite the existence of structures that had been set up to listen to children's views:

> There are so many mechanisms and we are told we are supposed to be a critical friend and keep them informed, but when you do it...they say come to us with more evidence. So we give case studies and then they say, 'you are talking about individuals and you don't know the whole story. You don't have all the facts... Who is listening? Who doesn't want to hear?'

> (Jane, advocacy service manager)

In particular, advocates and parents or carers of children with disabilities tended to express criticism of bureaucratic procedures that were perceived as putting young people at a disadvantage; institutional indifference to young people's views; or a belief in the primacy of professional status:

> She was tremendous, because she had worked with deaf children and she understood their needs, but sadly her words weren't listened to. She had a huge battle on her hands because the other professionals just didn't want to know...

> (Anthea, parent)

In these circumstances, broader work to promote children's participation was identified by both advocates and social care professionals as more likely to have a positive impact on local authority policies and approaches to working with young people. These approaches to consulting with, or involving, children in decision-making were perceived as less likely to be received as an attack on the work of individual social work and other care professionals and as producing benefits to the local authority, in terms of clarification of problems in the delivery of children's services:

> I think the groups...are quite strong and you get a much clearer view of what the issues are and over time, the groups have formed a lot of confidence with the children's rights officer who goes down there, so it's a very useful way of hearing what is going on.

> (Laura, children's services manager)

A second factor advanced to explain the limited impact of advocacy at a strategic level was more positive in its implications. Advocacy was perceived by both social care professionals and advocates as having limited impact at a policy or strategic level where children's services that had already integrated a pro-participation perspective in their work. In this context, the contribution of advocates was described as one of 'keeping staff on their toes'.

Children's satisfaction with advocacy

Children's views and experiences represent an important dimension of the effectiveness of advocacy. But before exploring young people's satisfaction with advocacy, their reasons for contacting an advocacy service will be explored in some detail.

Reasons for contacting an advocate

Some young people, particularly care leavers, reported that they had utilised the support of an advocate to address multiple problems over a period of time. The most common reason reported by young people for contacting an advocate concerned placement issues (19%). In most cases, young people wanted support to prevent or reverse an unwanted move (Table 11.1). In two cases, young people's views might be interpreted as challenging accepted wisdom in social work practice, namely that young people are most likely to benefit from living with a relative, or from being looked after by a carer of a similar ethnic background:

> My old placement, I liked them very much. I wanted to stay there. I liked the place where I was living. And the stupid social worker said that because I'm mixed race and the carers were white that I had to go to someone who was Black... If I was the social worker, I'd say 'you can stay wherever you're happy', but she's [the social worker] got to be so stressful.

> (John, age 10)

In the total sample of young people interviewed, seven raised issues concerning child protection (15%). In part, this might be attributed to the inclusion of a child protection advocacy service in the sample of services for more detailed investigation. Problems in negotiating contact arrangements with family members were also common (13%). Additionally, bullying by other children in foster or residential care, including sexual harassment, emerged in five cases (10%), and racial harassment by a teacher in one case. Access to education was identified as an issue for five young people (10%). In five cases, young people made specific reference to their use of advocacy in

Table 11.1: What are the most common reasons why young people ask advocates for help? Percentage of young people citing the factors specified*

(n = 48)	%	n=
Placement issues	19	9
Child protection	15	7
Contact with family and friends	13	6
Complaints against social workers or residential care staff	10	5
Bullying in foster or residential care, at school, including sexual harassment	10	5
Housing problems	10	5
Legal problems, including immigration and child custody	10	5
Welfare benefits and other entitlements	10	5
Education issues	10	5
Health-related issues	8	4
Complaints against foster carers	4	4
Allocation of social worker	4	2
Adoption issues	4	2
Problems with a mental health care plan	4	2
Racial harassment at school	2	1

* Please note: percentages add up to more than 100% as some young people cited multiple reasons.

applying for welfare benefits and other entitlements (10%). Five young people requested help in dealing with housing problems after leaving care (10%). Four young people reported health-related problems as their reason for contacting an advocate, including the need for help in gaining access to counselling services and other health services.

> I used to have a drugs problem and I got really desperate. Social services wouldn't help me. [The advocate] was brilliant. I asked for help to get me into rehab. I was really desperate.

(Mary, age 21)

Two young people enlisted the support of an advocate in order to prompt their social services department to allocate a social worker to them (4%).

Complaints against social workers and residential care staff were cited on five occasions (10%) and complaints against foster carers slightly less so (8%). Legal problems, including help with immigration, court proceedings and child custody, were less common, but tended to be complex and time-consuming for young people (10%). Two cases concerned matters related to adoption (4%). In a further two cases, young persons, queried the terms of their mental health care plan (4%).

Children's perspectives

Children's overall satisfaction with advocacy (Table 11.2) was explored by asking them to rate their experience of advocacy on a scale of 1 to 10, where 1 was very dissatisfied and 10 was very satisfied. Of 48 children and young people interviewed, 36 responses were obtained to this question. The findings indicate that most young people were very satisfied with their experience of advocacy, and four of the young people interviewed reported that they would give advocacy 'more than ten' points.

Table 11.2: Young people's satisfaction with advocacy
Number and percentage of young people who rated advocacy on a scale
of 1 to 10 (where 1 = very dissatisfied and 10=very satisfied) (n= 48)

Number	%	Points awarded
17	35	10
8	17	9
6	13	8
2	4	7
2	4	5
1	2	3
12	25	No response*

* A number of factors contributed to this non-response rate, including unplanned interruptions to interviews and communication difficulties, particularly in circumstances where the child was very young, or where the respondent had severe learning difficulties.

Eight-six per cent of those who responded (65% of the whole sample) gave advocacy between 8 and 10 points. Young people were also asked to identify the reasons for their scores. Young people acknowledged that involving an advocate was not necessarily predictive of success. Some felt that they would have 'given up' without the support of an advocate to help them challenge a decision. Advocates were also valued for their support and encouragement in the face of a care system perceived as not genuinely willing to listen to young people:

> Social services don't want to listen. They do what they want to do. I had a meeting with [the advocate] and with the social worker and in the meeting I still said I didn't want to go, and they said they would think about it. Making me think there might a choice. But actually that was a play thing, because they had already arranged the move, which I didn't know about.

> (Laura, age 15)

Others felt that advocacy assisted service providers in learning to listen to young people, and that this represented a process, rather than a one-off event. One young person, for example, felt that the first child protection case conference she attended had not listened to her concerns and had failed to take any action. Later, social care staff were described as paying closer attention to her views:

> What happened was that I didn't want my mum's ex-partner to come around, not for him to live in the house. But they didn't take no action with that… I felt angry at first, but when we got to the second meeting, they were saying 'sorry', that it wasn't brought to their attention and stuff like that. But now it is…

> (Susan, age 11)

Emotional and practical benefits

Most young people were able to identify important emotional and practical outcomes of advocacy. Just under half (46%) of young people reported a range of emotional benefits, such as feeling more confident in meetings, 'feeling better in yourself' and lower levels of stress as a result of speaking to an advocate and believing that others had listened, and taken their views seriously.

Some young people also valued advocacy for facilitating access to groups for looked after children and children with disabilities. Young people reported that they received support and information from these groups on a wide range of issues, such as bullying, racism, and the rights of children seeking asylum. Opportunities to socialise with their peers were reported as reducing social isolation, reducing stress, and affecting the child so they were 'not feeling so alone with my problems'.

> I was happy with the way things got sorted out. [The advocate] told me about the group [for looked after children]…and they talk about bullying and other things as well. It helps because I feel I can talk about my views, and no one will be laughing at me.

(Peter, age 14)

Equally important, many young people could identify practical outcomes of advocacy. Thirty-eight per cent of young people reported that their requests had been fully met, and these achievements were important and far-reaching. They include, for example, keeping custody of a baby, achieving contact with family and friends, remaining in the placement of their choice, tracing siblings, obtaining information on decision-making processes, and obtaining access to housing, counselling and welfare benefits. One young asylum seeker, for example, had been separated from his disabled brother who was moved to another borough without his knowledge. The advocacy service was reported as helping the two brothers to locate and sustain ongoing contact:

> We didn't know how to get in contact with him, so she made a search. She found out where he was and she sent some letters because he had a right to see his brother… It's good because at least we have contact with him and if he is not well, we can speak to him. Before, we didn't even know where he was.

(Mustafa, age 20, and his partner)

Just under a fifth (19%) reported that they got some of what they had asked for. Advocates were reported as assisting young people to reach a negotiated settlement, based on compromise, sometimes with unanticipated benefits, such as feeling more secure and therefore more able to concentrate on their education. Some young people reported that advocacy went further than responding solely to the original problem, and that advocates had helped them to obtain access to services that they would not otherwise have known about. Obtaining information on training and employment opportunities, welfare benefits, housing, counselling, and access to other support programmes and initiatives were identified as among the positive outcomes of advocacy:

> [The advocate] has done such a lot for me. He got money from the Prince's Trust charity…for the flat because the Council didn't help me… He's also helped me with Income Support, with college… I can't even think now of all the things whizzing around my head. It's because of him that I've been able to have so much access to things. I'm a single parent and have no family

so he helped me to get in touch with Sure Start. Also, I do classes now and my little boy goes to a creche. He helps me get resources I didn't think were within my reach.

(Tracey, age 22)

Some young people reported advocacy as having a positive impact on their lives in a broader sense. One young man, for example, thought that life at the respite care centre he attended had improved as a result of advocacy:

For example, we have a say in everyone who comes for a job at [the respite centre]. Before, we didn't have a say in who got jobs... I feel listened to more than before. Our views didn't count on things. If we didn't like anything, it was like it didn't count. Sometimes, it's like that at home as well, I think. It's better now than it used to be.

(James, age 16)

The three young people who rated their satisfaction with advocacy at five points or less (on a scale of 1–10) were all users of one advocacy service. In part, their dissatisfaction can be attributed to the refusal of social care professionals to meet their requests. Some of their frustration, however, was also directed at the advocate:

[The advocate] came to the review...because no one listens to me. I went there for the food and drink. When kids are in the review, it's only the adults talking and not the kids. So I wanted to butt in and say, 'this is my review, you should be listening to me!' [The advocate] sat there and listened.

(John, age 10)

One young person reported that she would give advocacy five points out of ten because, even though she achieved a change of placement, she believed that she was entitled to an apology from her former foster carer. Another young person had asked to be accommodated at age 16 following a period of living in a refuge. Despite the involvement of the advocate, the local social services department had refused to accommodate her. This failure was partly attributed to the young person's own lack of awareness of advocacy, but also to the implied passivity of the advocate:

So I got upset and gave up. [The advocate] came to my review, just taking notes, not talking. I didn't know how to use her, just asked her to come along, do the right thing... There was a lot of people I didn't know. Everybody was talking about me and I was just listening.

(Charlene, age 17)

Some of the comments made by young people who were dissatisfied with the outcomes of advocacy highlight the need for more rigorous training and supervision of advocates, and access to sources of ongoing professional development.

Conclusions

Advocacy seeks to make a positive difference to children and young people, particularly those in public care and children considered 'in need'. It is widely acknowledged that these groups of children have been failed by the care system and that, although care services may have improved in recent years, the gap between children in public care and children living with their families has widened over the past decade (DfES 2006). The study discussed in this chapter does not claim to offer a representative view of advocacy provision nationally, or a representative picture of the views of advocates, health and social care professionals, parents and carers, and children who have had contact with advocacy services. Nevertheless, the findings indicate that, at the level of the individual child, advocacy can indeed claim to produce wide-ranging benefits that, in the terms of Lee-Foster and Moorhead (1996), are both 'emotional' and 'instrumental'. There was a substantial measure of agreement among advocates, health and social care professionals, parents and carers, and children and young people that advocacy can lead to enhanced self-esteem, greater confidence and ability on the part of children to 'speak up' in meetings, improved packages of care, and the reversal of decisions not perceived to be in the interest of young people's wishes or welfare. Findings from interviews with all stakeholders also gave support to the claim that the process of advocacy can have a positive effect, even if a desired outcome is not achieved.

In particular, interviews with young people also gave support to the claim that advocacy can help young people to follow through their complaint or issue, and not give up in the face of institutional resistance. However, advocacy is not solely, or even predominantly, engaged in supporting children through formal complaints procedures. The advocacy role is far wider, having a key role to play in extending young people's horizons beyond their specific complaint or problem, to enabling them to gain access to needed services, such as leisure, education, health, and child care services, or sources of advice on employment and training.

It might be argued that individual casework advocacy can have only limited impact on individual children or the delivery of children's services more generally, and that collective forms of participation might be expected to improve the circumstances of a wider range and number of children. However, interviews with young users of advocacy services indicate that children place a high value on the advocacy relationship and the advocate's focus on their specific concerns, feelings and circumstances and that advocacy support can help to restore a sense of individuality to children in public care. Many reported that they felt 'passed around', uncared for, and unable to make themselves heard by adults working in the care system. It is, therefore, the individualism of advocacy that is one of its key strengths, at least in the eyes of children and young people.

Nevertheless, the impact of advocacy on strategic developments in children's services should not be overlooked. There was also a broad consensus among all stakeholder groups that, at a service level, a range of policy changes could be attributed to advocacy interventions. In those authorities that used casework advocacy as a form of internal audit, advocacy was credited with encouraging a range of new policy initiatives, including the allocation of pocket money, improved financial support for care leavers, a relaxation of procedures on overnight stays, raising the leaving care age from 16 to 18, and suspending care reviews while young people were sitting school examinations. In a more general sense, advocacy in these authorities was attributed with fostering cultural change towards the development of more child-centred services.

However, just over a fifth of advocates were also frustrated by local authorities' resistance to learning from the lessons of individual advocacy, and applying them to children's services on a strategic level. Barriers to achieving better outcomes for children were identified as an over-reliance on the part of social care professionals on bureaucratic procedures, and professional resistance to young people's participation in decision-making. Indeed, some social care professionals felt that broader participation work was more influential than casework advocacy in achieving improvements in the delivery of children's services. However, this view was most evident in local authorities that appeared to be unaware of, or unwilling to, use information from casework advocacy as a valid source of information on problems in service delivery.

Implications for policy and practice

Findings indicate that questions of organisational culture are critical to facilitating, or impeding, the effectiveness of advocacy in enhancing children's participation in decision-making. Some local authorities have made progress in developing a culture of listening to children and young people but positive change in this respect has been uneven. A key theme in children's accounts is the failure of adult services to 'listen' to them, and not just in a tokenistic or superficial way. It would appear that 'speaking', 'listening' and 'hearing' are three distinct dimensions of adult-child communication. Children expressed greatest frustration when they felt that adult 'listening' was a form of 'play acting'. The need for genuine receptivity on the part of care providers towards the value of listening to children's views and experiences was therefore highlighted.

Children's participation in decision-making speaks to wider debates concerning professional conceptualisations of 'care' and of the social construction of childhood, in which children are widely perceived to be less competent than adults to be involved in decisions that concern their 'welfare'. Attitudinal change may take some time to achieve. In the meantime, and on a more mechanistic level, providers of children's services could pay more attention to the potential benefits of casework advocacy in pinpointing aspects of service delivery that could be changed to benefit all children. Individual advocacy is also likely to have the greatest impact on children's services where it operates in synergy with broader participation strategies, and, ideally, adequate funding should be provided for both dimensions of advocacy practice.

Children and young people interviewed expressed a high level of satisfaction with advocacy and, in particular, with the energy and commitment demonstrated by advocates in their championing of children's views and wishes. As such, advocates might be thought of as supporting children to break through the barrier of professional resistance previously experienced by children as impenetrable. And, in most cases, advocates were successful in getting results for children, often in both tangible and emotional terms. However, some criticisms were also expressed and, while a minority view, such evidence suggests a need for closer attention to be paid to the management and supervision arrangements of advocates, and their professional development.

Advocacy services operate at the interface between children and service providers. As such, their work can illuminate some of the barriers and facilitators of the policy drive towards a closer partnership between health, education and social services on the individual and collective lives of children in public care and children 'in need'. It is perhaps too early to say whether the current emphasis on partnership working will compromise the development of child-focused services. At the very least, advocacy services could have a key role to play in ensuring children's voices, views, feelings and wishes are kept centre-stage, and not forced into the sidelines by the ever increasing number of professionals with an interest in, and responsibility for, the care of children and young people.

References

Boylan, J. and Wyllie, J. (1999) 'Advocacy and Child Protection.' In N. Parton and C.Wattam (eds) *Child Sexual Abuse: Responding to the Experiences of Children.* Chichester: Wiley.

Children's Commission for Wales (2003) *Telling Concerns: A Report of the Children's Commissioner for Wales' Review of the Operation of Complaints and Representations and Whistleblowing Procedures and Arrangements for the Provision of Children's Advocacy Services.* Swansea: Children's Commissioner for Wales Office.

Dalrymple, J. (2001) 'Safeguarding young people through confidential advocacy services.' *Child and Family Social Work 6*, 149–60.

DfES (2006) *Care Matters: Transforming the Lives of Children and Young People In Care.* London: DfES.

Henderson, R. and Pochin, M. (2001) *A Right Result? Advocacy, Justice and Empowerment.* Bristol: Policy Press.

Lee-Foster, A. and Moorhead, D. (1996) *Do the Rights Thing! An Advocacy Learning Pack.* London: Sense.

Oliver, C. (2003) *Advocacy for Children and Young People: A Review of Literature.* Understanding Children's Social Care Series No 7, London: Institute of Education, University of London.

Oliver, C., Knight, A. and Candappa, M. (2006) *Advocacy for Looked After Children and Children in Need: Achievements and Challenges.* London: DfES.

Simons, K. (1995) *'I'm Not Complaining, But…': Complaints Procedures in Social Services Departments.* York: Joseph Rowntree Foundation.

Willow, C. (1996) *Children's Rights and Participation in Residential Care.* London: National Children's Bureau.

Winn, Oakley, M. and Masson, J. (2000) *Official Friends and Friendly Officials: Support, Advice and Advocacy for Children and Young People in Public Care.* London: NSPCC.

Endnotes

1 See Chapter 2.

2 For more information on the methodology and other findings, see Oliver *et al.* (2006).

CHAPTER 12

Advocacy, Participation and Voice

Jane Dalrymple and Christine M. Oliver

The aim of putting together this book has been to offer a critical examination of advocacy for children and young people in the context of recent research, public policy and emerging practice. We are now in a position to consider different perspectives about the theory and practice of advocacy, to review its historical development, and to offer some thoughts about the future of advocacy for children and young people.

We can see from various contributors to this book that children and young people often find it hard to raise concerns or make a complaint, feel alienated and disengaged from the review process, experience child protection conferences as scary, find it difficult to discuss complex and painful issues in family group meetings, or may be excluded from participation in decision-making because they are disabled. The need for advocacy for children and young people is therefore relatively easy to understand. Furthermore, despite the fact that the United Nations Convention on the Rights of the Child recognises that children and young people are able to form and express opinions, participate in decision-making processes concerning their lives and influence solutions (Department of Health 2002; Welsh Assembly Government, 2003), and that children are being placed at the centre of new services developing in England and Wales, it has been suggested that these services are unlikely to be child-centred (Parton 2006). This makes it even more critical that we understand contemporary advocacy practice if it is to have an impact on the promoting the participatory rights of children and young people. To conclude therefore we will analyse the position of advocacy in the light of its historical development and current public policy before going to discuss the future of advocacy for children and young people.

Adult decision-making and children's voices

Advocacy has become established against a background of developing understanding about the construction of childhood, with varying perspectives on children's rights indicating the paradoxes that are apparent in promoting a positive rights agenda. With this in mind it is useful to remind ourselves of the impetus for the development of advocacy services and the core principles of advocacy that underpin the work of advocacy services from their inception.

The Children Act 1989 and the NHS and Community Care Act 1990 reflect a move away from paternalistic forms of welfare towards services that are more accountable to service users. Complaints procedures were incorporated into the legislation to facilitate an element of quality control in service delivery and are an effective way of enabling children and young people to have a voice. While legislation now recognises the need for young people to have advocacy support in complaints procedures, however, two issues remain. First, complaints procedures tend to be seen as a deterrent to bad practice in children's health and social care rather than a key element in the development of responsive, child-centred services. As a result, advocacy is more often associated with conflict and confrontation, rather than with the more constructive sense of supporting children and young people.

Second, despite legal reforms in support of children's participation, a key theme concerns the ways in which adult-organised bureaucratic processes that can be intimidating for young service users and thereby maintain adult hegemony in decision-making. Indeed, Parton (2006) argues that:

> In a period of increased anxiety about childhood, it is understandable that there is an emphasis on adults wanting to regulate the lives of children more and more. It takes considerable maturity to give the primary control to children and young people themselves so that they can report what they want, where and when, and how 'their concerns' should be addressed, so that they feel that they have a large degree of control about what happens to them. (p.186)

The initial impetus for setting up advocacy services for children and young people – the need for them to have access to independent support when expressing a concern or making a complaint (Timms 1995) – is therefore as relevant today as it was 20 years ago.

A key theme to emerge from several chapters in this book concerns the relationship between children's agency and adult-oriented decision-making structures. While the importance of children's agency (their capacity to influence events and the direction of their own lives) should not be underestimated, the constraints posed by the structures and procedures of care services should also be acknowledged. This resonates with other research studies which, as Parton (2006) notes, demonstrate that a range of contextual factors, such as age, gender and living circumstances, also has an impact on children's agency. This means that advocates need to understand the participation of children and young people in the wider context of their lives and suggests that a key advocacy skill is to recognise and understand these power relations and work with that understanding in a constructive way.

A key theme concerns the way in which advocacy can function as a mechanism to achieve a better balance of power between children and young people, and adult professionals. Jane Boylan notes in Chapter 3 that while young people did not talk explicitly about their own powerlessness, they knew that they were not always listened to or taken seriously and were aware that, when an advocate became involved, this dynamic appeared to change. This can be identified in case examples throughout the book. Furthermore, she points out, they recognised that the absence of power and authority was a significant barrier to their self-advocacy and effective participation. An interesting element from Christine M. Oliver's research (Chapter 11) is the fact that those young people who were dissatisfied with advocacy indicated that perhaps the advocate did not understand the power relations or feel able to challenge the attitudes of the professionals concerned.

Overall, evidence indicates that independent advocacy can offer an important means of redress for young people, and of holding services providers to account. Nevertheless, children's needs for support to facilitate their participation in decision-making may vary according to their individual circumstances or preferences. Depending on their own ability, the seriousness of a particular situation or a specific decision-making forum, some children and young people may find that they feel able to speak up for themselves. On occasion, they may express a preference for the support of an adult that they know well. However, within the context of contemporary practice in children's health and social care, a child or young person is more likely to need an advocate with an understanding of the systems and processes who is independent of the services involved to support them, particularly in complex situations.

Given the (sometimes limited) range of support options open to children and young people, a key theme concerns the relative effectiveness and appropriateness of independent as compared with informal forms of advocacy within bureaucratic decision-making processes. Evidence indicates that children and young people, as well as the adults involved in their lives, need to be aware of who might be able to undertake the advocacy role and how far they are able to offer the support children and young people need.

Research indicates that, while sharing difficulties is a key factor in enabling children and young people to develop coping mechanisms, they are careful about who they share information with, particularly adults. They often have a network of known and trusted adults that they might approach (Kelley 2002). Best friends, parents, siblings are the most likely confidantes – someone who can be trusted, and will keep their confidence – rather than professionals from formal agencies (Butler and Williamson 1994; Hallett, Murray and Punch 2003). However, while young people may have good relationships with key adults in their lives, such adults are not necessarily able or willing to act as their advocate. For example, in Chapter 5 we see that Alex's foster carers had been told not to intervene on his behalf. In family group conferences, family supporters can find it difficult to maintain the necessary element of independence from the situation that they are also a party to (Chapter 5). Similarly, a young person within the child protection system was very clear that family members all had their own point of view to put forward; she therefore placed a high value on the impartiality of her advocate (Chapter 4). In relation to services for young disabled people, some residential workers felt that advocates had more influence than they did (Chapter 7).

Clearly, informal advocacy support by trusted confidantes can offer an important element of support, where this is appropriate and desired by young people. However, many children and young people who work with independent advocates are in need of support because their 'natural' advocate – such as a parent or other significant figure – is absent or unable to do so. It is crucial, then, that the provision of advocacy services continues to be targeted at children and young people in the looked after system, who are invariably separated from the natural advocates in their lives.

In all the chapters presented in this book, independent advocates are people who have not worked with the children and young people concerned prior to the advocacy referral. Nevertheless, the close relationship that is established by many children and young people with their independent advocate is an important characteristic of advocacy practice. To some extent, this may be symptomatic of children's isolation and powerlessness within formal decision-making systems. Without the advocacy support, many children and young people experience situations where they would otherwise give up, or feel unable even to begin to voice their concerns or complaints. Nevertheless, the importance children and young people

DEVELOPING ADVOCACY FOR CHILDREN AND YOUNG PEOPLE

attribute to the advocacy relationship should not be underestimated. Young people who experience working with an independent advocate tend to see that person almost as a 'friend'. The core elements of this relationship are characterised by a number of components: trust, respect, confidentiality, reliability, independence and action. Clearly, the child-focused nature of advocacy is a key factor in creating positive advocacy relationships with children and young people.

The nature of the advocacy relationship with children and young people does not make an advocate any better than the professionals involved but it can be a cause for tension between advocates and professionals working in children's services. One of the more troublesome aspects of independent advocacy work is maintaining positive working relationships with other professionals while challenging decision-making and promoting participation. Findings indicate that, when professionals understand that advocates *stand in a different place* – that is, alongside the child or young person – then there is less resistance to advocacy and advocates (Chapter 2). A further factor concerns the professional power of social workers. It is therefore not surprising that social workers tend to perceive advocacy as detrimental, particularly in light of the historical link between advocacy and complaints procedures. While social workers are traditionally understood as having an advocacy role, only a few young people were positive about how far their social workers had supported them to make a complaint and others were critical of their social worker (Chapter 8).

Clearly, there are tensions between social work and the advocacy role, with advocacy described as 'a sometimes unwelcome and often awkward visitor to the world of work in children's services' (Chapter 7). Overall, the research discussed in this book does not present social workers as anti-advocacy or advocates as anti-social work – indeed, many social workers welcome the support of independent advocates, sometimes too enthusiastically as a source of generic support. However, social work practitioners who may wish to advocate for young service users can feel constrained by agency policies and procedures or by their responsibilities to act in the best interests of the child or young person concerned. Moreover, professionals in children's health and social care are in a powerful position both because they are invariably expected to make judgements that impact on the lives of children and young people, and because they control resources. Consequently, social workers are often unable to satisfactorily undertake the advocacy role.

Within decision-making processes relating to children and young people's health and social care, all those involved have an opinion – profes-

sionals, children, young people and their families. However, the power relations inherent in such settings can have the effect of isolating a child or
young person. While the right of children and young people to have a voice
in the decision-making processes concerning their lives is clearly stated in
policy and legislation, we need to remember that in the many investigations
concerning child deaths the voices of the children involved are silent. For
example, in relation to Victoria Climbié (Department of Health and Home
Office 2003), we know nothing about her probable experiences of being
frightened, confused and in pain during the time that she was living in
England (Cooper 2005). One of the reasons why we may not hear their
voices is that Victoria and children and young people in similar situations
may well bring out in adults mixed emotions, including fear and even disgust
at 'the smells, dirt and the notions of disorder' (Ferguson 2005, p.790)
which surround them. Understandably, the professionals involved are likely
to resist connecting with their pain. This may then cause conflict for concerned professionals who want to understand the situation of children and
young people while at the same time they are experiencing the 'feelings of
disgust which appear to judge and oppress people who are invariably already
subordinated' (Ferguson 2005, p.790). While silence may be a strategic
choice for some children, it is nevertheless of crucial importance that they
have access to an independent advocate, if they so wish.

Developments in children's advocacy services

The expansion of advocacy services by local authorities in various areas of
young people's lives is testament to the need for children and young people
in receipt of various services (especially those living away from home) to
have access to independent advocacy. However, as we have seen, the research
presented in this book tends to emphasise the relationship between
advocacy and various formal procedures (including reviews, child protection
conferences, family group conferences and complaints procedures). This
lends weight to the view that advocacy for children and young people is at
risk of becoming increasingly proceduralised and fragmented. It is a notable
feature of this book that six chapters investigate the relationship between
advocacy and formal decision-making procedures. Just as the provision of
welfare is split into different kinds of meetings and processes so the provision of advocacy would appear to be compartmentalised into those same
processes. The fragmentation of advocacy inevitably means that, while in
some respects this is governed by contractual agreements, it limits the
advocacy role to a specific setting.

However, we should also be cautious about assuming that the emphasis given to investigations of advocacy in relation to specific procedures is an accurate reflection of how advocacy is practised generally. It is possible that this focus is an artefact of the research commissioning process. Advocacy support in relation to complaints procedures is only part of a range of services that advocacy services offer to children and young people, and, indeed, evidence suggests that this may represent only a minor aspect of the work of advocacy services (Chapter 11). Indeed, we need to be aware that the strength of advocacy lies in its capacity to address children's immediate concerns and complaints, without necessarily resorting to formal procedures. Nevertheless, it is also possible that the duty placed on local authorities to provide advocacy for children making a formal complaint under the provisions of the 1989 Children Act has (possibly inadvertently) contributed to the narrowing of the focus and scope of advocacy activity (Oliver *et al.* 2006).

It is a cause for concern that advocacy may be becoming increasingly fragmented at a time when children's services are on a path towards closer integration. As partnership working between welfare, education, health and youth justice professionals becomes more prevalent, it has been suggested that advocacy may have an important role to play in maintaining a focus on the views and wishes of the child (Chapter 7). In this context, it is useful to remind ourselves of the core underpinning principles of advocacy practice.

Principles of contemporary advocacy practice

Two principle cornerstones – independence and confidentiality – have been significant in the development of advocacy services for children and young people.

Independence

The importance of independent advocacy (Smith and Ing 1996) is recognised in Standard 6 of the *National Standards for Agencies Providing Advocacy for Children and Young People* (Department of Health 2002; Welsh Assembly Government 2003). The advocacy service needs to make sure that its advocates are:

- free from all pressures or conflicts of interests which might affect their ability to advocate independently on behalf of individual children and young people
- able to demonstrate to children and young people from the outset of the relationship their complete integrity and independence.

This means that advocacy services should be able to show that they have secure funding, or funding from a source not directly affected by the outcomes of advocacy for individual young people; show they have no involvement in any of the systems affecting the child's life and provide advocates who can demonstrate that they are committed to children's rights and to following the instructions of the child or young person. Historically, in relation to complaints, the importance of independent support for children and young people making a complaint was recognised in debates of the Children Bill. One MP spoke out for independent investigation of complaints so that any children and young people in care who had

> serious complaints can be sure that they are heard by people who will listen fairly, who will not disbelieve them, and who will have no motive for wishing their version of events not to be true. Children need such independent representation.

> (quoted in Timms 1995, p.357)

We can see throughout the research presented here that it is valued by children and young people. The concept of organisational 'independence' though is one that is the subject of debate, and we see from the research in Chapters 2 and 8 that the issue is by no means straightforward.

Confidentiality

The need for confidentiality is the second principle, highlighted as important for children and young people when deciding who they might confide in (Hallett *et al.* 2003; Wattam 1999). The work of confidential helplines such as ChildLine indicates the importance of this principle for supporting children and young people to voice their concerns (McLeod 1996, 1999). Standard 7 of the National Standards emphasises the confidentiality principle although it has been contentious. Sir Ronald Waterhouse, at the launch of the National Standards in Wales (2003), encapsulated concerns about the need for a high threshold for breaking confidentiality, stating that the phraseology of this standard needs to be more robust to allow the advocate/child relationship to work. We see in Chapter 7 that young disabled people particularly valued access to talking to someone in confidence. However, while the concept of confidentiality was accepted in principle by adult carers and professionals, its relevance for disabled children was questioned. The researchers point out though that disabled young people's dependency on others for their care can make them more vulnerable to abuse and to the violation of their rights to be consulted about issues concerning their lives. This is not to deny the advocacy needs of other children in public care and those considered 'in need'. Arguably, all children and young people who are in situations where they need advocacy support are vulnerable. It is interesting to note that, despite being valued and identified (alongside independence) as a core feature of the work to be performed by children's advocacy services (Waterhouse 2003), it is not one that is addressed in any detail by contributors.

The future of advocacy – a wider participation strategy

Advocacy provision has developed in innovative ways to meet the different needs of children and young people, with committed and skilled staff providing advocacy services that gain general approval from young service users. The strength of different levels and forms of advocacy is that they can be complementary in meeting the varying needs of children and young people at different points in their lives. As we have noted above, however, there are problems with the current provision of advocacy services that relate to independence, competition, capacity of service providers, accessibility and consistency (Chapter 2).

The impact of good advocacy practice for *individual* young people is very clear – in fact it has been suggested that the individuality of advocacy is its key strength (Chapter 11). The research indicates that advocates and young people report the positive effects of having advocacy support, even if their desired outcome is not achieved. In particular, the psychological impact of enabling children and young people to gain confidence and self-esteem is a key component of much of the research. Bearing in mind that many children and young people who access advocacy are vulnerable – often in care or 'in need' – this is a positive factor that cannot be ignored. More practically, positive outcomes can lead to changes in young people's lives while involvement in decision-making restores faith in a system that has often let them down. Unanticipated benefits identified are the fact that if a child or young person feels more secure then the likelihood is that they are more able to concentrate on other elements of their lives such as education (Chapter 11). This is particularly significant in view of the statistics regarding the educational underachievement of looked after children and young people, for example. In this context, advocacy can have an important role to play in contributing to improving the lives of children and young people in line with the objectives of the *Every Child Matters* agenda (DfES 2004).

The typical case-based management of advocacy means that, while the impact of advocacy in relation to individual young people is evident, its impact on policy is less clear to quantify. Christine Oliver's research (Chapter 2) indicates that 56 per cent of policy changes could be attributed to advocacy, and the small study of Wiltshire child protection conferences identified local changes in relation to thinking about participation (Chapter 4). Overall, it would appear that, for advocacy to have a significant impact, it needs to form part of a wider participation strategy. This means that advocacy needs to be one of a range of services available to young people to enable their voice to be heard in different circumstances. Such a strategy also needs to recognise the systemic role of advocacy. While services are likely to continue to focus on case advocacy, collating information from individual situations provides the data needed to promote change in legislation, systems and policies. It could be seen as a positive that, when the impact of advocacy at a policy level was limited, children's services had already integrated a pro-participation perspective into their work (Chapter 11). Without a wider vision of children and young people's participation and rights, Anne Crowley and Andy Pithouse suggest that the dynamics of adult-child power relations are unlikely to change significantly, with independent advocacy being a 'blunt instrument' in ensuring the protection and empowerment of children and young people (Chapter 9).

Currently, there are barriers for many children and young people wanting information about or access to independent advocacy. There are variations in the way advocacy is provided, in the availability of advocacy across the country and in the way advocacy services are targeted for different groups of children and young people (Chapter 2). Clearly, there are children and young people who are excluded from decision-making processes, particularly, for example, disabled young people. While local authorities have a legislative mandate to provide advocacy services for children who want to make a complaint under the Children Act 1989, the complexity of advocacy provision means that children and young people's access to advocacy is more a matter of chance and there is need to consider radical changes to the way that children and young people are supported to participate within all public services. Arguably, to do this, young people need to be involved in determining service level agreements as a way of building in the flexibility needed 'to allow for a variety of different ways of giving young people what they want and deserve' (Clarke 2003, p.33).

In both England and Wales, there are proposals for change. In Wales, the debate is about a comprehensive advocacy service across all public services with advocacy commissioned by a consortia of local authorities, health trusts and partners (Welsh Assembly Government 2007). Proposals put forward by research into the provision of children's advocacy in England (Oliver *et al.* 2006) also recommend a more strategic approach, comprising (among other elements) a regional model for the commissioning of advocacy services. However, in England, recent proposals for improving services for children in public care (DfES 2006) show that, while children's need for advocacy is recognised, the advocacy role is confused with the role of independent visitor and does not equate to the definitions of advocacy set out in the National Standards (Department of Health 2002).

Key to contemporary debates is the question of how advocacy services should be funded. They continue to be funded through service level agreements, controlled by commissioners of services with the consequent likelihood of changes in advocacy service providers that make it difficult for long-term project planning and leave children feeling angry and let down (Chapter 8). While such arrangements may protect advocacy services from the potential of assimilation into mainstream service provision, it also means that they are dependent on the vagaries of the financial resources of commissioners who determine how or whether advocacy should be available. We hope that the research presented here will contribute to the debates about how advocacy is provided. However, it is crucial that we are not sidetracked by these debates away from issues and concerns about advocacy practice. Within the development of child-focused services, advocacy has a critical role to play in ensuring the centrality of children and young people within the bureaucratic structures that continue to epitomise service delivery.

Research has an important part to play in adding to our knowledge and understanding about advocacy, which in turn has an impact on practice and ultimately on the lives of children and young people. Some key questions have been posed by contributors to this book which we hope will enable advocates, commissioners of services and professionals to develop services that work for children and young people. Hearing the voices of children and young people is a crucial element in the provision of effective services, particularly within a policy agenda promoting ever increasing partnership working between social, health and education services. The role of advocacy, working at the interface between these services and children and young people, is critical in promoting the rights of children and young people to be heard. This means that we need to continue to research and evaluate the provision of advocacy to ensure that it avoids proceduralisation within service structures or assimilation into services, negating the ability that children and young people clearly have to shape their own lives.

References

Butler, I. and Williamson, H. (1994) *Children Speak: Children, Trauma and Social Work.* Harlow: Longman.

Clarke, P. (2003) *Some Thoughts About Advocacy. Setting the Standards.* Cardiff: Tros Gynnal.

Cooper, A. (2005) 'Surface and depth in the Vicoria Climbé Inquiry Report.' *Child and Family Social Work, 10,* 1–9.

Department for Education and Skills (2004) *Care Matters: Transforming the Lives of Children and Young People in Care.* London: The Stationery Office.

Department for Education and Skills (2004) *Every Child Matters: Change for Children.* London: Department of Education and Skills.

Department of Health (2002) *National Standards for the Provision of Children's Advocacy Services.* London: Department of Health Publications.

Department of Health and Home Office (2003) *The Victoria Climbie Inquiry: Report of an Inquiry by Lord Laming.* London: The Stationery Office.

Ferguson, H. (2005) 'Working with violence, the emotions and psychosocial dynamics of child protection: reflections on the Victoria Climbié case.' *Social Work Education, 24,* 781–795.

Hallett, C., Murray, C. and Punch, S. (2003) 'Young People and Welfare: Negotiating Pathways.' In C. Hallett, and A. Prout (eds) *Hearing the Voices of Children: Social Policy for a New Century.* London: Routledge Falmer.

Kelley, N. (2002) *Minor Problems? The Future of Advocacy and Legal Services for Children and Young People.* London: Office of the Children's Rights Commissioner for London.

McLeod, M. (1996) *Talking to Children about Child Abuse,* London: ChildLine.

McLeod, M. (1999) '"Don't Just Do It": Children's Access to Help and Protection.' In N. Parton and C. Wattam (eds) *Child Sexual Abuse, Responding to the Experiences of Children.* Chichester: Wiley.

Oliver, C., Knight, A. and Candappa, M. (2006) *Advocacy for Looked After Children and Children in Need.* Briefing Paper. London: Institute of Education. Also available at www.ioe.ac.uk/tcru and www.dfes.gov.uk/research (accessed 24 January 2008).

Parton, N. (2006) *Safeguarding Childhood: Early Intervention and Surveillance in a Late Modern Society.* Basingstoke: Palgrave Macmillan.

Timms, J. E. (1995) *Children's Representation: A Practitioners Guide.* London: Sweet and Maxwell.

Waterhouse, R. (2003) '*Lessons from "Lost in Care"'.* Setting the Standards.* Cardiff: Tros Gynnal.

Wattam, C. (1999) 'Confidentiality and the Social Organisation of Telling.' In N. Parton, and C. Wattam (eds) *Child Sexual Abuse, Responding to the Experiences of Children.* Chichester: Wiley.

Welsh Assembly Government (2003) *National Standards for the Provision of Children's Advocacy Services.* Cardiff: Welsh Assembly Government.

Welsh Assembly Government (2007) *Consultation on a New Service Model for Delivering Advocacy Services for Children and Young People.* Cardiff: Children's health and Social Care Directorate WAG.

Contributors

Jane Boylan is programme director of the social work course at the University of Keele. Her research interests include advocacy, looked after children and children's rights. For her doctoral thesis she undertook a critical analysis of looked after children's participation in their statutory reviews and the role of advocacy. Recent publications have included a series of articles for *Childright* based on the work of various advocacy projects co-authored with Dr. Jane Dalrymple from the University of the West of England.

Elaine Chase is a Senior Research Officer at the Thomas Coram Research Unit, Institute of Education, University of London. Over the past 17 years she has worked extensively in the fields of health promotion, public health and health-related research, both in the UK and internationally. Her work is primarily concerned with young people's health and well-being, with a particular focus on young people at risk of marginalisation.

Anne Crowley is a consultant researcher. Her research interests include child rights, advocacy, participation, looked after children and child poverty and exclusion. Anne has worked on a number of policy-related research projects with Cardiff University including a review of advocacy services in Wales (2005) and a review of the use of specialist placements for children in Wales (2003). Prior to becoming a consultant in 1995, Anne worked with young people as a social worker and probation officer. In 1991 she established the first dedicated advocacy service in Wales for looked after children and children in need. More recently she was an adviser to the Parliamentary Welsh Affairs Select committee for their enquiry into *Empowering Children and Young People in Wales.*

Jane Dalrymple is a senior lecturer at the University of the West of England. Prior to this she was the Director of a national advocacy service. She has undertaken a number of evaluations of local advocacy services and her doctoral thesis was entitled *Constructions of Advocacy: An Analysis of Professional Advocacy in Work with Children and Young People.* She contributed to the literature review for a study of Advocacy in Wales commissioned by the Welsh Assembly Government and recent publications have included a series of articles for *Childright* based on the work of various advocacy projects co-authored with Dr. Jane Boylan from the University of Keele.

Hilary Horan works for Barnardo's South West as the regional Children's Services Manager for family group conferences (FGCs) and Advocacy. She has helped to set up eight family group conference services in the area. The Wiltshire Project was the first in the UK to routinely offer independent advocates to young people having an FGC. Over the past four years she has helped to set up and develop the Child Protection Advocacy Service in Wiltshire and more recently in Swindon. Hilary previously worked as an independent chair of child protection conferences and as a guardian ad litem.

Perpetua Kirby in an independent research consultant (Director of PK Research Consultancy Ltd). Her main research interests are the participation of children and young people. She undertakes research for local and national government departments, health authorities and the voluntary sector. Recent publications have examined building cultures of participation across organisations, children's participation in policy and in research, young children's participation and evaluating children's participation internationally.

Abigail Knight is a Research Officer at the Thomas Coram Research Unit, Institute of Education, University of London. Previously a social worker, she has worked as a researcher for 11 years. Her research interests include issues affecting disabled children and young people in the care system. Her current doctoral studies are in the field of childhood studies.

Sophie Laws leads evaluation and policy work for Coram, a charity that aims to develop and promote best practice in the care of vulnerable children and their families. She has written widely on children and young people's participation and rights, including a guide to children's ethical and meaningful participation in research for the UN Study on Violence against Children. She is Honorary Research Fellow at London Metropolitan University and author of *Research for Development: A Practical Guide* (Sage 2003).

Christine M. Oliver is a Senior Researcher at the Thomas Coram Research Unit where she has worked for the past ten years. She has researched a wide range of topics in children's health and social care, with a particular emphasis on children's perspectives on their social worlds. She has investigated advocacy provision for adults and children and recently completed the first national study of advocacy for children and young people in England, prepared for the Department of Health and the Department for Education and Skills. The first stage of the research comprised a review of the literature on advocacy (Oliver 2003) and the final summary report is entitled *Advocacy for Looked After Children and Children in Need: Achievements and Challenges* (Oliver *et al.* 2006). A full report on the study will be published by Jessica Kingsley Publishers in 2008.

Andy Pithouse has researched and published extensively in child and family social work. He is a member of the inter-disciplinary Childhood Studies Research Group at Cardiff University where he lectures in theory, policy and research in child and family services. He led the recent Welsh Government funded national survey of children's advocacy services, the results of which have led to far-reaching policy proposals about both change and expansion to advocacy in Wales.

Maureen Winn Oakley is a practitioner working in two positions involving the promotion of children's rights and advocacy. She works for the National Youth Advocacy Service (NYAS) as Children's Rights Commissioner in Sandwell and is also employed as Birmingham Children's Rights Officer. She was NSPCC Senior Research Fellow at Warwick University Law School for nine years and is co-author of *Out of Hearing: Representing Children in Court* (Wiley 1999) and *Official Friends and Friendly Officials: Independent Visitors and Advocacy* (NSPCC 2000), *Protecting Powers: Emergency Intervention for Children's Protection* (NSPCC/Wiley Series in Protecting Children 2007).

Subject Index

Author Index